What if Ireland Defaults?

"Beautifully written and surprisingly easy to digest, this book digs deep into the default debate. The insights into the consequences of default for Ireland are compulsory reading for the mandarins in Finance and the false gods of the NTMA. The detached views of such a distinguished cast of characters offer far more enlightenment than you would find at the Cabinet table."

Shane Ross, independent TD, author and business editor of the
Sunday Independent

"This is a significant and timely written symposium from a very broad spectrum of opinion holders on the crucial issues for Ireland in respect of the viability of the ECB–IMF bailout and the consequences of its possible failure. Whether one hopes for failure or believes in success, and regardless of whether one agrees with some or none of the contributors, the articles are a must-read for citizens of an embattled society facing difficult but inescapable choices on the future of their Republic, and they will be quoted for years to come in the ongoing debate upon which we are launched."

Michael McDowell, barrister and former Minister for Justice

"Sober, balanced, comprehensive, and heavy with facts, *What if Ireland Defaults?* is necessary reading for anyone who wants to understand how the world will deal with a future of fiscal crises and moral hazard."

Dan Mitchell, senior economist with the Cato Institute

"Rather than hide behind the sofa every time the word 'default' is mentioned, we need an intelligent discussion of what it means and doesn't mean for economies, societies and citizens. This book brings together a wide range of perspectives and fact-based analyses on a topic that will dominate policy debates for years. Read this, agree or disagree with the contributors, but let's start acknowledging that debt is an over-riding political issue."

Michael Taft, research officer with UNITE

What if Ireland Defaults?

edited by

BRIAN LUCEY, CHARLES LARKIN AND
CONSTANTIN GURDGIEV

ORPEN PRESS

Published by
Orpen Press
Lonsdale House
Avoca Avenue
Blackrock
Co. Dublin
Ireland

e-mail: info@orpenpress.com
www.orpenpress.com

Paperback ISBN 978-1-871305-48-7
ePub ISBN 978-1-871305-52-4
Kindle ISBN 978-1-871305-53-1

Printed in the UK by the MPG Books Group

Brian – *To my wife, Mary, my support in all*
Charles – *To my parents and Jane for their help and support*
Constantin – *To my wife, Jennifer Hord, for her infinite patience and support*

We would like to acknowledge our contributors, editors and all those who made this book possible.

Please note that all dollar amounts are in US dollars unless stated otherwise.

Table of Contents

List of Acronyms... ix

About the Contributors... xi

Introduction 1

Setting the Scene... 5
1. Debt, Crises and Default from a Parliamentary
    Perspective... 7
    Sean Barrett
2. Crises and Contagion: A Survey 17
    Anzhela Knyazeva, Diana Knyazeva and Joseph Stiglitz

Ireland 51
3. Debt Restructuring in Ireland: Orderly, Selective and
    Unavoidable 53
    Constantin Gurdgiev
4. Ireland's Public Debt – Tell Me a Story We Have
    Not Heard Yet ….. 69
    Seamus Coffey
5. A very Irish Default, or When Is a Default
    Not a Default? 87
    Stephen Kinsella
6. How to Survive on the *Titanic*: Ireland's Relationship
    with Europe.. 99
    Megan Greene

Country Studies... 109
7. The Russian Crisis and the Crisis of Russia 111
   Constantin Gurdgiev
8. Iceland: The Accidental Hero 135
   Elaine Byrne and Huginn F. Þorsteinsson
9. Irish Public Debt: A View through the Lens of the
   Argentine Default... 149
   Tony Phillips
10. Coring out the Big Apple: New York's Fiscal Crisis 173
    Sam Roberts
11. When Cities Default 187
    Marc Tomljanovich

Perspectives... 197
12. A Market Participant's Perspective on Debt and
    Default.. 199
    Peter Brown
13. A Mortgage Broker's Perspective on Debt and
    Default.. 207
    Karl Deeter
14. The IMF and the Dilemmas of Sovereign Default........ 217
    Gary O'Callaghan
15. A Politician's Perspective on Debt and Default............ 235
    Peter Mathews
16. A Financial Journalist's Perspective on Debt and
    Default.. 245
    John Walsh
17. A Behavioural Economist's Perspective on Debt and
    Default.. 253
    Michael Dowling
18. A Political Activist and Businessperson's
    Perspective on Debt and Default 265
    Declan Ganley

Index 279

List of Acronyms

BIS	Bank for International Settlements
CADTM	Committee for the Abolition of Third World Debt
CBI	Central Bank of Iceland
CIS	Commonwealth of Independent States
COMECON	the common trade area of the former Warsaw Pact
DCU	Dublin City University
ECB	European Central Bank
EFSF	European Financial Stability Facility
EFSM	European Financial Stability Mechanism
ESM	European Stability Mechanism
FÁS	Irish National Training and Employment Authority
FDI	foreign direct investment
GDP	gross domestic product
GGD	general government debt
GKOs	Russian state-issued short-term bills
GNI	gross national income
GNP	gross national product
HIPC	Heavily Indebted Poor Countries
HIRC	Highly Indebted Rich Countries
IBRC	Irish Bank Resolution Corporation
IMF	International Monetary Fund
ISK	Icelandic krona
LTV	loan to value
MAC	Municipal Assistance Corporation (New York)
MNC	multinational corporation
NAMA	National Asset Management Agency
NPRF	National Pension Reserve Fund

NTMA	National Treasury Management Agency
NYC	New York City
OECD	Organisation for Economic Co-Operation and Development
PSI	private sector involvement
S&P	Standard and Poor's
SDRM	Sovereign Debt Restructuring Mechanism
UCD	University College Dublin
UDC	Urban Development Corporation (New York)
WPPSS	Washington Public Power System Supply

About the Contributors

Brian Lucey is professor of Finance in Trinity College Dublin and a prolific author and commentator on financial and banking issues. He has worked at Trinity since 1992. Prior to that he was an economist at the Central Bank of Ireland (1987–1992), and before that an administrative officer in the Department of Health (1985–1992). He has a BA in Economics from Trinity College Dublin (1985), an MA in International Economics, Trade and Politics from University College Dublin (1988) and a PhD in Finance from Stirling University (2003).

Charles Larkin is a research associate and adjunct lecturer in the School of Business, Trinity College Dublin, as well as at the National University of Ireland, Maynooth, and at the ESC Toulouse School of Business, France. Charles is also a special adviser on economic policy matters to Senator Sean Barrett. Charles' main areas of research are political economy and public policy. He was awarded his PhD in Economics from Trinity College Dublin in 2008. He is a regular contributor to the Irish media and is co-author with

Professor Colm Kearney of *The IMF and Nicaragua: Development Where People Matter*.

Constantin Gurdgiev is the head of research for St. Columbanus AG, a Swiss-based asset management firm, and the adjunct professor of Finance in Trinity College Dublin. He currently serves as the chair of the Ireland Russia Business Association, and holds non-executive appointments on the investment committees of GoldCore Ltd (Ireland) and Heinz Global Asset Management LLC (US). Constantin also lectures in the Smurfit Graduate Business School, University College Dublin and serves as a visiting professor of Finance in the Russian State University. In the past, Constantin served as the head of macroeconomics with the Institute for Business Value, IBM, director of research with NCB Stockbrokers Ltd, and group editor and director of *Business & Finance* Publications. Born in Moscow, Constantin was educated in the University of California, Los Angeles, University of Chicago, Johns Hopkins University and Trinity College, Dublin. He writes a daily blog at trueeconomics.blogspot.com and a number of regular columns in the international and Irish press.

Sean Barrett is the current senior lecturer in the Department of Economics, Trinity College Dublin and has enjoyed a distinguished career in academic circles along with holding high-ranking positions outside of the college, many of which have had a direct effect on transport policy and the tourism industry of Ireland. After graduating from University College

Dublin in 1973, Sean went on to obtain a Masters at the highly regarded McMasters University in Canada before returning to UCD to gain his PhD in Economics. Following the completion of his studies, Sean took up the post of lecturer in the Department of Economics in Trinity College Dublin in 1977 and has gone on to enjoy a 34-year-long career in the college. Over the course of his career Sean has made a reputation for himself as one of the foremost economists in Ireland. With over eighty-five different publications, mostly on his expert topics of transport and social policy, he is one of the most published economists in Ireland. However his achievements in economics have not just been limited to academic discourse, as he has been a key figure in legislation, most notably in his role as director of Bord Fáilte in 1984, where he was instrumental in the successful deregulation of Irish airlines, and his role as a vital member of the National Economic and Social Council since 2005. He was elected to Seanad Éireann by Trinity College graduates in April 2011.

Peter Brown is former chief dealer and head of the treasury team in Barclays Bank. He is also the co-founder of the Irish Institute of Financial Trading. Peter is currently the main lecturer in the Irish Institute of Financial Trading, specialising in trading courses. His media profile as a financial commentator has led to him being highly sought after by media in Ireland, the UK and continental Europe. Peter gained his extensive trading knowledge working in Citi Bank, Banque National de Paris, Ulster Bank and ten years in Barclays Bank. He experienced firsthand the British pound crisis of 1990s, giving him deep insight as to how the markets will react to the current Eurozone debt crisis.

Elaine Byrne is an adjutant lecturer at the Department of Political Science at Trinity College Dublin, where she has taught Irish Politics and Comparative Political Reform. Elaine has acted as a consultant for the United Nations, the World Bank, Transparency International and Global Integrity. Her first book, *Political Corruption in Ireland 1922–2010: A Crooked Harp* (Manchester University Press), was published in 2012. Elaine is a regular political columnist and her by-line has featured in the *Irish Times, Sunday Times, Sunday Business Post, Sunday Independent, The Times* and *The Guardian*. She is a regular contributor to Irish and international radio and television on Irish political affairs. Elaine combines her academic and media work as a political reform campaigner. Her advocacy work can be accessed at www.politicalreform.ie (co-editor) and from the deliberative democracy initiative www.wethecitizens.ie (co-founder). Her portfolio can be accessed at www.elaine.ie.

Seamus Coffey is a lecturer in the School of Economics in University College Cork. His teaching ranges across undergraduate and post-graduate courses with a particular emphasis on the relationship between government and the economy for undergraduates and applied statistical techniques for postgraduates. He is the programme director for the MSc in Health Economics, which has been running since 2007. His primary research area focuses on access to and utilisation of health services in Ireland and he is currently undertaking a PhD on this topic with the University of Manchester. He is a frequent contributor to the broadcast and print media on the ongoing crisis in the Irish economy.

Karl Deeter is a native of Los Angeles who now calls Ireland home. He has spent his career in financial services, having started in insurance and then moving to retail brokerage and accountancy. He is known for mortgage commentary on behalf of Irish Mortgage Brokers. He is also the head of client advice at accountancy firm Advisors.ie. Karl is a qualified financial advisor; he holds a Mortgage Diploma and a Certificate in Compliance, he is a part-qualified accountant, and he is also working towards a qualification in Islamic Finance. Prior to professional qualifications he studied at Dublin Institute of Technology, obtaining a Certificate and Diploma in Management.

Michael Dowling is a lecturer in Finance in Dublin City University since 2011, with previous employment including positions in the University of Essex and Trinity College Dublin. He holds a Masters in Banking and Finance from the University of Stirling, and a PhD, awarded in 2007, in Behavioural Finance from Trinity College Dublin. His research concentrates on psychological influences on investors and companies, and exploring how culture plays a role in societal and individual economic decision making. Among his publications include research published in the *International Review of Financial Analysis, Journal of Economic Surveys* and *Journal of Multinational Financial Management.*

Declan Ganley is an Irish entrepreneur and is chair and CEO of Rivada Networks, a communications and technology business with operations in the US and Europe. He is co-founder of the Swiss-based asset management company St Columbanus AG. Over the course of his career he has built a number of businesses in emerging markets in the forestry and telecommunications sectors. He founded Libertas as a think tank and later a political movement to promote the cause of a democratic, transparent, accountable and strong European Union. He is a frequent op-ed contributor on the subject of European reform. He is a recipient of the Louisiana Distinguished Service Medal, which was awarded for what was cited as his life-saving actions in the aftermath of Hurricane Katrina. He has received various awards for entrepreneurship and public advocacy, including the Frode Jacobsen Prize for courage in Denmark and the Michal Tosovsky Prize in the Czech Republic.

Megan Greene is the head of the Western Europe macroeconomics team at Roubini Global Economics and one of the leading voices in interpreting developments in the Eurozone crisis. At RGE, Megan conducts and coordinates macroeconomic forecasts on the Eurozone's most significant economies and responds to policy decisions (or the lack thereof) in Greece, Portugal, Ireland, Italy, Spain and Germany as well as at the EU level. She regularly appears in print and broadcast media, including the *Financial Times* and *Newsnight*. From 2007 to 2011 Megan worked as the Eurozone crisis expert at the Economist Intelligence Unit. Prior to working as an economist, Megan was an investment banking analyst at JP Morgan Chase and an advisor to the Liechtenstein royal family on eradicating money laundering from the principality's financial services industry. Megan received a BA in Political Economy from Princeton University and an MSc in European Studies from Nuffield College, Oxford University. You can read some of her analysis at www.economistmeg.com and follow her on Twitter (@economistmeg).

Stephen Kinsella is a lecturer in Economics at the University of Limerick. His interests are in macroeconomic modelling, banking and regulation, and the Irish economy. He has published in the *Cambridge Journal of Economics, Journal of Banking Regulation, Journal of Policy Modeling, Financial Regulation International,* as well as in four books. His first PhD is from the National University of Ireland, his second from the New School for Social Research. He recently won an INET grant to build a stock flow consistent macroeconomic model for Ireland. Stephen is a research fellow at the Geary Institute at University College Dublin and a research associate at the Institute for International Integration Studies, Trinity College Dublin.

Anzhela Knyazeva is assistant professor of Finance at the Simon School of Business, University of Rochester. She holds a PhD from New York University. She has worked on issues related to boards of directors, dividend behaviour, firm locations, bank lending and ownership reforms. Her work has been published in the *Journal of Financial Economics* and *Journal of Banking and Finance*. She teaches courses in International Finance and Investments and has been included on the Simon Teaching Honor Roll.

Diana Knyazeva is assistant professor of Finance at the Simon School of Business, University of Rochester. She earned her PhD at New York University's Stern School of Business. She has research interests in corporate finance, governance and banking. Her papers have examined corporate boards, payout policy, investment behaviour and analyst following. Her most recent work was published in the *Journal of Financial Economics*. She teaches Capital Budgeting and Financial Institutions. She has been repeatedly placed on the Simon Teaching Honor Roll.

Peter Mathews was educated at Gonzaga College and University College Dublin, where he obtained a B. Comm. and an MBA from UCD's Smurfit Graduate Business School. He is a qualified chartered accountant with extensive experience in audit, taxation and consultancy with Coopers and Lybrand Dublin (now PricewaterhouseCoopers) in the 1970s. In 1979 he joined ICC Bank in Dublin and managed the enterprise development, hi-tech and FDI lending sections of the bank. In 1983 he was appointed to develop and manage the property development, construction and investment lending section, a successful specialist area of lending for the bank. In 1999 he set up an independent banking (property and finance) consultancy practice in Dublin, consulting on the financing of property-related deals and also advising on loans as well as zoning and planning matters. Peter was elected to Dáil Éireann in the 2011 general election. He is a member of the Oireachtas Joint Committee on Finance, Public Expenditure and Reform.

Gary O'Callaghan was educated at CBS Mitchelstown, Co Cork and graduated with a Bachelor of Commerce degree from University College Cork in 1981. He also earned a Masters in Economic Science from UCC and a PhD in Economics from George Mason University in Virginia, US. He joined the International Monetary Fund in Washington DC in 1990 and, as a member of the European Department, worked to assuage the fallout from the ERM crisis of 1992–1993. He switched to assisting post-socialist economies after 1994 and spent a year in Bosnia in 1996–1997. He was IMF Resident Representative to Croatia from 1997 to 2001 and then moved to Montenegro as an advisor to the Prime Minister. Having settled in Dubrovnik, he formally left the IMF in 2003 but still works as an economic advisor to governments in the region. He became professor of Economics at Dubrovnik International University in 2010.

Anthony George Phillips was born in Dublin and is currently resident in Buenos Aires, Argentina. He has worked in more than twenty countries on four continents. He is a journalist and analyst in political economics and ecology, and editor of the online magazine *DensidadRegional.org*. He is currently completing a Masters in Economics in the University of Buenos Aires on the subject of financing alternative energy policy and other alternative developments using autochthonous finance. He is a researcher on international public finance and debt-related issues in South America and holds a BSc in Mathematics, Information Sciences and Geology from University College Dublin.

Sam Roberts is the urban affairs correspondent of the *New York Times*. He is the co-author of a biography of Nelson Rockefeller, the author of *Who We Are: A Portrait of America* (1994), *Who We Are Now* (2004), *The Brother: The Untold Story of the Rosenberg Atom Spy Case* (2001) and *A Kind of Genius*, about making government work (2009). An anthology of his podcasts, titled *Only in New York*, was published in November 2009. He is the editor of *America's Mayor: John V.*

Lindsay and the Re-Invention of New York (2010). He is the host of the *New York Times Close Up*, an hour-long weekly news and interview programme on New York 1, the all-news cable channel.

Joseph E. Stiglitz is university professor at Columbia University, the winner of the 2001 Nobel Memorial Prize in Economics, and a lead author of the 1995 Intergovernmental Panel on Climate Change report, which shared the 2007 Nobel Peace Prize. He was chair of the US Council of Economic Advisors under President Clinton and chief economist and senior vice president of the World Bank from 1997 to 2000. In 1979 Stiglitz received the John Bates Clark Medal, awarded biennially to the American economist under the age of 40 who has made the most significant contribution to the subject. He was a Fulbright Scholar at Cambridge University, held the Drummond Professorship at All Souls College, Oxford, and has also taught at MIT, Yale, Stanford and Princeton. He is the author most recently of *Freefall: Free Markets and the Sinking of the Global Economy*.

Marc Tomljanovich is an associate professor of Economics at Drew University, a liberal arts college in the United States. Marc's research focuses on applied macroeconomic issues, including the impact of monetary policy structures on financial markets, the influence policy makers have on regional and national economic growth, and the effects of options listings on underlying financial instruments. Marc's work has appeared in numerous peer-reviewed journals, including *American Economic Review, Southern Economic Journal, Journal of Futures Markets, Empirical Economics* and *Contemporary Economic Policy*. Marc also is a regular weekly contributor to the *Wall Street Journal*. In 2006 he was the recipient of a National Sciences Foundation grant that helped fund an annual national workshop for macroeconomics research at liberal arts colleges. In 2010 he was chosen as teacher of the year at his institution.

Huginn Freyr Þorsteinsson is a philosopher of science and adjunct professor at the University of Akureyri. In the aftermath of Iceland's financial meltdown he became the adviser to Iceland's Minister of Finance from 2009 to 2011. He is currently the adviser to the Icelandic Minister of Economic Affairs and the Icelandic Minister of Fisheries and Agriculture.

John Walsh is the editor of *Business & Finance Magazine*. He took up this position in March 2008 after serving as deputy editor since 2006. Prior to joining *Business & Finance*, Walsh had been in London for over seven years. He trained as a journalist with the publishing firm Incisive Media. Subsequent positions included economics/markets reporter with Bridge/Reuters, sub-editor with the *Financial Times* and corporate correspondent with the energy news service Argus Media. Walsh has also worked for the BBC on its flagship current affairs programme *Panorama* and the *Today* programme on BBC Radio 4.

Introduction

Brian Lucey, Charles Larkin and Constantin Gurdgiev

Brian is professor of Finance, Trinity College Dublin and a columnist with the Irish Examiner. He blogs at brianmlucey.wordpress.com. Charles is research associate, School of Business, Trinity College Dublin. Constantin is adjunct professor, School of Business, Trinity College Dublin, and a director of St Columbanus AG, a Swiss asset management company. An internationally syndicated newspaper columnist, he blogs at trueeconomics.blogspot.com.

The Irish financial, fiscal, banking and economic crisis of 2008–? has already been a defining event in modern Irish history. For the first time the state was required to seek the assistance of the IMF and the ECB/EU, finding itself locked out of the financial markets. From a position as the poster-boy of Europe, a good example, it slipped in three short years to being a basket case, financially a horrible warning.

The essays collected in this book represent a cross-section of views on how, why, and on whose watch this crisis emerged, as well as a varied discussion on how best to emerge from it. The concentration here is primarily macro-financial. That is to say, we for the most part do not see essayists discussing the very real unemployment, competitiveness or other economic issues, except *en passant*. That is not to suggest that the authors are either unaware of or indifferent to these, rather that the focus here is on the interplay of the two aspects which precipitated the loss of Irish sovereignty: the banking and sovereign debt crises.

The overriding sense from reading the essays is of an economy on a knife edge. Given favourable economic circumstances, especially in regard to a variety of external factors which will influence exports, given a favourable political climate in the EU with regard to dealings with the legacy bank debt, and given domestic economic growth, then the debt levels which Ireland now faces are sustainable, in that a default is not probable. However, as will become clear, we consider, in reading these essays, these conditions are by no means guaranteed, and in that case restructuring of debts may become inevitable. Reading the essays by Gurdgiev and Coffey in the section on Ireland, one is struck by two factors. First, the authors are in broad agreement on the underlying macroeconomic trajectories and, second, they are at some variance on the implications. The sense of a narrow path, one side of which leads to default the other to a long grinding haul is palpable. Kinsella and Greene complete this section by examining the role that Europe has had and will likely have in the resolution of the Irish crisis. Both emphasise the central role of the bank guarantee and the role of the European context, and both conclude, reluctantly it seems, that given where we are now it is better to 'stay the course' than to default.

How we got here is discussed in the prologue to many of the essays, but a good overview of the particulars of the Irish case can be found in the scene-setting essay by Barrett, while the Irish crisis is contextualised in terms of previous research and international findings by Stiglitz. From Stiglitz we see that the Irish crisis can almost be seen as a 'stylised fact', with almost every feature found elsewhere in crises found here, while in other crises some but not all of these features are present. A clear reading of this will show the importance of a historically informed research sense in policy making. Barrett, for long a critic of excessive deficits and government inefficiency, has a strong scene-setting piece, where a plea for better governance is loud and consistent

What if we do default? Gurdgiev, in his discussion on Russia, Phillips on Argentina, Roberts on the New York fiscal crash of the mid-1970s and Tomljanovich in discussing municipalities all show that this is by no means costless. Increased poverty, reduced services, a longstanding scar on the financial psyche of the population, and political casualties are the common denominators of the short term after a default or crisis. In the medium and long term the removal of the debt burden can be beneficial, but again this requires the good governance discussed by Barrett to be implemented. An ongoing experiment in partial default, the Icelandic banking situation, is discussed by Byrne, with the conclusion that, akin to the possibly apocryphal story of the Chinese general's view on the effect of the French Revolution, 'it is too early to tell'. What this does show us however, is that there are always alternatives, there is never only one game in town, and that politicians of courage who are in tune with the desires of their voters can take nations through crisis situations which would derail other polities.

In the section on perspectives we find a wide variety of views. Mathews, who has been one of the foremost critics of how the banking crisis has been handled, renews his call for debt writedowns, noting the combined debt levels across public and private sectors are of a level that runs the risk of crushing the economy. Having commented for years from the perspective of a banking consultant, his views now have added force as those of a parliamentarian. Walsh critiques the way in which the media handled, or was collusive in ramping up, the bubble and muses on the ability of the Irish media to 'step up to the plate' in fostering a robust and honest debate on issues around debt and default. Dowling draws on behavioural and sociological perspectives on finance, noting that community and community strength are conducive to economic as well as personal well-being and suggesting that one unexpected upside of the crisis is likely to be a resurgence of this spirit. Deeter echoes in his discussion the concerns of Mathews regarding mortgage issues, and notes that the experience of other countries is, as noted in Phillips, that lending conditions, including mortgages, generally deteriorate. Brown draws on a lifetime's experience in the markets, laying out in very stark terms the way in which market traders perceive the Euro. He is not sanguine about the survival of the Euro in its present form but again the common theme of the book emerges

– default (which in his analysis would be alongside any breakup of the Euro) is neither simple nor painless. O'Callaghan details the extreme pragmatisim of the IMF in his analysis, concluding that debt discussions are not a morality play and that any decisions on default or restructuring must be conducted with the ultimate aim of rapid restoration of normal economic activity. Finally, Ganley draws lessons from early US federal history, and suggests that the banking and federalist perspectives of Alexander Hamilton provide a template for an ever closer union in Europe.

Overall we trust that this book of essays will provide both an overview of the debate on the Irish crisis and stimulate further discussion. As editors we have individual viewpoints on the default versus restructuring versus working out process. What is important in Ireland now is that viewpoints are aired, and discussed in a calm and respectful manner, and that the political system becomes more engaged with the debate. We hope this book will assist in that process.

SETTING THE SCENE

Debt, Crises and Default from a Parliamentary Perspective

Sean Barrett

Sean is a professor of economics at Trinity College Dublin, represents Trinity College, University of Dublin in the Irish upper house of parliament (the Seanad) and is whip of the university senators in parliament.

Introduction

The membership of parliament in Ireland changed radically in the 2011 elections following the International Monetary Fund/European Union/European Central Bank (IMF/EU/ECB) bail-in late 2010. Of the 166 seats in the Dáil or lower house, 77 ~~ent)~~ were held in late 2011 by members who were not in the ~~previous~~ parliament. Of the 60 seats in the Seanad or upper house, 42 (70 per cent) were held in late 2011 by members who were not in the previous Seanad.

The crises in banking and the public finances illustrated by the bank rescue of 2008 and the national bailout of 2010 resulted in the reduction of seats held by the outgoing government from a majority of 83 (December 2010) in the previous Dáil to 19 seats in late 2011 held by the Fianna Fáil party and the elimination of its coalition partner, the Green Party, from any parliamentary representation. Fianna Fáil had dominated Irish public life for eight decades before the 2011 election.

The lessons for government in Ireland from the years 2008–2011 are that capture of politicians by the construction sector for over a decade leading to the property bubble and the capture of the government by the banking sector in 2008 are now opposed by the overwhelming majority of the public. The election results are loud and clear.

The lessons for governance are more complex and largely unaddressed. Widespread reforms are required if Ireland is to be rescued from its massive debt burden. Failures of corporate governance in the private and public sectors require institutional reform, and progress to date has been minimal. The main emphasis to date has been on solving the Irish debt problem by increasing taxation rather than addressing either expenditure or institutional reform issues. Table 1.1 shows that the adjustment of the current budget over the IMF/EU/ECB rescue period is dominated by tax increases. There are legitimate fears that by the end of the rescue period the institutions and policies which caused the crisis will remain unreformed. The massive rejection of the politicians associated with the Irish economic collapse will have been futile.

Table 1.1: Current Budget Adjustment, Ireland, 2011–2015 (€ billions)

	2011	2015	Change
Tax revenue	34.5	43.3	+8.8
Net current expenditure	48.7	46.5	-2.2
Current budget balance	-11.7	-1.7	-10.0

Note: Non-tax revenue is forecast to fall from €2.6 billion to €1.5 billion during this period
Source: Department of Finance, *Medium Term Fiscal Statement*, November 2011, Table 3.2.

Capture and Lobbying

On the night of 29/30 September 2008 four Irish banks and two building societies secured government guarantees to underwrite their entire network. Murphy and Devlin[1] wrote that 'Guaranteeing the banks was an extraordinary step. It meant that if any bank discovered it had unmanageable bad loans, the taxpayer would be liable.'

The bank guarantee was heavily criticised because of the costs involved, the failure to address moral hazard, the failure to consult other members of the EU and the Eurozone, the failure to address the causes of the financial problems of Irish banks and their failed regulatory regime, and the failure to convene a normal Cabinet meeting on the guarantee.

The Cabinet meeting was incorporeal on the basis that a meeting of all ministers could not be convened in time. This latter excuse is unconvincing. Several ministers lived within a few miles of Government Buildings. Ireland is a small country with a good motorway network. The government was represented in its dealings with the lobbying bankers by the Taoiseach, the Minister for Finance, the Attorney General and the Governor of the Central Bank.

Byrne and Þornsteinsson[2] state, 'the capture of the state by an oligopolistic financial sector, due to excessive risk taking without consequence, was complemented by the failure of political institutions to anticipate the collapse.' The decision of the overnight incorporeal Cabinet meeting to bail out the banks without full Cabinet participation is merely another lapse in scrutiny and checks and balances in Irish public finances. Ireland has a rigid parliamentary whip system in which dissenters, three in 2011, are expelled from parliamentary parties. The Department of Finance lacked the competences required to assess banking policy. The Wright Report[3] found that only 7 per cent of the staff of the Department had a qualification at Master's level or above in Economics. The post of Governor of the Central Bank was filled from the Department of Finance repeatedly during the build-up to the crisis in 2008. Cooper[4] notes that 'throughout 2008 and early 2009 both the then Central Bank governor and financial regulator publicly defended the lending policies of Irish banks on many occasions, endorsed the strength of their balance sheets and decried suggestions that the banks might have walked themselves into trouble.'

Kinsella[5] notes that 'the liabilities of the banking system in Ireland are roughly four times the yearly income of the nation.'

Phillips[6] estimates that 'the end result of the rescue was the generation by various mechanisms, including bank guarantees, of what Standard and Poor's estimate at €90 billion in new sovereign debt (counting likely future losses in NAMA [the National Asset Management Agency]).'

Banks and Borrowing

As Mathews[7] points out, 'at 494 per cent of national income, Irish combined debt levels are the most crushing in the world.' This burden comprises, as a proportion of national income respectively, government debt at 137 per cent, household debt at 147 per cent and corporate debt at 210 per cent. As Phillips states:

> Reckless financing in the Irish construction industry combined with a lack of enforcement of national banking regulations with cheap Eurozone credit financed twenty years of Irish economic expansion .... When the bubble burst the overextended construction sector collapsed, defaulting on its loans. This destabilised the Irish financial sector, resulting in the insolvency of almost all Irish private banks.[8]

The Economist House Price Index 1997–2007 showed Ireland with the highest house price index increase, at 251 per cent, or almost double the average for the fourteen observations in the Organisation for Economic Co-Operation and Development (OECD) countries surveyed.[9] The highest price rise in Ireland was for second-hand houses in Dublin, from an average of €104,000 in 1997 to €512,000 in 2007. Ireland illustrates the quote from Paul Volcker in Roberts' chapter:[10] '"we borrow and borrow and continually spend and, so long as people are willing to lend, there is not sufficient pressure to do something about it in a timely way."'

Ireland illustrates also the consequences of easily available borrowing. Fiscal discipline is undermined. The distinction between capital and current spending becomes blurred and items are labelled 'capital' in order to bypass a current budget constraint. Capital expenditure appraisal techniques, hardly at the frontier of economics today, were notably absent from the large Irish public capital programme.[11] Ireland experienced the problems of both Niskanen's bureaucracy and Baumol's disease.

The *Report of the Special Group on Public Service Numbers and Expenditure Programmes*[12] (better known as the Bord Snip Nua Report) found an increase of 82 per cent in higher management staff in the civil service between 1997 and 2007 compared to a 27 per cent increase in civil service staff as a whole. The Irish system of social partnership increased the governance roles of senior civil servants, public service trade union leaders and public expenditure lobbyists at the expense of parliament. Centralised wage bargaining under social partnership increased the costs of public services by neglecting productivity increases in return for increases in public pay, and by extra awards for senior public servants through a now discredited system known as bench-marking, under which public pay at the higher levels in Ireland exceeded that in the countries from which Ireland sought rescue finance in 2010.

Lack of discipline in the Irish public finances is illustrated in the account by Brendan Drumm of his five-year term as the first chief executive of the Health Service Executive: 'Between 1997 and 2005, Ireland's annual health service budget tripled from €3.7 billion to €11.5 billion. Despite this, in 2006 Ireland was ranked 25th among the 26 countries included in the Euro Health Consumer Index'.[13] Over a twenty-year period the number of health service staff doubled to 112,000 in 2007. Problems of productivity and value for money were not confined to direct employees however, but extended to successful rent seeking by suppliers to the sector such as pharmacists and drug companies. Efforts to reduce drug costs were opposed by the industry and 'by politicians from all political parties' in 2007:

> It seemed to go unnoticed that the Health Service Executive team was representing the interest of the taxpayers in trying to reduce expenditure on drugs, which was out of line with most comparable

countries and which was resulting in a reduction in other frontline services.[14]

The European Dimension

Ireland and the other peripheral states illustrate the basic design faults in the Eurozone project, such as the lack of an exit mechanism, the one-size-fits-all prescription and the vulnerability of small economies to massive capital flows from the larger states. An early enthusiast for the Euro, Jacques Delors, is quoted in late 2011 saying that 'the Euro project was doomed from the start'.[15] Ireland lost the exchange rate and interest rates as policy instruments. The exchange rate was used successfully in the 1990s in the recovery from the debt crisis in the 1980s. Ireland's interest rate needs were contrary to those of the larger German economy, but the rates themselves were in tune with German requirements, and so were countercyclical in the Irish case. The warnings of Friedman on the adverse consequences of joining the Euro for Ireland[16] were ignored. Ireland joined the Euro as a full employment solvent country but had to be rescued in 2010 and as of January 2012 has over 14 per cent unemployment. Ireland also failed to face the issue of joining the Euro while its major trading partner, the United Kingdom, remained outside. Ireland also failed to understand the impact on Irish asset prices of capital flows from the larger EU economies. The EU before the single currency made substantial fiscal transfers to Ireland in structural funds and agricultural price supports. These promoted rent seeking by Ireland from the EU and weakened the incentive for balancing the public sector budget. The prospect of 'free money from Brussels' diverted Ireland from sound public finance. For example, EU money played a large role in spending €1 billion a year on FÁS, the state training body, in an economy which was at full employment. As Europe moves away from a common market and towards an extra layer of government the question arises whether extra government contributes to economic welfare or adds to overhead costs. Ganley's recommendation that we 'take the calculated but worthwhile risk to fully unite in a demo-cratic and federal union, or we will see this project fall apart' is therefore a high-risk strategy.[17] Europe operated successfully for several decades as a common market based on free trade rather than extra layers of governance.

Parliament and the Public Finances

Ireland illustrates many of the difficulties caused by laxity in the operation of national finances. Weak public expenditure controls lead to an expanded bureaucracy which is both expensive and difficult to reduce as required over the economic cycle. Weak public expenditure controls increase the rewards for lobbyists and rent seekers. The ease with which the bank lobby imposed massive costs on Ireland relative to GDP by securing the bank guarantee in September 2008 ranks as one of the most successful lobbying exercises ever. A further cost of weak public expendi-ture controls is the diversion of the banking sector from the skills of risk assessment of investment in the market economy to risk-free lending to governments and bodies with govern-ment guarantees. The success of lobby efforts was in part due to the lack of proper scrutiny of the political class by voters. The presentation of parliament to the citizens in the print media is dominated by image impressions to the virtual exclusion of matters of substance. Contact between the citizens and the many new members of parliament is more likely through social rather than print media.

Walsh criticises 'the failure of the media to put any brake on the frothy excesses of the boom years' and cites the case that 'most financial journalism is now PR driven. The news agenda is shaped by journalists rewriting press releases'.[18] In the boom years the Irish print media gained advertising revenues from the property price spiral. Many investigative journalists in Ireland continue to join PR companies in their later careers.

Parliament must also respond to the growth of the power of the bureaucracy. The chairman John McGuinness of the Committee on Public Accounts writes that:

> [O]ver the past 10 years or so, for various reasons, some to do with
> corruption, power has slipped through the fingers of politicians into
> the hands of the unelected, who devised and were allowed to oper-
> ate strategies to ensure they had to answer to the Dáil as little as
> possible. It is only in recent years that scandals in State and semi-
> State bodies have revealed the true cost of lack of governance and
> accountability.[19]

A Fiscal Responsibility Agenda

Ireland's debt problems must be tackled across the board. Fiscal
responsibility legislation must limit the borrowing powers of
governments. Borrowing is a tax on future generations not now
represented in parliament and they therefore require legal and
constitutional protection from governments borrowing now for
short-term political gains.

A register of lobbyists and their visits to government departments must be maintained by each house of parliament and
updated daily. The full Cabinet must deliberate on large appli-
cations for state intervention rather than the subgroup at the
incorporeal meeting of 29/30 September 2008. A two-thirds
parliamentary majority should be required in the case of large
rescue operations such as the Irish bank rescue and party whips
should not apply in such debates. There should be a new grade of
economist in the Irish public service in order to reduce the potential for control of public servants by lobby groups where public
servants lack the economic expertise to rebut lobbyists. Whis-
tle-blowers who report malpractice in public spending should
have legal protection in the wider public interest. Parliament
must assert control over the bureaucracy of the public service by
requiring measures of output and parliamentary evaluation of all
current spending programmes.

Each spending proposal must include an evaluation of the
results of past spending in the field and projections of future
returns from additional expenditure. Ireland requires greater

standards of accountability in corporate governance in both the public and private sectors. Senior bureaucrats should have a limited right of audience at parliamentary committees but should not retain the present system of passing notes to ministers while technically not present in parliament. The practice of senior civil servants passing notes or whispered advice to ministers in parliament – government by ventriloquist – should cease. A Central Office of Project Evaluation (COPE) should assume responsibility for all capital expenditure from spending departments. Its reports should be published at least one year before any expenditure is incurred and open to full independent scrutiny by parliament. Appointments of secretaries general in government departments and to state boards should be subject to parliamentary scrutiny. Citizens must have direct access to parliamentary debates rather than through image-based reporting. Proposals to transfer even more sovereignty to the EU should be put on hold until it is apparent that Brussels has any advantages over national governments in terms of efficiency and accountability.

The context for Ireland is that the state is spending more than the taxable capacity of the country and the willingness of foreign lending bodies to finance. Sam Roberts captures this context on pages 185–186: '"We didn't change the way we provide public services …. We simply shrunk the system."' The Culliton Review of Industrial Policy in Ireland decided not to endorse any extra spending as requested by various lobby groups.[20] 'Honey, I shrunk the agencies' was the slogan used then in a movement to restore sound public finances. That imperative is now essential.

Ireland has more new parliamentarians in both houses than in any previous parliament. We new parliamentary brooms must now sweep away the debris from widespread failures of governance which brought first the banks and second the entire country to bankruptcy. That is why we have elections.

Endnotes

[1] David Murphy and Martina Devlin (2009) *Banksters*, Dublin: Hachette Books Ireland, p. 7.

2   Chapter 8 of this book, 'Iceland: The Accidental Hero', p. 146.

3   Rob Wright (2010) *Strengthening the Capacity of the Department of Finance*, Dublin: Stationery Office, p. 44.

4   Matt Cooper (2009) *Who Really Runs Ireland*, Dublin: Penguin Ireland, p. 207.

5   Chapter 5 of this book, 'A very Irish Default, or When Is a Default Not a Default?', p. 95.

6   Chapter 9 of this book, 'Irish Public Debt: A View through the Lens of the Argentine Default', p. 154.

7   Chapter 15 of this book, 'A Politician's Perspective on Debt and Default', p. 244.

8   Chapter 9 of this book, p. 149.

9   'Houses Built on Sand', *The Economist*, 15 September 2007.

10   Chapter 10 of this book, 'Coring out the Big Apple: New York's Fiscal Crisis', p. 186.

11   Sean D. Barrett (2006) 'Evaluating Transport 21: Some Economic Aspects', *Quarterly Economic Commentary*, Winter, pp. 36–58.

12   Special Group on Public Service Numbers and Expenditure Programmes (2009) *Report of the Special Group on Public Service Numbers and Expenditure Programmes*, Dublin: Stationery Office, p. 43.

13   Brendan Drumm (2011) *The Challenge of Change: Putting Patients Before Providers*, Dublin: Orpen Press, p. 137.

14   *Ibid.*

15   James Kirkup (2011) 'Euro Doomed from Start, says Jacques Delors', *Daily Telegraph*, 3 December 2011.

16   Conor O'Cleary (2001) 'US Economist Expounds on Great Euro Mistake', *Irish Times*, 5 September 2001.

17   Chapter 18 of this book, 'A Political Activist and Businessperson's Perspective on Debt and Default', p. 274.

18   Chapter 16 of this book, 'A Financial Journalist's Perspective on Debt and Default', p. 250.

19   John McGuinness and Naoise Nunn (2010) *The House Always Wins*, Dublin: Gill and Macmillan, p. 209.

20   Jim Culliton (1992) *A Time for Change: Industrial Policy for the 1990s*, Report of the Industrial Policy Review Group, Dublin: Stationery Office.

2

Crises and Contagion: A Survey[1]

Anzhela Knyazeva, Diana Knyazeva and Joseph Stiglitz

Anzhela and Diana are assistant professors of Finance at the Simon School of Business, University of Rochester. Their corporate finance research has been most recently published in the Journal of Financial Economics. *Joseph is a Nobel Prize-winning economist and a university professor at Columbia University. He is a prolific researcher, commentator and author, whose books have been translated into more than thirty-five languages. His most recent book is* Freefall: America, Free Markets, and the Sinking of the World Economy *(2010). In 2011,* Time *named Stiglitz one of the 100 most influential people in the world.*

Introduction

Financial and economic crises and contagion are the subjects of a vast body of macroeconomic and finance research. Many recent interventions by national governments and multilateral institutions, such as the International Monetary Fund and the European Central Bank, sought to stem the spread of contagion. In September 2008, motivated by concerns about a run on the banking sector, the Irish government provided a two-year guarantee for the debt and deposits of major Irish financial institutions such as Anglo Irish Bank, AIB, Bank of Ireland, and several others. Major Irish banks, including Anglo Irish, had been experiencing deposit outflows and short-selling by institutional investors concerned about the spread of global financial turmoil and the crisis in the Irish property market. At the time financial regulators deemed it to be an illiquidity, not an insolvency, issue (*Wall Street Journal*, 2010).[2] The introduction of a government guarantee to the banking sector was expected to stem the confidence crisis and signal to capital markets a reduced chance of default, avoiding costly bank failures. The magnitude of the bad loan problem came to light in subsequent quarters. Amidst widening losses on property loans, the Irish government nationalised Anglo Irish Bank and subsequently provided capital to the bank. The Irish government formed the National Asset Management Agency (NAMA), which took land and construction loans off bank balance sheets in an effort to shore up major banks.[3] Over the next two years, the government would inject an estimated total of €46.3 billion into the banking system, including €29.3 billion into Anglo Irish Bank (*Wall Street Journal*, 2011). The costs of the bank sector rescue led Ireland to negotiate an ECB/IMF bailout. The final tally of bailout costs is likely to be larger due to recessionary pressures stemming from fiscal austerity measures (Stiglitz, 2010a).

Before assessing the effectiveness of interventions or designing a global financial architecture that limits the spread of contagion yet takes advantage of the benefits of integration, we need a rigorous understanding of the mechanisms behind crises and contagion. Below we provide a survey of the existing theories of financial crises and contagion. We conclude by discussing the implications of contagion for economies with open capital markets, illustrated by recent global financial crises in East Asia, the US and Ireland.

Economic crises are defined as a sudden downturn in the level of economic activity, accompanied by an increase in unemployment rate and bankruptcies. Financial crises are typically associated with a sudden fall in the exchange rate or stock market prices. Banking crises are characterised by credit contraction, increase in defaults, and even bank runs and bankruptcies. Typically, the various crises are related (both temporally and causally): an economic crisis (whatever the cause) typically leads to a stock market downturn and a weakening of the exchange rate; and banking and financial crises typically lead to economic crises.[4]

This survey is written from the vantage point of hindsight provided by the recent global financial crises. Several earlier theories of crises provide little insight into those crises, while other explanations have proven to be more relevant. In any case, the recent global financial turmoil provides a new lens through which one can see crises more generally. For instance, standard interpretations of the East Asian crisis emphasised weak institutions and a lack of transparency, and suggested American institutions as an alternative model, which presumably would reduce, if not eliminate, the incidence of crises. We now realise that whatever is meant by 'transparency' and 'good institutions' is more complicated than was widely thought at the time; in particular, it became evident that there were major deficiencies in governance and in transparency in American financial institutions, both the private institutions and the public ones that were supposed to regulate them. While some commentators had predicted a crisis, based on persistent global imbalances, the recent financial crises in the US and Ireland were not caused by those imbalances, but at least precipitated by the bursting of the housing bubble. For years the Celtic Tiger growth had been backed by solid fundamentals, including investments in infrastructure and human capital, and productivity growth. Like the US and many other markets, Ireland also witnessed a property boom facilitated by low interest rates and easy access to bank loans. As long as investors pursued leveraged bets on the real estate sector, helping to sustain the growth in residential and commercial property prices, default rates on loans remained low. Consequently, banks enjoyed rising equity valuations and low yield spreads. However, as interest rates increased and investor sentiment weakened with the onset of the global financial crisis, the property market collapsed, bank loan losses mounted and major banks became undercapitalised.

Standard models based on previous crises attempting to predict vulnerability to crises would have suggested that the US and Western Europe were not vulnerable. This is, in a sense, in keeping with the long tradition of crises, where each crisis seems attributable to factors that were not singled out as 'explaining' the previous. Indeed, according to the conventional wisdom, where flawed macroeconomic and monetary policies were often cited as playing a key role in the generation of crises, the US and Europe were given high marks.

There is a large literature on crises and contagion. This survey focuses on the theory, and in particular on how to reconcile crises with standard neoclassical theory and macroeconomics. Crises present a number of puzzles for standard economic theory. While some of the models discussed below resolve some of these puzzles, none to date does so in a fully satisfactory way, or at least in a way which is consistent with much of prevailing finance and macroeconomics:

- A distinguishing feature of most financial crises is a sudden change in the exchange rate. While outside observers may have expressed continuing worries, say about an overvalued exchange rate, the exchange rate adjustment process does not appear to work smoothly (in contrast to standard forward-looking models with rational expectations, where individuals gradually revise expectations in light of the steady inflow of information; typically, there is no new information of a magnitude that should have led to a readjustment of exchange rates of the magnitudes observed). This is an example of the more general puzzle of crises: large changes in outcomes that seem incommensurate with the scale of changes in the underlying state variables (see Stiglitz, 2011; United Nations, 2010).

- Standard models suggest that diversification – the spreading of risk around the world – should have led to a more stable economic system. The 2008 crisis suggested the contrary: diversification helped spread the crisis. There is a growing consensus that diversification may reduce the exposure to small crises, but increase that to larger ones. As more countries liberalised their capital markets, global capital and interbank linkages became more prevalent. Countries around the world experienced spill-overs from the US financial crisis. Irish banks had relied heavily on global interbank loans prior to the crisis. When short-term interbank lending froze up in the third quarter of 2008, Irish banks faced significant funding constraints.

- Conventional theories imply that even in markets where there is some irrationality, all that is required to make markets work well (to make markets reasonably stable and efficient) is that there be enough (and enough may be a relative notion) rational market participants.[5] The empirical evidence (buttressed by this crisis) is that rational participants exploiting the irrationality of others may make the markets highly volatile.

- After the crisis there is a focus on contagion – on how interdependence can lead a crisis to move from one country to another; but before the crisis there is an emphasis on the benefits of diversification, on how interdependence enhances stability. None of the prevailing models integrates coherently these opposite forces (with the exception of Stiglitz, 2010b, 2010c).

- Policy frameworks have been equally incoherent. The standard response to contagious diseases is quarantine – the equivalent of capital controls. But many in the international community have resisted the imposition of capital controls, even in the event of a crisis.

- Policy decisions have often entailed interventions in the market that are announced to be (or believed to be) temporary, but it is argued that they will have long-run effects, shifting the equilibrium in the countries suffering from contagion. Why such temporary interventions would have long-run effects is often not clear (Stiglitz, 1999a).

A central thesis of this survey is that understanding crises requires an understanding of market imperfections – and especially of the constraints, for instance, on borrowing, imposed by imperfect information – and how those market imperfections interact with irrationalities on the part of market participants and imperfections in the regulatory environment.

In the discussion below, we follow the literature on crises through its various stages, motivated by the series of crises the world has experienced in the last three decades. In retrospect, however, there is a basic taxonomy:

- Models in which the shock giving rise to the crisis is exogenous, and those in which it is endogenous

- Models in which markets are fully rational, and those in which they are not

- Models in which there are multiple momentary equilibria, and models in which there is a unique momentary equilibrium

- Models in which there is a unique steady state (long-run) equilibrium, and models in which there are multiple long-run equilibria

The logic of crises is simple: if there are multiple momentary equilibria, then the economy can suddenly switch from one to the other without any large change in any state variable (other than beliefs, which themselves are treated as state variables). If there are multiple steady state equilibria, then a shock to the state variables of the economy (whether endogenous or exogenous) can act as a tipping point, bringing the economy into a different 'orbit of attraction'.

So too, the mathematics of crises is simple: under the convexity assumptions made in most economic models diversification spreads risks and reduces their impact. But, as Stiglitz (2010b, 2010c) points out, non-convexities are pervasive (bankruptcy, learning, etc.), and with non-convexities diversification can amplify systemic risk.

This paper is divided into three sections. The first surveys the literature on what causes crises; the second on contagion and the effect of interdependence in amplifying crises; the third on the role of government. Not surprisingly, theories which stress the efficiency and stability of markets look to government as the source of the problem; stability is attained by government not interfering in the natural workings of the market. Theories which see the economy as inherently inefficient and unstable look to government to help correct market failures.

Ascertaining which of these theories is correct is not easy, and beyond the task of this short survey. One of the reasons for the difficulties is that there are elements of many of the alternative approaches present in every crisis. No one could look at the recession of 2008 or the Irish banking crisis without noting market irrationalities. But does that mean we could not have had a crisis in the absence of such irrationalities? The major shock was an endogenous one – a housing bubble; the shock was not an exogenous event ('a once in a hundred year flood'), but there were exogenous (at least to the economic system) events that perhaps could have triggered a major downturn, reflected in the spike in oil and food prices.

What Causes Financial Crises?

The earliest approaches to the onset of currency and financial crises – the first generation of crisis models – focused on fundamental macroeconomic imbalances and adherence to a monetary policy incompatible with the maintenance of an exchange rate peg (for example, Krugman, 1979).[6]

The 1994–1995 Mexican crisis led policy makers to ask what accounted for the sudden onset of a market panic. Although fundamental macroeconomic problems, including overvalued exchange rates, current account deficits and rising short-term foreign currency government debt, were present, the peso's devaluation alone did not quickly stem the crisis.[7] The crisis (like many before it) posed several questions: (a) why did it occur when it did? The fundamental imbalances had long been recognised, and (b) the large immediate fall in the exchange rate, which many thought should have equilibrated the market – leading to what might be viewed as an equilibrium exchange rate – didn't stem the crisis. Why not?

The peso crisis led researchers to turn their attention to information flows and trader behaviour around market panics, which
formed the second generation of theories of currency crises (for
example, Sachs, Tornell and Velasco (1996); and Agenor and
Masson (1999); and more informal discussions by Furman and
Stiglitz (1998); and Stiglitz (2010b)).

Multiple Equilibria

The 'second generation' literature explored one possible explanation for the sudden large change in the exchange rate (beyond
what can be explained by changes in the shocks to the economy,
including new information) and the failure of the exchange rate
to equilibrate.

The peso crisis precipitated a massive loss of confidence in the
currency and a full-on market panic. Though the importance of
confidence is often mentioned, traditional macro models do not
include independent variables that quantify confidence. Those
that have tried to do so show that confidence can have significant
explanatory powers, but few models incorporate confidence in a
formal way.

One way of doing so is to assume that there are multiple equilibria.[8] Models of multiple equilibria (sunspots) that formally
incorporated 'confidence' suggest that a change in confidence
can move the economy from one equilibrium to another. In the
case of debt crises, Brazil (and perhaps Greece) provide examples: with low interest rates the country can easily service the
debt, so it is rational that interest rates are low; but if interest
rates become high, the country cannot service the debt, and it is
rational that the interest rate is high to compensate for the risk of
default (Greenwald and Stiglitz, 2003).The idea of a self-fulfilling market panic originated in the context of a run on a bank.
In Diamond and Dybvig (1983), banks have relatively illiquid
assets; in other words, if a bank has to sell assets on short notice
it sacrifices a part of the asset value in the process. Every period
some customers withdraw money from the bank to meet their

spending needs. In a perfect world, all others keep their money in the bank. However, customers are aware that withdrawals will not be honoured if the bank runs out of money (no deposit insurance scheme exists). As they observe other customers' withdrawals, they could decide to take their own money out as well in anticipation of a bank run. Such self-fulfilling panics can leave everybody worse off.

Market Frictions

A third generation of models of crises focused on how various market frictions contribute to the onset of a financial crisis, amplifying (rather than dampening) shocks (for example, Kiyotaki and Moore, 1997; Caballero and Krishnamurthy, 2001; and Mendoza, 2010). Moreover, in these models what would normally be equilibrating adjustments to the shocks can be destabilising. While the importance attributed to specific financial frictions varies from model to model, a common theme in these theories of financial crises is the role of market imperfections in explaining both the fast pace of diffusion and the large extent of amplification of negative economic shocks, providing a recipe for a sudden crash.

Market frictions (information asymmetries, costly state verification, costs of contract enforcement, and bankruptcy (see Greenwald and Stiglitz, 1993a)) limit the extent to which firms can use equity or hedging contracts.[9] As a result, firms have to rely on debt, while remaining exposed to risk, and firms act in a risk-averse manner.[10] Optimal financial structures lead effectively to constraints on debt–equity ratios, so that a decrease in firm equity reduces its ability to borrow. The macroeconomic consequences of these micro imperfections are severe, with investment (including inventory accumulation), for instance, expanding in booms by a multiple of the change in equity (the financial accelerator), and the converse happening in downturns (for example, Greenwald and Stiglitz, 1993a; Bernanke, Gertler and Gilchrist, 1996). Not only are the effects of shocks amplified, but they can persist over time.

Other imperfections in financial markets can similarly trigger crises. Many borrowers face collateral constraints that limit borrowing capacity. Contract enforcement is complicated and lenders have only partial information. A collateral requirement can act both as a selection and incentive device (Stiglitz and Weiss, 1986) and can help manage default risk. For example, in Kiyotaki and Moore (1997) creditors cannot force repayment or seize the borrower's human capital, so borrowers can strategically default on the debt. Collateral-based borrowing constraints tied to the value of the firm's real assets become necessary.[11] As a result, the maximum amount of debt the firm can take on, assuming collateral of a given value, is limited. Even a temporary shock to the value of collateral translates into reduced borrowing ability. Thus a shock sets in motion a feedback effect that decreases investment and the rate of growth for several years. Credit-constrained firms are forced to reduce investment, resulting in further declines in net worth, which in turn lead to tighter borrowing constraints and additional investment cuts.

Greenwald and Stiglitz (1993a) explain how with unindexed debt contracts a macroeconomic shock (for example, monetary policy tightening) that leads to lower than expected prices results in decreased equity, with real effects that are amplified by the financial accelerator. Non-convexities in the relationship between equity and investment also imply that a distributional shock (for example, an increase in the price of oil) has macroeconomic consequences, with the contraction in the losing sector exceeding the expansion in the benefiting sector.[12] These financial constraints cause one-time shocks to persist and result in widespread insolvencies.

The banking system itself can amplify especially large downturns. Banks can be viewed as highly leveraged firms (Greenwald and Stiglitz, 2003), so that, when their equity is diminished, they reduce their lending. Institutional features and regulatory design can increase the extent to which this is prevalent. Excessive reliance on capital adequacy requirements can result in a built-in destabiliser; countercyclical prudential regulations or appropriately designed policies of regulatory forbearance may be able to offset the effects (see Helmann, Murdoch and Stiglitz (2000) and the various essays in Griffith-Jones, Ocampo and Stiglitz (2010)). Regulation of maturity and currency mismatches in banks and the firms to which they lend can reduce the vulnerability of the banking system – and thereby the economy – to shocks.

During the Irish financial crisis, property developers facing declining real estate valuations were unable to refinance existing loans or obtain new loans. Asset write downs resulting from losses on property loans constrained the banks' ability to raise new financing, in turn limiting loan provision. Business and consumer credit reductions exerted downward pressure on the rate of new investment and consumption growth.

Other institutional rules and policies (in both home and foreign countries), such as the weakening of automatic stabilisers (for example, safety nets), can make countries more sensitive to shocks. Delegating authority of risk evaluation to rating agencies and imposing constraints on what pensions can invest in can contribute to volatility – a sharp downgrade by the rating agencies (as happened in Thailand in 1997) can precipitate a crisis (see Ferri, Liu and Stiglitz, 1999). In Ireland and other GIIPS (Greece, Ireland, Italy, Portugal and Spain) countries, downgrades of sovereign and bank credit ratings limited capital market access, causing a credit contraction and exacerbating recessionary pressures.

Systemic Crises

In the third generation models just described, financial constraints (operating through collateral requirements, debt–equity constraints or real balance effects), especially in the context of imperfectly indexed debt contracts, can lead to the amplification and persistence of shocks. While research on systemic shocks began well before the Great Recession, the recession has enhanced impetus for this work (see, for example, Haldane, 2009;

and Haldane and May, 2011). Greenwald and Stiglitz (2003) and Allen and Gale (2000) describe bankruptcy cascades – how the bankruptcy of one firm can lead to that of others. The extent to which this occurs depends on financial interdependence. Pecuniary externalities arising in the presence of incomplete risk markets and imperfect information imply that the set of privately profitable contracts will not in general be socially optimal (Greenwald and Stiglitz, 1986). In fact, managerial contracts implicitly based on relative performance can lead to excessively correlated risk taking (Nalebuff and Stiglitz, 1983). Moreover, there are strong incentives, especially for large banks, to become excessively interdependent and correlated, so that in bad outcomes they will be bailed out (Stiglitz, 2010a; Acharya and Yorulmazer, 2008; etc.).

Market and Individual Irrationalities

In the original Diamond–Dybvig (1983) model, customers have no information about the bank's default risk. In real life, some depositors could have information about the bank's financial health. However, even when customers are able to assess the bank's financial condition, they sometimes end up ignoring their private knowledge and copying the actions of others, which is known as herding (see, for example, Banerjee, 1992; and Bikhchandani, Hirshleifer and Welch, 1992). As a result, bank runs or sudden market crashes can occur even when only a few investors or depositors possess negative information. Such herding may be rational.

In addition to the rational reasons for herding, many have argued that irrationality plays a crucial role in both the onset and the creation of the conditions for and the spread of financial crises (for example, Stiglitz, 1999b, 2004; and Hirshleifer and Teoh, 2009). For instance, as Kindleberger, Aliber and Solow (2005) note, changes in the sentiment of borrowers and creditors over time can explain the well-known cyclical nature of bank lending. (Such changes in sentiment also play an important role in Minsky cycles and credit crises.) Increases in loan supply can be attributed to optimism in good times, while decreases in credit can be linked to pessimism in bad times. Irrational investor pessimism causes rapid declines in lending, asset prices and exchange rates, typically seen during crises. Investor irrationality can stem from the inability to correctly process available data, compounded by behavioural biases that cause investors to make suboptimal decisions based on the beliefs they have formed (see Barberis and Thaler (2003) for a detailed survey).[13] The resulting overreaction to economic news can cause small negative shocks to trigger large-scale market panics that spread across national borders.

When bubbles break (or when panics lead to irrationally depressed prices), there are large real balance effects and the other effects delineated above arising from the financial accelerator, and these can give rise to a macroeconomic crisis. The devastating consequences of a burst housing market bubble have been seen in the recent US and Irish financial crises.

In open economies with firms that have substantial foreign currency debt (with mismatches in the currency and maturity structure of assets and liabilities), large changes in exchange rates similarly can have dramatic effects on equity values or lead to large increases in collateral requirements, precipitating a crisis, for instance, as firms make large cutbacks in investment. During the 1997–1998 Asian financial crisis, firms with foreign currency liabilities and home currency assets were vulnerable to depreciation of the home currency (Stiglitz, 2001; Cespedes, Chang and Velasco, 2004).

In standard dynamic stochastic general equilibrium models the sources of crises are exogenous shocks, but the most important crises involve the breaking of bubbles, most of which can be attributed to internal market dynamics. Housing prices, for instance, rise to the point where further increases are not sustainable given the constraints imposed by the institutional and regulatory system (even with mild forbearance). When home prices can no longer increase at the rate that has been anticipated, demand for housing decreases suddenly with the follow-on effects described above. This pattern, repeated historically, presents a challenge to rational expectations models. There are two possibilities. One is that with short-sighted market participants the economy can evolve in a manner that is consistent with inter-temporal arbitrage equations for a very long time, before a (say, non-negativity) constraint becomes binding (for example, Shell and Stiglitz, 1967). The other is that there is uncertainty about the date of unravelling of the process, and a bubble can then be consistent with rational expectations for an extended period of time (Abreu and Brunnermeier, 2003).

We suspect though that it is challenging to fully reconcile bubbles with perfect rationality. In the US, Irish and most other bubbles (Gurdgiev, Lucey, Mac an Bhaird and Roche-Kelly (2011) discuss the Irish property bubble), large numbers of investors recognised that there was a very high probability of a bubble (and took short bets), even if others believed it was not the case. The question is, why couldn't those who knew better correct the market irrationality? Note that the analysis of such situations requires the construction of models in which individuals have different beliefs, and even as they extract information from the market, they do not converge to the same beliefs. Recent models focusing on the consequences of short sale restrictions for asset bubbles have provided insights, since those who are more optimistic are given more weight during booms than during recessions (for example, Scheinkman and Xiong, 2003). This gives rise to higher market volatility, with real consequences of the kind that we noted earlier in this essay.

In practice, delineating rational and irrational causes of crises can be hard not only because investors face imperfect markets, but also because rationality and irrationality interact: there are rational actors willing to exploit the irrationality of others (and imperfections in the regulatory framework). While standard models assume that such rational exploitation of market irrationality stabilises the economy, in fact that often does not seem to be the case. The crisis of 2008 serves as an example. The lending during the housing bubble illustrates a high level of irrationality on the part of market participants. Incentive distortions led to excessive risk taking in mortgage provision. In the end, it was rational for major institutions to make contracts with each other which amplified risks and made them less transparent, because it ensured (under the assumption of too-big-to fail) large and sustained government subsidies.

Destabilising Market Processes

The collapse of the exchange rate may restore the market equilibrium (by increasing exports and reducing imports), but it may sometimes have the opposite effect on the economy. If domestic firms have foreign currency denominated debt, the change in exchange rates has large real balance effects (Greenwald and Stiglitz, 1993a), which leads to large changes in behaviour – production, investment, inventory holdings, etc. – and can precipitate an economic downturn. It affects the ability to repay loans, and that in turn affects banks' ability to lend. Limited access to credit and weak balance sheets impede the normal foreign exchange adjustment mechanism. A decline in the exchange rate can weaken aggregate demand and exacerbate the downturn.[14]

This is but one example of how economic processes that in simplistic models help the economy equilibrate may, in more realistic models, have just the opposite effect. In a recession, wage and price declines weaken aggregate demand, exacerbating the gap between supply and demand and the economic downturn.[15]

Trend Reinforcement and 'Orbits of Attraction'

Battiston, Delli Gatti, Greenwald and Stiglitz (2007) describe a variety of other destabilising circumstances where there is a process of *trend reinforcement*, that is, a negative shock is followed by consequences that worsen the firm's (or the economy's) future prospects. Consider the evolution of a firm's net worth as a stochastic process. A negative shock increases the likelihood that the firm will go bankrupt (reach the zero boundary at an earlier date), but that means that lenders will demand higher interest rates, increasing the pace at which a firm with negative drift moves downward.

There can exist a range of state variables (here, net worth) such that in one set of conditions the firm (economy) converges to bankruptcy (crisis), while in another it does not. Shocks can move the economy from one 'orbit of attraction' to another.

How Crises Spread

We have provided a brief and by no means exhaustive overview of finance and macroeconomics research into the causes of financial crises. As Stiglitz (2010b) notes, the mechanisms behind shock amplification can help explain not only the onset of crises but also the spread of crises across countries. As countries remove restrictions on international capital flows, crises that arise when small shocks snowball due to market frictions increasingly involve multiple economies. In today's global financial and banking marketplace, the issue of propagation of shocks and crises across countries is arguably of predominant importance. Therefore, we next turn to the role of contagion[16] and other factors contributing to the spread of financial crises.

It should be obvious that substantial trade or capital linkages can contribute to the spread of crises. But that does not mean that the linkages exacerbate crises. They may dampen the crisis in one country, while at the same time bringing about a downturn in another. Had the US not exported so many of its securitised mortgages leading up to the recent crisis, arguably the US crisis would have been worse. In standard models, however, the global aggregative effect is reduced through interdependence. The worry, however, is that financial interdependence leads to the opposite effect, in a process which is called contagion, by analogy to the spread of disease, where interaction amplifies the overall incidence of the disease.

Of course, even if diversification leads to better overall global economic performance, countries may worry about their own exposure to risks. The last section explained how, as a result of financial constraints, economic systems may amplify shocks; and the costs of offsetting and managing risks may be significant, and not worth the benefits of increased integration. Stiglitz (2006) has, for instance, discussed the high costs associated with reserves that countries maintain to enable them to better manage the shocks that they face.

Financial linkages can take on several forms:

- A reduction in foreign direct investment, as a result of either financial constraints in the investing country or in the markets for which the goods to be produced are destined

- A decrease in financial inflows, not adequately offset by actions of domestic monetary authorities, that leads to financial constraints and/or higher cost of capital

- A reversal of financial flows – from inflows to outflows – which typically is associated with large changes in exchange rates

While these changes in exchange rates would, in the standard trade models, enhance aggregate demand through an increase in net exports, balance sheet effects (especially important when debt is denominated in foreign currencies) often dominate. Moreover, the changes in financial flows can be motivated either by changes in information or beliefs (investors suddenly realise that the risk of investing in foreign countries is greater than they had previously believed), by changes in financial constraints or by real shocks amplified through financial constraints. The financial constraints can arise from regulation or institutional/informational imperfections. Finally, investor actions can bring about a correlated onset of crises, if investors update their views about the likelihood of a crisis based on witnessing a crisis in another market or if investors (including banks) have exposure to several different markets through their portfolios.

One example of what is sometimes called 'pure contagion' involves investors fleeing a country after observing a crisis in another economy that has no trade or capital ties to the original economy. The idea that investors can infer an economy's prospects from crises in other economies is central to the information contagion view (Chen, 1999; King and Wadhwani, 1990; etc.) Intuitively, falling asset prices in one market can convey information about the value of securities in other markets if the two markets share some common risks.[17] Imperfectly informed investors learn about the odds of a crisis in their economy by observing crisis episodes overseas.

The caveat about investor rationality applies here as well. The explanations above focused on rational investors. Often at least some degree of irrationality is involved in investor panics. If investors overreact to news or make other mistakes when drawing inference from other crises, contagion can spread faster as a result of investor irrationality. Even if investors do not perceive a dramatic shift in risk, an expectation that other investors will update their beliefs about risk may be sufficient to spur a sell-off.

The channels through which pure contagion exerts its effects are all of those described in the previous section, including the impact of prices (especially through fire sales) on borrowing constraints and real balances.

Several studies focus on the role of direct financial linkages in shock diffusion. Financial linkages can take the form of risk-sharing arrangements or balance sheet exposure to distressed countries or financial institutions. In a series of papers, Battiston et al. (2007), Gallegati, Greenwald, Richiardi and Stiglitz (2008), and Stiglitz (2010b, 2010c) ask when will it be the case that such risk-sharing arrangements exacerbate rather than reduce systemic risk. Gallegati et al. (2008) model diffusion of shocks among interlinked financial institutions. (Linkages can be, for example, viewed as loans extended to other banks.) Interbank loans allow individual banks to diversify away idiosyncratic shocks to their loan portfolios, reducing the likelihood of failures. However, when economic tides turn, bank failures are more likely to be systemic in nature if banks are interconnected. Moreover, bank managers who have incentive conflicts or who do not fully internalise the spill-overs of bank failures tend to establish too many interbank links.

Several other papers explain how the interconnectedness of bank balance sheets can facilitate the spread of shocks affecting an individual bank to other financial institutions. Allen and Gale (2000) provide a model of balance sheet contagion in the banking sector. Contagion occurs due to overlapping claims between different banks. Liquidity shocks to one bank lead to losses at other banks in the economy because their claims on the troubled bank decline in value. This channel can augment the effects of relatively small shocks and lead to contagion and financial fragility in the banking system. Wagner (2010) similarly concludes that banks motivated by the diversification of idiosyncratic risk can contribute to systemic risk. Haldane (2009) shows that these interlinkages may reduce the risk of failure when there are small or uncorrelated shocks, but increase the risk of failure when there are large and correlated shocks.

The analysis of the consequences of financial linkages across countries is, in many ways, parallel to that of interlinkages among banks (or banks and firms) within a country (Greenwald and Stiglitz, 2003; Stiglitz, 2010c). In the international finance setting, capital flows between countries can serve as a similar risk-sharing mechanism (Stiglitz, 2010b). Capital market integration allows individual countries to smooth country-specific shocks to output. Assuming a high level of country-specific risk and a cost of such variability to consumers, risk sharing through international capital flows is beneficial. On the flipside, a major adverse event that affects a single economy has the potential to cause a systemic failure in all economies interlinked through capital markets.

The underlying intuition behind these seemingly perverse results is that in the presence of non-convexities risk sharing may lower expected returns. Non-convexities are pervasive – they arise whenever there are information constraints, bankruptcy costs or learning processes.[18] The process of trend reinforcement described earlier implicitly entails a non-convexity. In that model, with a negative drift to the stochastic process when equity falls below a critical level, increases in risk increase the chance that the firm escapes the death trap.

Cross-border financial flows may exacerbate financial constraints, and therefore increase the magnitude of the global consequences of shocks and imply that much of the burden of a shock to a given country is experienced by countries with which it is financially integrated. For instance, creditors may impose more stringent collateral requirements on foreign borrowers because of the greater information asymmetries. In Caballero and Krishnamurthy (2001) contractual distortions in the treatment of domestic and international collateral can induce fire sales (presumably that are worse than those that would have arisen if cross-border lending was limited), resulting in liquidation of assets at a significant discount in the event of a shock. In a related vein, in Mendoza (2010) information costs, high leverage and borrowing constraints combine to cause fire sales. Traders facing high debt levels and borrowing constraints can be forced into fire sales of assets to less informed foreign buyers, even though the shock is only temporary. Such fire sales can precipitate rapid shutdowns of external capital markets (i.e. countries facing these fire sales lose access to foreign funds) and large consumption contractions.[19] Stiglitz (2002) described how these effects served to deepen the East Asia crisis of 1997–1998.

The spread of crises to economies that have the same creditors or investors (such as global banks or hedge funds) as the economy in crisis constitutes another channel for the transmission of shocks. Creditors or investors that suffered losses in a crisis in one economy are likely to modify their lending or investment strategy with respect to seemingly unrelated economies. When banks face loan defaults, they are likely to scale back lending to all borrowers, even those unaffected by the initial adverse event, due to capital requirements or balance sheet effects. The worse the effect of defaults on the bank's financial health and ability to raise equity, the more pronounced the cutbacks in lending to other borrowers. Because of information asymmetries, lending cuts may be disproportionately large for foreign borrowers.

Chava and Purnanandam (2011) find empirical support for the role of lender portfolios in the transmission of shocks to previously unaffected firms in a study of borrowers dependent on bank debt around the 1998 Russian financial crisis. Rashid (2011) similarly finds that foreign banks play an important role in the transmission of shocks across borders.

Similarly, investors who lose money in one market might liquidate their positions in other economies (to cover losses or meet margin requirements). Shocks, therefore, can be transmitted as a result of portfolio rebalancing by investors with stakes in multiple markets (Kodres and Pritsker, 2002). Investors are expected to respond to shocks that affect a given market by modifying portfolio exposures to shared macroeconomic risk factors. Such cross-market linkages are likely to spread shocks faster during bad times and in the presence of high levels of foreign debt, as was the case for emerging economies in the Asian financial crisis. But even if there are no shared macroeconomic risks, globally diversified investor portfolios can also speed propagation of individual country shocks to other economies through investor wealth effects (Kyle and Xiong, 2001; Goldstein and Pauzner, 2004). A crisis in one country leads to a reduction in the wealth of those invested in that country. The decline in wealth causes investors to rebalance portfolios, and possibly even to act in a more risk-averse manner, so they scale back holdings of risky assets in other countries, even when those other countries share no ties or risk factors with the original economy in crisis.

Finally, crises can be transmitted via the real sector, for example, through trade ties and competitive (terms-of-trade) effects. Shocks affecting developed countries eventually affect developed countries' trade partners. The recent US economic downturn resulted in a slowdown in gross domestic product growth and a reduction in import demand, adversely affecting many developing economies that traditionally exported to the US (Stiglitz, 2010b). Adverse exchange rate effects would, in the standard model, be viewed as purely redistributive – one country gains what the other country loses – but with financial constraints, as we have noted, the aggregative effect may still be negative (see also Paasche, 2001.)

In this section we have discussed several alternative theories of financial contagion. Of the various theories, the pure contagion models are the least plausible. As Stiglitz (1999b) notes, while Brazil and Russia had few risk factors in common with Southeast Asian economies, both countries saw significant capital flight in the immediate aftermath of the Asian crisis. Similarly, Brazil suffered in the aftermath of the Russian crisis. In those cases, the effects arose from financial institutions and hedge funds with portfolio exposures to multiple emerging markets both within and outside of Asia, and especially from the financial constraints faced by those firms. More recently, disproportionate contractions in lending by banks in the crisis-affected countries helped spread crises to Eastern Europe and emerging markets.

Our discussion of the circumstances that precipitate contagion and spread of shocks to multiple economies has important policy implications for countries with significant international capital market linkages, including Ireland, which we discuss in the next section.

Contagion and Financial and Capital Market Liberalisation

Short-Run Exchange Rate Interventions

A standard response to the threat of contagion includes an international bailout package, the essential ingredient of which is a commitment of large amounts of financial support, some of which is used immediately for intervention to support the currency, and the rest is left to convince the market that more support will be provided, should the need occur. As Stiglitz (1999a) has commented, there are two things that are odd about these interventions, which often are ineffective (for example, in Russia in 1998, in East Asia in 1997 and in Argentina in 2001). First, why should a temporary intervention in the market have persistent effects? Moreover, if the crisis conveyed information about Mexico's fundamentals that are relevant to Argentina's situation, then even if the IMF intervention stabilised Mexico's exchange rate, it would not change market perceptions of the underlying weaknesses in Argentina's economy. Only if market participants were naïve enough just to look at the exchange rate (the outcome of market processes *and* intervention) would the intervention work.[20] And secondly, why should an intervention in Mexico have any effect on Argentina? On the contrary, *if* the market thought that intervention was necessary but that intervention on behalf of Argentina was less likely than in the case of Mexico, an intervention in Mexico, even if successful in supporting the Mexican exchange rate, could have an adverse effect on Argentina.

There are two sets of models in which such temporary interventions might make sense. The first is in the presence of deep market irrationalities – where market participants are truly naïve and only look at exchange rates, not what brings them about; where they have simple beliefs about contagion – that a crisis in one country is like a communicable disease, and if we cure the symptoms in one country, it can affect its spread to others. The other is that there are multiple equilibria, and interventions help to move the economy from the 'bad' equilibrium to the 'good' one. A third explanation, which is a variant of the second explanation, is that markets are often prone to overshooting and interventions are an attempt to prevent that. Given the real consequences of overshooting discussed earlier, such interventions may make sense. Note that in each of these explanations market processes on their own are assumed to lead to sub-optimal outcomes. But the advocates of these interventions at the international financial institutions, which typically have placed strong confidence in the efficiency and stability of market processes, need to provide a clear delineation of the circumstances in which markets can be relied upon and those in which they cannot. Critics might argue that in the case of crises the market inefficiencies are so large that they simply can't be ignored, but they are likely present at other times as well (Greenwald and Stiglitz, 1987).

More broadly, however, the models that we have delineated in this paper provide a rationale for such exchange rate interventions. Markets with rational expectations but imperfect and asymmetric information are typically not efficient; even more so if markets are subject to irrational pessimism. Then the effects of such irrationalities (even if relatively small) can be large and persistent; markets may exhibit excessive volatility, and there can be *real* benefits to government efforts at stabilisation.

Optimal Financial Architecture

Stiglitz (2000, 2002, 2006, 2010b, 2010c) analyses the optimal design of international financial architecture given both the benefits of financial integration in achieving diversification and smoothing of negative consumption shocks and the costs of adverse spill-overs across markets due to financial contagion. Financial integration raises the overall risk of spill-overs of large negative shocks (Stiglitz, 2010c). Stiglitz (2010b) examines the trade-off between contagion and diversification associated with open capital markets in a risk-sharing context. He shows that risk-sharing arrangements can become a negative-sum game in the presence of bankruptcy costs and other commonly accepted financial market frictions. In the absence of such frictions, diversification achieved through risk-sharing arrangements benefits risk-averse investors and consumers. However, a number of plausible market frictions can set in motion a financial accelerator effect that leads the initial shock to gain magnitude and persist. With bankruptcy costs, full diversification may result in lower aggregate output (net of such costs), so much lower that it more than offsets the benefits from diversification. Capital market integration could increase, instead of lower, the likelihood of a financial crisis in a given economy. Even if risk sharing does not initially increase the likelihood of a crisis but only increases the probability of a near-crisis state, the resulting increase in borrowing costs accounts for trend reinforcement, which raises the odds of a crisis in the long run.[21]

One analogy is with fuller integration of electricity grids, which saves on generating capacity but increases the risk of a broader systemic failure. In practice, well-designed electricity networks make use of circuit breakers. In international finance capital controls serve as such circuit breakers.

If well-designed capital controls could be incorporated to prevent contagion during crisis episodes without compromising the risk-sharing benefits of integration, integration would always be preferred. However, designing and implementing such a mechanism is very challenging in practice. Therefore, the choice of integration depends on the likelihood of a large shock (and ensuing systemic failure) relative to the level of country-specific risk and the costs associated with variability. Moreover, the types and severity of informational and other frictions present in different countries must be considered for a complete assessment of the trade-offs and benefits of capital market integration.

In their analysis of the Asian financial crisis, Furman and Stiglitz (1998)[22] and Stiglitz (2004) argue that while the adverse events affecting East Asian economies were at least to some extent exogenous (irrational investor perceptions, sudden changes in investor willingness to bear risk, interest rate increases in industrialised countries), the rapid liberalisation of capital flows and integration of domestic markets into global financial markets in the absence of a sound bank supervisory and regulatory framework contributed to the severity of the crisis. They find evidence that rapid growth in unhedged short-term debt exposures made East Asian markets vulnerable to sudden capital outflows and heightened the magnitude of the subsequent crisis. Moreover, financial integration limited the flexibility of the macroeconomic policy response because of the concern that interest rate reductions would exacerbate capital flight. In the aftermath of the Asian financial crisis and the Great Recession, the highly volatile, short-term, speculative nature of international capital movements has led many emerging market governments to reconsider the benefits of full liberalisation of capital flows (Calvo and Mendoza, 2000). Recently, the IMF has also argued that certain restrictions on cross-border capital flows may be desirable and included such restrictions in some of its recent programmes (for example, in Iceland).

Financial liberalisation refers to the opening of a country's financial system to banking institutions (and other financial institutions) from abroad. Research conducted before the crisis suggested that it provided one mechanism for the spread of a crisis from one country to others; as we have noted, the Great Recession reinforced these findings. One policy response is to question the single market principle, under which a bank that is regulated by one jurisdiction is allowed to operate freely in other jurisdictions. There is now a growing consensus that countries have to regulate all financial institutions operating within their jurisdiction (regardless of ownership) and that they should be organised as subsidiaries (not branches), to ensure that there is adequate capital within the country (United Nations, 2010).

Extensive work on crises and their propagation can be used to understand the history of financial crises, to draw inferences about the origins and spread of the recent financial crisis, and to devise policy frameworks to reduce the occurrence and magnitude of future crises. We have identified a number of mechanisms leading to crises and their contagion. Most of the plausible mechanisms require us to go beyond the standard macroeconomic frameworks based on rational agents with rational expectations operating in well-functioning financial markets. What is needed now is a comprehensive model that integrates various crisis transmission channels and provides a coherent set of policy recommendations both to reduce the magnitude and frequency of shocks, to stem contagion and to respond to the crises that nonetheless occur.

Endnotes

[1] The authors thank Charles Larkin, Brian Lucey and Constantin Gurdgiev for their helpful suggestions.

[2] As we note below, this was a mistake, which is not uncommon in the presence of supervisory failures.

3   There were major institutional flaws in the design of NAMA which under-
    mined its ability to fulfil its mission. These are not the subject of this
    paper.

4   We say typically because there are exceptions: in the Great Recession,
    though precipitated by the US banking crisis, the US appeared to be a
    safe haven, and its exchange rate appreciated. The subsequent low inter-
    est rates and depressed wages helped (at least temporarily) to buoy stock
    market prices, even though economic activity languished.

5   That this is not so in general—that markets with even large numbers of
    well-informed participants may look markedly different from those in
    which *all* are well informed—is one of the central messages of Salop and
    Stiglitz (1976). Grossman and Stiglitz (1980) showed that uninformed
    market participants could extract some, but not all, of the information
    from the prices generated by informed traders.

6   The essential insight was that with an overvalued exchange rate the coun-
    try would generate a trade deficit, which foreign exchange reserves could
    only finance for a limited amount of time. Of course, if markets antici-
    pated this, with rational expectations, the crisis would occur well before
    foreign exchange reserves were finally exhausted.

7   There is some evidence that normal trade adjustments, spurred in part by
    devaluation, were central to the resolution of the crisis; the bail-out, by
    temporarily leading to an exchange rate that was higher than it otherwise
    would have been, may in fact have impeded adjustment.

8   In these models, there is no way that market participants can anticipate
    when the economy might shift from one equilibrium to another.

9   See also the earlier work of Myers and Majluf (1984) and Greenwald,
    Stiglitz and Weiss (1984).

10 Either because managers are forced to bear some risk, as part of optimal
    incentive contracts, or because of bankruptcy costs. See Greenwald and
    Stiglitz (1990).

11 Moreover, the value of firm equity can change rapidly, and there may be
    many claimants.

12 Similarly, Miller and Stiglitz (2010) use a model with collateral require-
    ments to demonstrate how shocks can turn into crises in the presence of
    high leverage and overvalued assets.

13 More recent research has emphasised that individuals discount informa-
    tion that is inconsistent with their priors, and overweight information
    that is consistent. If a bubble is forming, they tend to weigh more heav-
    ily the information that is consistent with their beliefs. There can be

equilibrium frictions, where they 'rationally' believe that there is a bubble (see Hoff and Stiglitz, 2010).

14   Traditional economic theory – and economic policy – has taken ambiguous positions about these destabilising adjustments. It has been standard fare to worry about 'overshooting'. Excessive exchange rate adjustments, it is thought, impede the adjustment of the market economy to the new (or 'correct') equilibrium, and this provides justification for interventions to reduce the magnitude of the exchange rate adjustment. In some cases, there is evidence that such interventions actually impede the adjustment process. Indeed, one set of studies suggests that it was the normal foreign exchange adjustment mechanism which restored Mexico's growth, and that attempts to dampen the foreign exchange correction (driven by concerns about impact on foreign creditors) slowed down adjustment. In particular, if there had been larger foreign exchange adjustments accompanied by debt restructuring, the economy arguably would have recovered more quickly (Lederman, Menendez, Perry and Stiglitz, 2001, 2003).

15   Standard macro theories are of two minds about the role of wage and price rigidities. While the Hicksian IS-LM tradition focuses on wage and price rigidities, the Fisherian tradition revived by Greenwald and Stiglitz (1993a, 1993b, and the articles cited there) emphasises that with imperfectly indexed debt contracts wage flexibility may exacerbate economic downturns. In a model where both wages and prices are flexible, but imperfectly so, the economy can have sustained unemployment (see Solow and Stiglitz, 1968).

16   Although many sources mention contagion, no consensus has emerged on the precise definition of contagion (see, for example, Gallegati, Greenwald, Richiardi and Stiglitz, 2008). In the broadest sense, contagion involves spill-overs of economic events from one country to other countries (or, in the context of lending, from one borrower to other borrowers). A narrower view, more specific to crisis episodes, defines contagion as an increase in correlations among two countries in bad times or, in the words of Dornbusch, Park and Claessens (2000, p. 178), 'a significant increase in cross-market linkages after a shock to an individual country, as measured by the degree to which asset prices or financial flows move together across markets relative to this co-movement in tranquil time.'

17   Bank decisions in anticipation of contagion can increase the level of systemic risk. For example, Acharya and Yorulmazer (2008) consider the lending decisions of banks affected by common as well as idiosyncratic shocks. If one bank fails, investors update their assessment of other banks.

Investors are unable to tell if the bank failed for bank-specific or systemic reasons, so they become more reluctant to invest in the remaining banks. Anticipating such investor actions, banks try to minimise unfavourable information spill-overs of bank failures by investing in more highly correlated loans. Thus, the expectation of contagion causes banks to herd, which aggravates systemic risk and the magnitude of contagion occurring ex post. Nalebuff and Stiglitz (1983) examine the role of incentive conflicts in explaining herding.

[18] See, for instance, Radner and Stiglitz (1984).

[19] The general theory is set forth in Korinek (2008).

[20] Alternatively, if contagion occurred through 'real' channels – Mexican purchases of Argentinean goods were enhanced as a result of exchange rate support, because real balance effects are more important than relative price effects – then the Mexican intervention could reduce spill-over effects. These effects did not play an important role in the discussions preceding most of the bailouts.

[21] Stiglitz (2010c) uses a life cycle model to show that capital market liberalisation may actually reduce the scope for inter-temporal risk sharing, and thus lower the long-term present discounted value of expected utility.

[22] After each crisis of the 1980s and 1990s, policy makers identified a factor that seemed to be pivotal as the source of a crisis: an overvalued exchange rate, excessive public indebtedness, insufficient private savings, lack of transparency. But the analysis was ad hoc and had little predictive power. Mexico's problems in 1994 were markedly different from those of Latin America in the early 1980s. East Asian countries had high savings rates and low public indebtedness. The last set of countries to suffer from a financial crisis before the East Asian crisis were those of Scandinavia, generally viewed as the most transparent in the world. Furman and Stiglitz (1998) attempt to identify econometrically the factors that contribute to an economy's vulnerability to a financial crisis. Needless to say, their results confirm the lack of predictive power of the standard explanations of vulnerability to a crisis.

References

Abreu, D. and Brunnermeier, M. (2003) 'Bubbles and Crashes', *Econometrica*, Vol. 71, No. 1, pp. 173–204.

Acharya, V. and Yorulmazer, T. (2008) 'Information Contagion and Bank Herding', *Journal of Money, Credit, and Banking*, Vol. 40, No. 1, pp. 215–231.

Agenor, P.-R. and Masson, P. (1999) 'Credibility, Reputation, and the Mexican Peso Crisis', *Journal of Money, Credit, and Banking*, Vol. 31, No. 1, pp. 70–84.

Allen, F. and Gale, D. (2000) 'Financial Contagion', *Journal of Political Economy*, Vol. 108, No. 1, pp. 1–33.

Banerjee, A. (1992) 'A Simple Model of Herd Behavior', *Quarterly Journal of Economics*, Vo. 107, No. 3, pp. 797–817.

Barberis, N. and Thaler, R. (2003) 'A Survey of Behavioral Finance', in G. Constantinides, R. Stulz and M. Harris (eds.), *Handbook of the Economics of Finance*, Amsterdam: North-Holland, pp. 1053–1121.

Battiston, S., Delli Gatti, D., Greenwald, B. and Stiglitz, J. (2007) 'Credit Chains and Bankruptcy Propagation in Production Networks', *Journal of Economic Dynamics and Control*, Vol. 31, No. 6, pp. 2061–2084.

Bernanke, B., Gertler, M. and Gilchrist, S. (1996) 'The Financial Accelerator and the Flight to Quality', *Review of Economics and Statistics*, Vol. 78, No. 1, pp. 1–15.

Bikhchandani, S., Hirshleifer, D. and Welch, I. (1992) 'A Theory of Fads, Fashion, Custom, and Cultural Change as Informational Cascades', *Journal of Political Economy*, Vol. 100, No. 5, pp. 992–1026.

Caballero, R. and Krishnamurthy, A. (2001) 'International and Domestic Collateral Constraints in a Model of Emerging Market Crises', *Journal of Monetary Economics*, Vol. 48, No. 3, pp. 513–548.

Calvo, G. and Mendoza, E. (2000) 'Rational Contagion and the Globalization of Securities Markets', *Journal of Economic Theory*, Vol. 51, No. 1, pp. 79–113.

Cespedes, L., Chang, R. and Velasco, A. (2004) 'Balance Sheets and Exchange Rate Policy', *American Economic Review*, Vol. 94, No. 4, pp. 1183–1193.

Chava, S. and Purnanandam, A. (2011) 'The Effect of Banking Crisis on Bank-Dependent Borrowers', *Journal of Financial Economics*, Vol. 99, No. 1, pp. 116–135.

Chen, Y. (1999) 'Banking Panics: The Role of the First-Come, First-Served Rule and Information Externalities', *Journal of Political Economy*, Vol. 107, No. 5, pp. 946–968.

Diamond, D. and Dybvig, P. (1983) 'Bank Runs, Deposit Insurance, and Liquidity', *Journal of Political Economy*, Vol. 91, No. 3, pp. 401–419.

Dornbusch, R., Park, Y. and Claessens, S. (2000) 'Contagion: Understanding How It Spreads', *World Bank Research Observer*, Vol. 15, No. 2, pp. 177–197.

Ferri, G., Liu, L.-G. and Stiglitz, J. (1999) 'The Procyclical Role of Rating Agencies: Evidence from the East Asian Crisis', *Economic Notes*, Vol. 28, No. 3, pp. 335–355.

Furman, J. and Stiglitz, J. (1998) 'Economic Crises: Evidence and Insights from East Asia', *Brookings Papers on Economic Activity*, Vol. 29, No. 2, pp. 1–136.

Gallegati, M., Greenwald, B., Richiardi, M. and Stiglitz, J. (2008) 'The Asymmetric Effect of Diffusion Processes: Risk Sharing and Contagion', *Global Economy Journal*, Vol. 8, No. 3, Article 2.

Goldstein, I. and Pauzner, A. (2004) 'Contagion of Self-Fulfilling Financial Crises Due to Diversification of Investment Portfolios', *Journal of Economic Theory*, Vol. 119, No. 1, pp. 151–183.

Greenwald, B. and Stiglitz, J. (1986) 'Externalities in Economies with Imperfect Information and Incomplete Markets', *Quarterly Journal of Economics*, Vol. 101, No. 2, pp. 229–264.

Greenwald, B. and Stiglitz, J. (1987) 'Keynesian, New Keynesian and New Classical Economics', *Oxford Economic Papers*, Vol. 39, No. 1, pp. 119–133.

Greenwald, B. and Stiglitz, J. (1990) 'Asymmetric Information and the New Theory of the Firm: Financial Constraints and Risk Behavior', *American Economic Review*, Vol. 80, No. 2, pp. 160–165.

Greenwald, B. and Stiglitz, J. (1993a) 'Financial Market Imperfections and Business Cycles', *Quarterly Journal of Economics*, Vol. 108, No. 1, pp. 77–114.

Greenwald, B. and Stiglitz, J. (1993b) 'New and Old Keynesians', *Journal of Economic Perspectives*, Vol. 7, No. 1, pp. 23–44.

Greenwald, B. and Stiglitz, J. (2003) *Towards a New Paradigm in Monetary Economics*, Cambridge: Cambridge University Press.

Greenwald, B., Stiglitz, J. and Weiss, A. (1984) 'Informational Imperfections in the Capital Market and Macroeconomic Fluctuations', *American Economic Review*, Vol. 74, No. 2, pp. 194–199.

Griffith-Jones, S., Ocampo, J.A. and Stiglitz, J. (2010) *Time for a Visible Hand: Lessons from the 2008 World Financial Crisis, Initiative for Policy Dialogue Series*, Oxford: Oxford University Press.

Grossman, S. and Stiglitz, J. (1980) 'On the Impossibility of Informationally Efficient Markets', *American Economic Review*, Vol. 70, No. 3, pp. 393–408.

Gurdgiev, C., Lucey, B.M., Mac an Bhaird, C. and Roche-Kelly, L. (2011) 'The Irish Economy: Three Strikes and You're Out?', *Panoeconomicus*, Vol. 58, No. 1, pp. 19–41.

Haldane, A. (2009) 'Rethinking the Financial Network', speech given at the Financial Student Association on 28 April 2009.

Haldane, A. and May, R. (2011) 'Systemic Risk in Banking Ecosystems', *Nature*, Vol. 469, pp. 351–355.

Helmann, T., Murdoch, K. and Stiglitz, J. (2000) 'Liberalization, Moral Hazard in Banking and Prudential Regulation: Are Capital Requirements Enough?' *American Economic Review*, Vol. 90, No. 1, pp. 147–165.

Hirshleifer, D. and Teoh, S. (2009) 'Thought and Behavior Contagion in Capital Markets', in T. Hens and K. Schenk-Hoppe (eds.), *Handbook of Financial Markets: Dynamics and Evolution*, Amsterdam: Elsevier, pp. 1–56.

Hoff, K. and Stiglitz, J. (2010) 'Equilibrium Fictions: A Cognitive Approach to Societal Rigidity', *American Economic Review*, Vol. 100, No. 2, pp. 141–146.

Kindleberger, C., Aliber, R. and Solow, R. (2005) *Manias, Panics, and Crashes: A History of Financial Crises*, fifth edition, Hoboken, NJ: John Wiley and Sons.

King, M. and Wadhwani, S. (1990) 'Transmission of Volatility between Stock Markets', *Review of Financial Studies*, Vol. 3, No. 1, pp. 5–33.

Kiyotaki, N. and Moore, J. (1997) 'Credit Cycles', *Journal of Political Economy*, Vol. 105, No. 2, pp. 211–248.

Kodres, L. and Pritsker, M. (2002) 'A Rational Expectations Model of Financial Contagion' *Journal of Finance*, Vol. 57, No. 2, pp. 769–799.

Korinek, A. (2008) 'Regulating Capital Flows to Emerging Markets: An Externality View', working paper, University of Maryland.

Krugman, P. (1979) 'A Model of Balance-of-Payments Crises', *Journal of Money, Credit, and Banking*, Vol. 11, No. 3, pp. 311–325.

Kyle, A. and Xiong, W. (2001) 'Contagion as a Wealth Effect', *Journal of Finance*, Vol. 56, No. 4, pp. 1401–1440.

Lederman, D., Menendez, A., Perry, G. and Stiglitz, J. (2001) 'Mexico—Five Years after the Crisis', in B. Pleskovic and N. Stern (eds.), *Annual Bank Conference on Development Economics 2000*, Washington, DC: World Bank, pp. 263–282.

Lederman, D., Menendez, A., Perry, G. and Stiglitz, J. (2003) 'Mexican Investment after the Tequila Crisis: Basic Economics, "Confidence" Effect or Market Imperfection?', *Journal of International Money and Finance*, Vol. 22, No. 1, pp. 131–151.

Mendoza, E. (2010) 'Sudden Stops, Financial Crises, and Leverage', *American Economic Review*, Vol. 100, No. 5, pp. 1941–1966.

Miller, M. and Stiglitz, J. (2010) 'Leverage and Asset Bubbles: Averting Armageddon with Chapter 11?' *Economic Journal*, Vol. 120, No. 544, pp. 500–518.

Myers, S. and Majluf, N. (1984) 'Corporate Financing and Investment Decisions when Firms Have Information That Investors Do Not Have', *Journal of Financial Economics*, Vol. 13, No. 2, pp. 187–221.

Nalebuff, B. and Stiglitz, J. (1983) 'Prizes and Incentives: Towards a General Theory of Compensation and Competition', *Bell Journal of Economics*, Vol. 14, No. 1, pp. 21–43.

Paasche, B. (2001) 'Credit Constraints and International Financial Crises', *Journal of Monetary Economics*, Vol. 48, No. 3, pp. 623–650.

Radner, R. and Stiglitz, J. (1984) 'A Nonconcavity in the Value of Information', in M. Boyer and R. Khilstrom (eds.), *Bayesian Models in Economic Theory*, Amsterdam: Elsevier Science Publications, pp. 33–52.

Rashid, H. (2011) 'Credit to Private sector, Interest Spread and Volatility in Credit-Flows: Do Bank Ownership and Deposits Matter?', working paper, United Nations.

Sachs, J., Tornell, A. and Velasco, A. (1996) 'The Mexican Peso Crisis: Sudden Death or Death Foretold?' *Journal of International Economics*, Vol. 41, Nos. 3–4, pp. 265–283.

Salop, S. and Stiglitz, J. (1976) 'A Theory of Sales', working paper, Stanford University.

Scheinkman, J. and Xiong, W. (2003) 'Overconfidence and Speculative Bubbles,' *Journal of Political Economy*, Vol. 111, No. 6, pp. 1183–1219.

Shell, K. and Stiglitz, J. (1967) 'Allocation of Investment in a Dynamic Economy', *Quarterly Journal of Economics*, Vol. 81, No. 4, pp. 592–609.

Solow, R. and Stiglitz, J. (1968) 'Output, Employment and Wages in the Short Run', *Quarterly Journal of Economics*, Vol. 82, No. 4, pp. 537–560.

Stiglitz, J. (1999a) 'Reforming the Global Economic Architecture: Lessons from Recent Crises', *Journal of Finance*, Vol. 54, No. 4, pp. 1508–1521.

Stiglitz, J. (1999b) 'Knowledge for Development: Economic Science, Economic Policy, and Economic Advice', in B. Pleskovic and J. Stiglitz (eds.), *Annual World Bank Conference on Development Economics 1998*, Washington DC: World Bank, pp. 9–58.

Stiglitz, J. (2000) 'Capital Market Liberalization, Economic Growth, and Instability', *World Development*, Vol. 28, No. 6, pp. 1075–1086.

Stiglitz, J. (2001) 'From Miracle to Crisis to Recovery: Lessons from Four Decades of East Asian Experience', in J. Stiglitz and S. Yusuf (eds.), *Rethinking the East Asian Miracle*, Oxford: Oxford University Press, pp. 509–526.

Stiglitz, J. (2002) *Globalization and Its Discontents*, New York: W.W. Norton & Company.

Stiglitz, J. (2004) 'Capital Market Liberalization, Globalization, and the IMF', *Oxford Review of Economic Policy*, Vol. 20, No. 1, pp. 57–71.

Stiglitz, J. (2006) *Making Globalization Work*, New York: W.W. Norton & Company.

Stiglitz, J. (2010a) *Freefall: America, Free Markets, and the Sinking of the World Economy*, New York: W.W. Norton & Company.

Stiglitz, J. (2010b) 'Contagion, Liberalization, and the Optimal Structure of Globalization', *Journal of Globalization and Development*, Vol. 1, No. 2, Article 2.

Stiglitz, J. (2010c) 'Risk and Global Economic Architecture: Why Full Financial Integration May Be Undesirable', *American Economic Review*, Vol. 100, No. 2, pp. 388–392.

Stiglitz, J. (2011) 'Preface', in D. Coats (ed.), *Exiting from the Crisis: Towards a Model of More Equitable and Sustainable Growth*, Brussels: European Trade Union Institute, pp. 9–16.

Stiglitz, J. and Weiss, A. (1986) 'Credit Rationing and Collateral', in J. Edwards, J. Franks, C. Mayer and S. Schaefer (eds.), *Recent Developments in Corporate Finance*, Cambridge: Cambridge University Press, pp. 101–135.

United Nations Commission of Experts of the President of the United Nations General Assembly on Reforms of the International Monetary and Financial System (2010) *The Stiglitz Report: Reforming the International Monetary and Financial Systems in the Wake of the Global Crisis*, New York: The New Press.

Wagner, W. (2010) 'Diversification at Financial Institutions and Systemic Crises,' *Journal of Financial Intermediation*, Vol. 19, No. 3, pp. 373–386.

Wall Street Journal (2010) 'Ireland's Fate Tied to Doomed Banks', *Wall Street Journal*, eastern edition, 10 November 2010.

Wall Street Journal (2011) 'Ireland's Banks Get Failing Grades', *Wall Street Journal*, eastern edition, 1 April 2011.

IRELAND

3

Debt Restructuring in Ireland:
Orderly, Selective and Unavoidable

Constantin Gurdgiev

*Constantin is adjunct professor at the School of Business, Trinity College Dublin,
and a director of St Columbanus AG, a Swiss asset management company. An
internationally syndicated newspaper columnist,
he blogs at trueeconomics.blogspot.com.*

Ireland's Road to Debt Restructuring

In a 2011 research paper titled 'The Real Effects of Debt', Bank for International Settlements (BIS) researchers S. Cecchetti, M. Mohanty and F. Zampolli provide analysis of the long-term effects of debt on future growth. The authors use a sample of eighteen Organisation for Economic Co-Operation and Development (OECD) countries, not including Ireland, for the period of 1980–2010 and conclude that 'for government debt, the threshold [beyond which public debt becomes damaging to the economy] is in the range of 80 to 100% of GDP [gross domestic product].' The implication is that 'countries with high debt must act quickly and decisively to address their fiscal problems.' Furthermore, 'when corporate debt goes beyond 90% of GDP, [the] results suggest that it becomes a drag on growth. And for household debt, ... a threshold [is] around 85% of GDP.' Combined private non-financial and public debt in excess of circa 250 per cent of GDP exerts a long-term drag on future growth.

These effects were present during the benign environment of the Age of Great Moderation, the period from the mid-1990s through 2007, when low inflation and cost of capital spurred above-average global growth. More significantly, the effects were present while the Baby Boom generation was at its prime productive age, rapid expansion of information and communication technology (ICT) drove productivity in manufacturing and services, and innovations in logistics revolutionised retailing (the so-called Wal-Mart effect).

In other words, despite all the positive push forces lifting the growth rates the negative pull force of building debt overhang was still econometrically traceable. Eurozone economies posted average growth rates of 2.0 per cent per annum in 1991–2007, well below the less indebted group of smaller advanced economies[1] that posted average annual growth rates of over 4.2 per cent.[2]

From the Irish perspective, the impact of debt overhang on long-term growth in the advanced economies presents a clear warning. Ireland's robust growth in the 1990s and through to 2007 represents not a long-term norm but a delayed catching up with the rest of the advanced economies. In other words, even disregarding the negative effects of the severe debt overhang we experience today, Ireland's average growth rates in the foreseeable future will be close to the average growth for smaller open economies in the Eurozone. That rate, according to the IMF's latest forecasts, is unlikely to be significantly above 2.0 per cent.

But Ireland's debt overhang, when it comes to debt types analysed by Cecchetti, Mohanty and Zampolli (2011), is beyond severe. It is outright extreme, as shown in Figure 3.1. Across the eighteen advanced economies, weighted average real economic debts stood at 307 per cent of GDP at the end of 2010 and are expected to rise to circa 310–312 per cent of GDP or gross national product (GNP) by the end of 2011. Ireland's real economy debt to GDP ratio is likely to reach close to 400 per cent of GDP and, more importantly, close to 480 per cent of GNP.

Below, we show that this level of debt overhang can be expected to permanently reduce the potential rate of growth in the Irish economy to that consistent with deflationary stagnation.

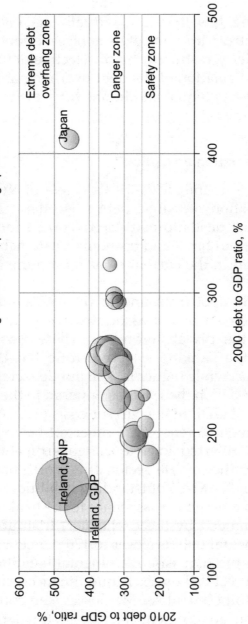

Figure 3.1: Debt Overhang, 2000–2010

Size of bubble = change 2000–2010, percentage points

Sources: Department of Finance; Central Statistics Office; Cecchetti, Mohanty and Zampolli (2011); and author's own calculations.

In addition, we also show that the internal devaluation option is not likely to produce meaningful debt reductions at these levels of debt overhang. It is, therefore, virtually inevitable that Ireland will need to restructure some of its debts. We conclude by showing that an orderly restructuring of selective debts can result in simultaneous alleviation of the debt overhang and its effects on growth, creating potential conditions for a swift recovery from the insolvency crisis.

Is Internal Devaluation an Option?

Irish experience in the 1980s–1990s – one of the few cases of successful deflation of public debt – is often presented as an example of what needs to be done to correct for current insolvency. This path to fiscal and economic sustainability, however, is simply invalid in the current crisis for a number of structural reasons.

Firstly, public debt overhang in the 1980s – as severe as it might have been – was not associated with simultaneous debt overhangs in the private economy. There was no structural insolvency in the banking system during the 1980s and Irish debt–GDP ratios, while higher for the public sector debt at under 120 per cent of GDP in the 1980s as opposed to the expected peak of 116 per cent of GDP in the current crisis (ex-NAMA (National Asset Management Agency) and other off-balance sheet liabilities commonly referred to as quasi-governmental debt), were much lower for the private sector. It is worth noting, however, that inclusive of NAMA's outstanding liabilities and the Central Bank of Ireland emergency assistance to the banking sector (both explicitly guaranteed by the Exchequer) Irish government and quasi-governmental debt is closer to 170 per cent of GDP. While the majority of these quasi-governmental liabilities are unlikely to generate a direct call on Exchequer finances, some, especially those relating to potential NAMA losses, can constitute a direct cost to the Irish government. Private sector debts back in the 1980s peaked at about 50 per cent of GDP and these currently stand, as variously estimated, at between 210 per cent and 289 per cent of GDP. Furthermore, while servicing costs on government debt managed to reach almost 10 per cent of GDP and 35 per cent of tax revenue back in the 1980s, servicing costs of the government debt this time around, courtesy of the troika agreements, can be expected to reach circa 4.7–6.5 per cent of GDP, depending on the underlying European Central Bank (ECB) rate assumptions, which is far less than in the past. However, the real carrying capacity of this economy is no longer measured by the actual GDP and should be benchmarked instead to GNP. In these terms, financing costs of the public debt, especially including promissory notes, can be as high as 8 per cent of GNP. The combined private and public debt burden on the economy in the 1980s was around 14 per cent. At current levels, using the lower estimate for total public and private debt, the Irish economy is spending circa 15 per cent of GDP or 18 per cent of GNP on interest payments on the non-financial debt.

Secondly, unlike in the 1980s and the 1990s, Irish policy makers no longer have control over interest rates and currency valuations. Thus, Ireland no longer can avail of surprise devaluations, similar to those that took place in 1986–1987 and subsequently.

Thirdly, unlike in the 1990s, the core twin drivers for growth, namely robust external demand and catching up with EU-average levels of capital stock and infrastructure, are no longer present today. The former cannot be expected to contribute significantly to Irish growth because our main trading partners – the US, UK and Eurozone – are currently facing long-term deleveraging of their own economies. The latter is unlikely to happen because our internal as well as global financial systems – transmitters of global savings into investment – are in the need of structural repairs that will take years. In addition, significant structural funds made available to Ireland during the 1990s by the EU are also out of our reach today.

Fourthly, Irish institutional competitiveness – especially as expressed in terms of legal, regulatory and policy frameworks international rankings, as compared to our core trading competitors – is no longer a given. Back in the 1980s and early 1990s, Ireland's relative rankings in terms of institutional quality were low. However, the gains in Irish institutional competitiveness in the early to mid-1990s were made against relatively less dynamic competition from Ireland's peers. This allowed Ireland to act as a leader in institutional innovation and precipitated significant comparative advantages to Ireland as a location for foreign direct investment (FDI), equity investments, and mergers and acquisitions. Today, Ireland is no longer ahead of the curve on institutional innovation and much of its institutional capacity is hard-wired into internationally less competitive European frameworks. This makes it more difficult for Ireland to compete for FDI and in the trade arena on the basis of superior gains in overall institutional environments.

In short, the option of deflating via growth and devaluation our debt overhang is closed. Common referencing of the 1990s Celtic Tiger boom as the benchmark to which Ireland naturally moves during the current crisis adjustments is a superficial *deus ex machina* for blindly stumbling toward a disorderly collapse of the debt-ridden economy. This is so because, as argued above, we no longer possess the same starting conditions for policy innovation and economic growth that made the Celtic Tiger of the 1990s feasible. It is also true because the global conditions of rapid growth in global FDI and lower competition pressures from the Asia Pacific region and Eastern Europe, which facilitated the development of the Celtic Tiger in the 1990s, are no longer present.

Scoping the Problem

Using the model estimates by Cecchetti, Mohanty and Zampolli (2011) and updating their results to include Ireland, the core problem faced by the Irish economy is clearly that of debt overhang. Using the study estimates, the potential reduction in Irish GDP growth over the long-term horizon arising from the combined debt overhangs can be as high as 2.1 per cent of GDP. The largest impact from debt overhang for Ireland arises from corporate debt, followed by household debt. Despite this, the Irish government's core objective to date has been to deleverage banks and to contain government debt explosion. In doing so, the government is opting for loading more debt onto households by reducing disposable after-tax incomes and refusing to implement significant savings in current public expenditure.

Ireland's debt levels are extreme. Again referencing the BIS study we see that Ireland sports the highest level of debt to GNP ratio, the second highest debt to GDP ratio and the fastest increases in 2000–2010 in both ratios in the developed world. At this junction in time, Ireland has two options: either attempt to deliver significant – close to double-digit – current account (external) surpluses to pay down the debt over time (with required surpluses of close to the interest costs required to cover debt maintenance, or some 10–12 per cent of annual GDP growth over the next ten years plus), or restructure its debts. In other words, it's either a default on growth, with all economic activity going to finance debt repayments, or a default on debt with all debt-financing resources of the economy going to finance growth.

Exports-Led Growth and Debt Overhang

The exports-driven recovery options for Ireland are, of course, superficial. In reality, Ireland is unlikely to be able to generate significant enough surpluses on its current account to deliver growth-based debt pay downs. In the previous decade, the Irish economy ran a cumulative current account deficit amounting to 19.5 per cent of its GDP. The average current account deficit in 2000–2009 in Ireland was -2.35 per cent, and even during the boom years of the 1990s the average current account surplus achieved by the Irish economy was just 1.74 per cent of GDP – not enough to cover interest costs on combined private and public sector debts.

As the Eurozone economies pursued populist agendas of 'social' services and subsidies expansion throughout the 1990s and 2000s, some (indeed the majority) of the European economies stagnated, implying a diminished capacity to sustain subsidies transfers within the European Union.

To see this, look no further than the links between the current account deficits (external imbalances across the entire economy, public and private) and government deficits (fiscal imbalances), as well as structural deficits (fiscal imbalances corrected for recessionary impacts).

Figure 3.2 shows cumulated current account deficits for twelve years since 2000 as well as cumulated structural deficits.

Figure 3.2: 2000–2011 Cumulated Current Account and General Government Structural Deficits

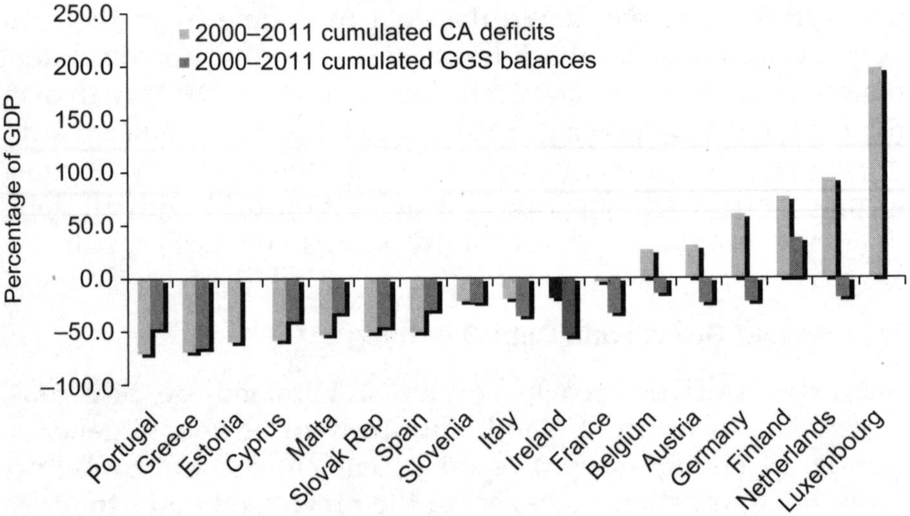

Source: IMF WEO (2011) and author's own calculations.

The striking feature of Figure 3.2 is that over the twelve years' horizon, only six countries of the Eurozone have managed to post a cumulative external surplus, while only one country (Finland) has managed to live within its means both in terms of external balance and fiscal balance.

Another striking feature of the graph is that France was running dual external and fiscal deficits. Germany – another paragon of 'stability' – ran structural deficits on the fiscal side, i.e. spent beyond its means when it comes to government expenditure outside what is needed to correct for recessionary imbalances. Ditto for the Netherlands.

For Ireland, 'exports-led growth' is, alas, historically not an engine of external balances. The cumulated current account deficit for the country is -19.5 per cent of GDP. Reversing twelve years of that experience will require re-wiring our economy, preferences, political and institutional structures, etc. – all long-term and exceptionally hard to achieve measures.

The fact is, deficits are sticky and thus very hard to reverse. Past deficit experience shapes much of the future performance, as illustrated in Figure 3.3.

Once you are insolvent for a decade (1990s) you are highly likely to remain insolvent for the next decade as well (2000s). And the headwinds against Ireland reversing that and moving into strong surpluses in its current account in years ahead are strong. If we look at the transition from the 1990s external balance position to the 2000s position, the following holds for the Eurozone:

• Finland and the Netherlands stand out as the only two countries that managed to improve their surpluses on the current account side between the 1990s and 2000s averages.

• France, Belgium and Luxembourg are the only three countries that managed to retain surpluses, but their performance weakened between 1990s and 2000s.

• Malta was the only country that managed to reduce its external deficits between the 1990s and 2000s in terms of averages.

• Portugal, Greece, Estonia, Cyprus, the Slovak Republic, Spain, Ireland, Slovenia and Italy all saw average deficits of the 1990s deepening in the 2000s.

• Only two economies, Austria and Germany, managed to reverse previous deficits (in the 1990s) to surpluses in the 2000s.

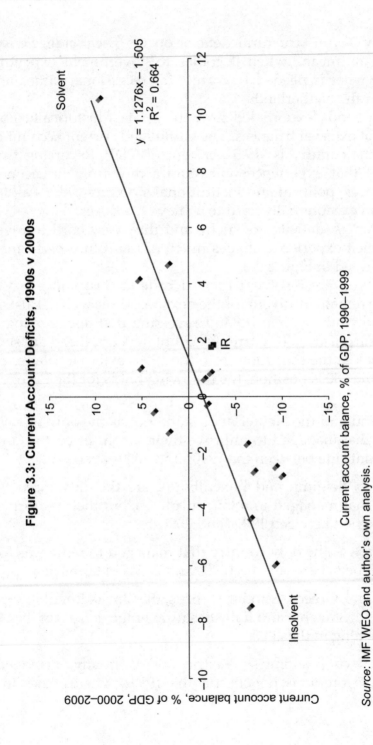

Figure 3.3: Current Account Deficits, 1990s v 2000s

$y = 1.1276x - 1.505$
$R^2 = 0.664$

Solvent

Insolvent

IR

Current account balance, % of GDP, 2000-2009

Current account balance, % of GDP, 1990–1999

Source: IMF WEO and author's own analysis.

That means that, historically, the chance of reversing an average current account deficit in the previous decade to a surplus in the next decade is 2 to 17 or less than 12 per cent. Not an impossible feat, but an unlikely one.

Current account deficits do appear to correlate closely to general government deficits and structural fiscal deficits. Thus insolvency of the deepest (across all three measures) variety was the domain of ten out of seventeen member states when it comes to the last twelve years of Eurozone history. Another five member states are insolvent by two out of three criteria. Lastly, only two member states – Finland and Luxembourg – have actually been fully solvent since 2000.

And, of course, Ireland stands out once again, with:

- Relatively solvent external balances averaging 1.74 per cent of GDP in 1990–1999 (fourth strongest) yielding to an average annual current account deficit of 2.35 per cent over 2000–2009 period (seventh worst performer in the Eurozone)

- Mildly insolvent public finances in 1990–1999 (with average general government deficits of 0.90 per cent of GDP; third best performance in the Eurozone) yielding to a 1.02 per cent average deficit in 2000–2009 (twelfth best performance in the Eurozone)

- Substantial structural deficits in the 1990–1999 period (with an average structural deficit of 3.09 per cent; the eleventh highest in the Eurozone) yielding to a 6.14 per cent average deficit in the 2000–2009 period (second highest after Greece)

It is worth noting that in the 1990s Irish current account surpluses were subject to potentially higher tax revenue capture than they are today. A combination of lower corporate tax rates and increased reliance on multinational corporations to produce these surpluses (evidenced by Ireland's widening GDP/GNP gap – the gap that reflects outflows of payments from Irish-based multinational corporations) suggest this much.

Selective Restructuring as the Only Option

Put against the requirement for double-digit current account surpluses in order to deflate the current debt overhang in the Irish economy, the above historical record is not encouraging. Growing out of debt is unlikely to be a sustainable strategy for Irish economy.

The traditional tool-box for dealing with balance sheet recessions includes:

- Growth-supporting external demand

- Availability of cheap investment financing from abroad

- Devaluation-driven improved cost competitiveness

- Deep and swift institutional reforms

- Significant excess capacity for absorption of FDI

Hardly any of the above tools are available to Ireland today.

From this vantage point, restructuring of Irish debts appears to be no longer a policy choice, but a policy necessity. The only remaining question, therefore, is how such restructuring can be configured to minimise adverse effects on the Irish economy.

Given the analysis above, it is clear that the options available to Ireland are:

- Option 1: Restructure official government debt, which is expected to peak at circa 116 per cent of GDP in 2013–2014

- Option 2: Restructure banking sector debts, especially those that represent quasi-governmental liabilities, such as the promissory notes to the Irish Bank Resolution Corporation (IBRC, formerly Anglo Irish Bank), amounting to under €30 billion

- Option 3: Restructure household debt

- Option 4: Restructure private corporate debt

Option 4 can be ruled out from the start as it will constitute a market-distorting support for incumbent enterprises. In addition, corporate debt restructuring can be dealt with through both normal liquidation and receivership processes. Furthermore, absent independent monetary policy capacity, restructuring corporate debts in a systemic fashion will have the most adverse impact on the banking sector balance sheets and will lead to significant debt transfers from the private sector to the Exchequer. It is perhaps revealing to note that the Irish government's approach to resolving the banking crisis to date, exemplified by NAMA, attempted exactly this type of restructuring with NAMA purchasing only business loans related to land, development and property investments.

Option 1, while attractive from the fiscal short-term sustainability point of view, carries substantial costs for any Exchequer that is running deep (greater than 1–2 per cent) structural deficits. The requirement for securing external funding to finance gradual adjustments to fiscal deficits means that this option is de facto shut for Ireland.

This suggests that the only two options open for Ireland are Options 2 and 3: restructuring of some banking sector debts and some household debts. The two options are not only feasible, they are actually complementary. This complementarity implies an overall reduced cost of undertaking such restructuring and is driven by the fact that much of the household debt in Ireland is held on domestic banks' balance sheets. Further complementarity is implied by the fact that some of the banking sector debts are directly linked to the government debt – via the promissory notes and NAMA bonds which have been used as collateral for borrowings from the Central Bank of Ireland and the ECB. In other words, restructuring banking sector debts by reducing sector liabilities to external lenders will free resources to draw down some of the assets written against the households and the Exchequer.

The upside to such a drawdown is to reduce the probability of future defaults by the households and to bring loan-to-value

(LTV) ratios closer to the level where any foreclosures that might still arise will be carried out at no loss to both the banks and the households. Core benefits, however, are much broader. Restructuring current household debt levels will reduce the overall rates of mortgage default and will simultaneously compensate households for the greater burden of recent banks bailouts and public debt increases.

Mortgages arrears and pressures on household budgets arising from the income and wealth effects of increasing costs of mortgage financing and the continued deterioration in asset values in the Irish property sector are immense. Per the latest data available to us, in Quarter 3 of 2011 there were 773,420 outstanding mortgages in Ireland. Of these, 62,970 mortgages were in arrears more than 90 days, up 55.6 per cent on same period a year ago. In addition, 36,376 mortgages were 'restructured' but are currently 'performing' – in other words, paying at least some interest. Adding together all mortgages in arrears and repossessions, plus those mortgages that were restructured but are not in arrears yet, 100,230 mortgages (13 per cent of the total), amounting to €18.3 billion (or 16 per cent of the total outstanding mortgage amount), are currently at risk of default, are defaulting or have defaulted. Given the trend to date, we can expect that by the end of 2011 there will be some 107,000–110,000 mortgages in distress in Ireland. By the end of 2012 this number may rise to over 161,000 or some 21 per cent of the total mortgage pool in the country. When considered in the light of demographic distribution and vintages, mortgages that are likely to be in arrears around the end of 2012/the beginning of 2013 can account for up to 30 per cent of the total value of mortgages outstanding. This is a simple corollary of the fact that the mortgage crisis is now impacting most severely families in their 30s and 40s, with more recent and, thus, larger mortgages signed around the peak of the property bubble. These households are facing three pressures in today's environment.

Firstly, they are experiencing above-average unemployment and income pressures. Per the Quarterly National Household Survey, in Quarter 2 of 2011, the unemployment rate for persons aged 25–34 was 16.5 per cent and the unemployment rate for those aged 35–44 was 12.4 per cent; both well ahead of the 8.95 per cent average unemployment rate for older households. By virtue of being more concentrated in the middle class earning categories, they are also facing higher tax burdens than their lower earning younger and more asset rich older counterparts.

Secondly, they are facing higher costs of living, further depressing their capacity to repay these mortgages. In September 2011, the prices of petrol and diesel were some 15 per cent above their levels a year previously, and bus fares were up 10.8 per cent. Since the time these families bought their houses (circa 2005–2007), primary and secondary education costs increased 21–22 per cent, and third level education costs rose 32 per cent. On average, larger families require greater health spending, the cost of which rose 16 per cent above 2005–2007 levels. The three categories of costs described above comprise circa 20 per cent of the total household budget for an average Irish household and above that for mid-aged households with children.

Thirdly, as their disposable incomes shrink and mortgage costs rise (mortgage-related interest costs are up 17.2 per cent year on year and 11 per cent on 2006), the very same households that are hardest hit by the crisis are also missing vital years for generating savings for their old age pension provisions and the most active years for entrepreneurship and investment.

In short, courtesy of the crisis and the government policy responses to it to date, Ireland already has a 'lost generation' – the most economically, socially and culturally productive one. And this generation is now at the forefront of the largest homemade crisis we are facing – the crisis of mortgage defaults and personal bankruptcies. Against this backdrop, the forthcoming Personal Bankruptcies Bill should form a cornerstone of the government's policy.

Bringing household debt to sustainable (growth-support-ive) levels in the case of Ireland implies a write-down of circa €40–50 billion and can be financed via a direct write-down of the banks' borrowings from the Central Bank of Ireland. In addition, restructuring bank-held government promissory notes to zero coupon 30-year notes will achieve Exchequer savings of circa €44–50 billion over the ten years' horizon, depending on the various estimates of the total cost of these notes financing. Finally, taking a direct write-down of 20–25 per cent of Irish banks' borrowings from the ECB will allow for the write-downs of the mortgage debts to the scenario that would bring them in line with the situation where the maximum extent of the current negative equity for primary residences will be no larger than 15 per cent. The combined measures will reduce the overall debt levels of the Irish Exchequer closer to more sustainable 80 per cent of GDP levels (relative to 2010–2012 GDP) and household debts to 90 per cent of GDP.

In the current global economic environment and given the severity of the total real economy debt overhang in Ireland, the above restructuring, which does not involve any non-banking sector participation by private investors or public debt holders, is the lowest cost feasible solution for the crisis. Given the extremely low probability of the Irish economy being able to achieve sutained levels of growth that would be required to 'grow out' of the current debt crisis, it is virtually inevitable that some debt restructuring will take place sooner or later. The longer such a restructuring is delayed, the more severe will be the cumulative losses sustained by the economy in the periods prior to the restructuring and the weaker will be the economy to re-start growth post-restructuring. It is, therefore, imperative that the Irish government leads the markets with a concerted policy response designed to reduce our real economy's debt overhang.

Endnotes

[1] Comprising the group of countries defined by the IMF as 'other advanced economies' (advanced economies excluding G7 and Eurozone), see WEO database.

[2] All data from IMF World Economic Outlook, September 2011 database, unless specified otherwise.

4

Ireland's Public Debt –
Tell Me a Story We Have Not Heard Yet …

Seamus Coffey

Seamus is a lecturer in the School of Economics in University College Cork.

There has been an ongoing, and at times confusing, debate about what Ireland's public debt will be in 2015. This chapter aims to look at some of the different elements of Irish public debt and the factors that can pull us away from the precipice of a sovereign default. This would be relatively straightforward if there was a universally accepted definition of public debt; there is not.

Economists are at heart storytellers. As storytellers, economists decide what matters for their purposes; they are, in a word, selective. By appreciating economists as storytellers, the general public can perhaps appreciate better why economists disagree. The spectre of default in Ireland is an exemplar of storytelling and how appreciating the choices the economist as storyteller makes is crucial in enabling the reader of such stories entering into that economist's imaginative world. So, let me tell you a story of default.

As a starting point we will use the general government debt (GGD) measure as defined in the Maastricht Treaty of 1992. This is the measure used by Eurostat when compiling EU data and is also commonly used by the International Monetary Fund (IMF) and the Organisation of Economic Co-Operation and

Development (OECD). The GGD is the consolidated gross total of all liabilities of general government.

In the GGD no allowance is made for any assets that may offset some of these liabilities. The GGD is simply the total of all general government liabilities. The Maastricht Treaty laid out the rules for entry and participation in the single currency. One of these was that the GGD could not exceed 60 per cent of a country's nominal gross domestic product (GDP). At the end of 2011 only four Eurozone countries satisfied this limit: Finland, Luxembourg, Slovakia and Slovenia. All other countries were in excess of the 60 per cent limit.

At the end of 2011, Ireland's GGD was €166 billion. The composition of this debt is shown in Table 4.1. Although we are still awaiting the final figure it is likely that 2011 nominal GDP will be around €155 billion. This means our debt to GDP ratio is probably 107 per cent.

Table 4.1: General Government Debt, December 2011

Item	Amount
Government bonds	€85 billion
Promissory notes	€28 billion
Retail debt	€14 billion
EU/IMF loans	€33 billion
Other	€6 billion
Total	*€166 billion*

Source: National Treasury Management Agency

It is also important to note that there was €13 billion of cash in the Exchequer Account at the end of 2011 which is not offset when determining the GGD.

Just as there is no single definition of public debt, there is no universally accepted threshold of where this debt becomes unsustainable with a default viewed as inevitable. The 60 per cent threshold was chosen for the Maastricht Treaty simply because this was viewed as a 'safe' level of public debt. At the time of the introduction of the Euro in 1999, original members of the Euro-zone such as Belgium and Italy already had debt that was above 100 per cent of GDP.

Recent studies have shown that a public debt in excess of 80 per cent of GDP has a negative effect on economic growth, but this is not the same as saying the debt is unsustainable. In a European context it is likely that a debt ratio in excess of 120 per cent puts a country in grave danger of seeing its debt spiral out of control.

At the end of 2011 the Greek debt ratio was well in excess of this level at 160 per cent, with Italy right on threshold at 120 per cent. In 2011, Ireland, with a debt of 107 per cent of GDP, was below this threshold and while there are some (including me) who envisage the debt ratio stabilising and subsequently falling away from these levels, there are many who see the debt ratio breaking through this threshold and continuing to rise. In one view default can be avoided; in the other it is inevitable.

To see why the choice of these thresholds is not universal we simply have to look at the example of Japan. At the end of 2011, the Japanese GGD was 230 per cent of GDP. This is more than twice the Irish ratio but there is no one writing books stating that Japan is on the verge of default. At the end of 2011 the yield on ten-year Japanese government bonds was less than 1 per cent. Investors in Japanese bonds do not think they will default either.

There are a myriad of reasons as to why Japanese debt is sustainable at 230 per cent of GDP while default is the only outcome for Greece with a debt of 160 per cent of GDP. The key one is that the Japanese government controls the Bank of Japan, which can simply print more yen to repay their debts. Greece cannot avail of anything like this facility with the European Central Bank (ECB).

The debt ratio is a straightforward calculation that puts the total debt in the numerator and the level of GDP in the denominator. Changes in either will bring about changes in the ratio.

$$\frac{Debt}{GDP} \sim \frac{Interest\ Cost\ \&\ Primary\ Deficit}{Economic\ Growth\ \&\ Inflation}$$

In order for the debt to be sustainable it is necessary that the average interest rate on the debt is less than the sum of the growth and inflation rates unless the government runs a sufficiently large primary surplus. The primary balance is the budget balance excluding interest payments. If a country is running a primary deficit and the interest rate is greater than the nominal growth rate the debt ratio will rise unsustainably.

At the time of the Budget in December 2011 the Department of Finance estimated that nominal growth in 2012 would be 2.3 per cent and that there would be a primary deficit in 2012 of 4.1 per cent of GDP. In both cases we miss the debt sustainability criteria. The interest rate on our debt is more than double the growth rate and there is no primary surplus to offset this interest cost. In 2012 the GGD is forecast to rise from 107 per cent to 114 per cent of GDP.

Over the coming years the nominal growth rate is forecast to rise to around 4 per cent a year, though changes to real growth or inflation will affect this. This will still be below the average interest rate on our debt, which is forecast to be 5.2 per cent in 2015, so in the absence of a sufficiently large primary surplus the debt ratio will continue to rise.

The primary balance is forecast to move from a deficit of 4 per cent of GDP in 2012 to a surplus of 3 per cent in 2015. It is this improvement in the public finances that will stabilise the debt ratio. If these conditions are satisfied in 2015 the debt will fall from 117 per cent to 114 per cent of GDP over the year.

This dynamic was improved considerably by the EU decision in July 2011 to reduce the interest rate on loans provided as part of the EU/IMF programme. This decision reduced the average interest rate on Irish debt by about 1 per cent and substantially increased the impact of a primary surplus on the debt ratio. If these interest rate reductions were not granted it is unlikely that the debt ratio would have been contained.

To see why this debt sustainability story is plausible we are going to do two things. First, we will explore how the GGD got to €166 billion by 2011; and second, what it will rise to by 2015.

At the end of 2007, Ireland's GGD was €47 billion. This is the debt level we brought into the crisis, which was largely a result of the previous crisis in the public finances in the 1980s. In general governments do not repay debt, rolling it over instead by borrowing anew. From 2007, the debt then increased by €119 billion in just four years.

From 2007 to 2009, the cash balances in the Exchequer and other accounts increased from just under €4 billion to almost €17 billion. During 2008 and 2009 the National Treasury Management Agency had the foresight to borrow funds on international markets to build up these cash balances before Ireland was shut out of the bond markets in late 2010. This increase in our cash buffer accounts for about €13 billion of the rise in the government debt.

Financing the services provided by government in these four years required €59 billion of borrowing. This was necessary to fill the gap that emerged between government revenue and government expenditure and to ensure that the government could meet its pay, pensions, social welfare and interest outgoings. Interest expenditure over the four years was €13 billion.

Separately, there is the money that has been used for the bailout of our delinquent banking system. By the end of 2010, the Exchequer had contributed around €9 billion directly to the banks. This was evenly split between borrowed money paid into the National Pension Reserve Fund since 2007 that was subsequently used as part of the initial recapitalisations of AIB and Bank of Ireland, and direct contributions from the Exchequer to Anglo, Irish National Building Society (INBS) and EBS.

There was also the creation of €31 billion of promissory notes given to Anglo, INBS and EBS in 2010. These are a promise by the state to pay this money to the banks, but the payment will be spread out over an extended period. The first instalment of €3.1 billion was made in March 2011 and these will continue well into the next decade until the full amount, plus accrued interest, is paid to these zombie institutions. The final cost of repaying the promissory notes has been estimated at €48 billion and if these repayments continue to be made with borrowed money the total cost of the promissory notes will exceed €80 billion by 2030.

We will look at Anglo and INBS in more detail in a later section but it is important to remember that the cost of the promissory notes and the cost of the recapitalisation are not the same thing. The repayments on the promissory notes include €17 billion of interest. This is being paid to Anglo Irish Bank and INBS, which are state owned. They in turn are using the promissory notes to avail of emergency liquidity from the Central Bank of Ireland. They are paying interest to the Central Bank for this facility. The Central Bank will make a profit on this and will return the interest to the Exchequer as part of its annual surplus. The interest on the promissory notes is not a cost to the state as much of it will be returned.

In 2011 there was a further stress test and subsequent recapitalisation of the other four covered banks: AIB, Bank of Ireland, EBS and Permanent TSB. The Central Bank estimated that the four banks would need to be recapitalised by €24 billion in order to be in a position to absorb the losses projected over the next three years by the consulting firm BlackRock.

Significant haircuts undertaken with subordinated bondholders in the banks provided about €5 billion of this amount. Some asset disposals by the banks and private sector investment in Bank of Ireland reduced the amount to be covered by the state to just under €17 billion. Of this, €10 billion came from the further liquidation of the assets built up in the National Pension Reserve Fund so the additional debt from the bank recapitalisation was around €7 billion.

The €119 billion increase in the GGD from 2007 to 2011 can be broken down as follows:

- €13 billion to build up cash balances

- €59 billion to fund government services

- €47 billion for the bank bailout

Although it attracts the most attention, the banking disaster has contributed just 40 per cent of the increase in the GGD over the past four years. The next issue is where the debt level is going to go over the next four years.

At this stage the only thing certain to increase the debt over the next four years are the annual deficits. Some steps have been taken to try to control the deficit but it remains at very high levels. Between 2012 and 2015 it is estimated that a further €40 billion will be required to finance the annual deficits across all areas of government. The deficits for the four years are forecast to be €13.6 billion, €12.4 billion, €8.6 billion and €5.1 billion. This will put the debt at €206 billion in 2015.

This is substantially lower than some earlier estimates of our 2015 debt. For example, in early 2011 the IMF were forecasting that the 2015 debt would be €225 billion and debt sustainability was only possible if some very optimistic growth projections were used. However, since then there have been some positive developments for Ireland's debt dynamics.

The original EU/IMF programme set aside a €35 billion 'worst case scenario' contingency fund for the recapitalisation of the banks, of which €17.5 billion was going to be borrowed. As we now know the 2011 recapitalisation required less than €7 billion of additional borrowing. The reduction in the EU interest rates will reduce the forecast by around €3 billion while there was a €4 billion reduction in the starting point because of a 'double counting error' in the Department of Finance revealed in November 2011.

The IMF also used 2014 as an endpoint for the programme meaning their 2015 deficit is on a no policy change basis. This put their original 2015 deficit forecast about €3 billion higher than will be the case as the budgetary adjustment programme is now extended in 2015.

In total, these developments over the past year mean that the IMF's forecast of Ireland's 2015 GGD can be reduced by more than €20 billion. After four years of almost unrelenting bad news and deteriorating projections it is encouraging to see that some forecasts are finally beginning to improve.

Of course, all these deficits, plus the rollover of existing debt will require substantial amounts of funding. Could it be the case that we will default because we will run out of money?

The current EU/IMF programme is designed to run until the end of 2013. Ireland needs €46 billion in 2012 and 2013 to fund the annual deficits, meet the payments on the promissory notes and repay the maturing of existing debt. We still have to draw down around €34 billion of loans as part of the EU/IMF programme. The remaining €12 billion is expected to come from state savings schemes, our existing resources and some market funding.

Ireland had €13 billion of cash in the Exchequer account at the end of 2011. Without additional funding the state can meet all its obligations through to the end of 2013. It is also forecast that €1.5 billion a year can be raised through the state savings schemes such as savings bonds, prize bonds and the national solidarity bond. In 2011 these raised €1.36 billion. If the €1.5 billion was achieved we would have around €4 billion left in the Exchequer account at the end of 2013. Without market funding this would be a very weak position to be in as there is a €12 billion bond maturing on 15 January 2014 and we will need €10 billion to fund the Exchequer deficit that year.

We could run out of money in January 2014 but that will not happen. The National Treasury Management Agency has already carried a bond swap that has pushed the maturity of about one-third of the January 2014 bond out to February 2015. This reduced the amount of funding we will need in 2014. It is hoped that the state will 'dip its toe' back into the bond market in late 2012/early 2013 to try to raise some new market funding. At this remove it appears unlikely that this will be able to raise the necessary amounts.

However, at the EU summit on 21 July 2011 it was agreed that programme countries would continue to be funded after the terms of the original agreements have ended. At the time, Michael Noonan said, 'there's a commitment that if countries continue to fulfil the conditions of their programme, the European authorities will continue to supply them with money, even when the programme concludes' and also 'if we're not back in the markets, the European authorities will give us money until we're back in the markets.' Ireland will not run out of money that will force it into a default.

There are other issues related to the banking collapse that are not included in the GGD. These are, the final outcome of the NAMA process, whether the shutdown of Anglo and INBS will require further injections of capital and how to unwind the €110 billion of liquidity the banks have taken from the European and Irish Central Banks. There is also the long-term hope that we will be able to sell off our stakes in the two 'pillar' banks to recoup some of the money swallowed by the bailout. There is a great deal of uncertainty about all these.

The NAMA process has seen the creation of €31 billion of bonds used to buy over €72 billion of developer loans from the banks with an average discount of 58 per cent. These bonds are a liability of the state but following a ruling of Eurostat they are not included in the GGD. It is impossible to know what the final outcome of the NAMA process will be. NAMA did create €31 billion of bonds to buy the developer debt, but it bought assets which also had a notional value of €31 billion as valued in November 2009. If these levels were to be maintained beyond the November 2009 valuation date, NAMA would have no effect on our net debt position. Of course, property prices have not been unchanged since November 2009 and in fact have tumbled ever downward. There are some estimates that the value of property backing the loans has fallen by a further €5 billion since the NAMA valuation date.

It is impossible to use this as a projection of possible NAMA losses. In most cases NAMA has control over the loans and not the assets. NAMA has been making substantial disposals for the past year but we are not told if the agency is making a loss or even possibly a profit on these transactions. These sales have allowed NAMA to begin repaying the bonds issued when the agency was formed. NAMA has the potential to make a call on the state's resources to cover a shortfall in its operations. Of the €31 billion of bonds created, €1.5 billion are subordinated bonds which will not be repaid if the agency generates a loss. Unless there is an almost complete collapse in asset values it is hard to see how this shortfall could be more than €5 billion, and it is likely to be substantially less than that.

The Irish Bank Resolution Corporation (IBRC) was formed with the merger of Anglo Irish Bank and the Irish Nationwide Building Society in September 2011. The IBRC is a wholly state-owned bank and its liabilities are equivalent to sovereign liabilities. In its last set of accounts, produced for the first six months of 2011 Anglo revealed it has outstanding liabilities of €51 billion, of which €41 billion was owed to the Central Bank of Ireland. There was around €6 billion of bonds and €4 billion of other liabilities. A summary of Anglo's last balance sheet is provided in Table 4.2. These liabilities could be included in the GGD and it is possible that a change to reflect this will be introduced.

Table 4.2: Anglo Irish Bank Balance Sheet, June 2011

Assets		Liabilities	
Promissory notes	€24 billion	Central Bank	€41 billion
Customer loans	€15 billion	Bonds	€6 billion
Loans for sale	€7 billion	Other liabilities	€4 billion
Other assets	€8 billion		
Total assets	€54 billion	Total liabilities	€51 billion
Total equity			*€3 billion*

Source: Anglo Irish Bank, *Interim Report*, June 2011

On the asset side we can see that half of these liabilities are already covered by promissory notes issued by the state and that there is €3 billion of equity in the bank. Consolidating the accounts would mean that about €20 billion of Anglo liabilities would be added to the GGD. The figure for the INBS part of the IBRC will be less than a quarter of this.

This change would increase the debt ratio by 15 per cent of GDP and push the debt ratio above 130 per cent of GDP. It is important to realise that this change would not put any additional cost on the Exchequer but would merely allow the GGD to better reflect the gross liabilities of the state.

There will only be an additional cost to the state if the assets on the balance sheet are not able to meet the liabilities to be paid (of which 80 per cent is owed to the Central Bank of Ireland). The IBRC has already disposed of some of these. The loans for sale category includes a €6 billion US loan book which was sold for around €5 billion in October 2011. This loss was provided for in the above accounts. This €5 billion was used to repay some of the emergency liquidity assistance the bank is availing of from the Central Bank of Ireland.

Customer loans amount to €24 billion, with €15 billion in Ireland and €9 billion in the UK. All US loans were classed as loans for sale. A loss provision of €9 billion on customer loans gives rise to the €15 billion figure used in the balance sheet. This is a write-down of around 40 per cent.

Figures on the loan book performance show that only 45 per cent of the loans are non-impaired. It is difficult to forecast what the recovery rate on non-performing loans will be but achieving 60 per cent of the nominal value of the loans seems probable. The bank does have around €3 billion of equity (which was provided by the state of course) but this means that a loan loss rate of greater than 50 per cent would be required before any additional state resources would be required.

The inclusion of the IBRC would increase the GGD but would not mean that additional state support for the bank is necessarily required. If no additional support to the bank is required the inclusion of the IBRC in the GGD cannot make debt sustainability any less likely. Only losses on the bank's customer loans above 40 per cent or on its other assets can cause that.

The €110 billion of Central Bank liquidity the banks have obtained is also backed by assets that have a nominal value well in excess of €110 billion. Outside of the IBRC, these are largely the customer loans the banks have issued. Between the NAMA process and the recent stress tests, €85 billion of loan losses have been accounted for in the covered banks. Other losses provided for in the banks' annual accounts (such as the €9 billion discussed in the Anglo accounts above) and covered by the former equity they held would bring this even higher. It is likely that well over €100 billion of loan losses in the covered banks have already been accounted for and there are no credible estimates that they will be higher.

The banks have substantial liabilities to central banks, bond-holders and depositors. Without state assistance they would not be able to meet these liabilities. The state has provided €63 billion to the banks to cover this shortfall. If the banks are not to meet their liabilities it would require losses above those already accounted for to materialise. There is little to suggest that this is the case. In time the covered banks can unwind their reliance on Central Bank funding. This will be achieved as loans are repaid or sold and by acquiring deposits, particular inter-bank deposits, as confidence in the Irish banking system is slowly restored.

What all the above shows is why there is such confusion about Ireland's public debt and why there is no hard rule on what constitutes an unsustainable level of debt. Ireland's public debt is massive and is set to grow over the next few years. However, it is very probable that the debt ratio can be controlled and, in time, will fall away from the extreme levels it is currently exhibiting.

Using the current definition, Ireland's GGD was €166 billion at the end of 2011. With nominal GDP of around €155 billion the debt was equivalent to 107 per cent of GDP. It is possible to get a number that is much larger than this.

If NAMA's €30 billion of liabilities are included the debt would be 124 per cent of GDP. If the consolidated liabilities of the IBRC are added the debt would be around 140 per cent of GDP. If we are just picking numbers out of the air we could add another 10 per cent of GDP for no good reason other than the banks have huge levels of Central Bank liquidity drawn down. As we're at it we could add in over €100 billion of unfunded pension liabilities that the state will face over the coming decades. In the space of a single paragraph we have gone from a high but manageable debt of 107 per cent of GDP to a huge and unsustainable debt of 220 per cent of GDP.

In fact, neither figure proves that the debt is manageable or unsustainable. What truly decides whether a debt mountain is sustainable or not is the interest burden it puts on the public finances. Japan can carry a debt of 220 per cent of GDP because it can borrow at less than 1 per cent interest over ten years. This keeps Japan's interest expenditure at manageable levels. As countries rarely repay public debt the decisive issue is not the size of the debt but the amount of government revenue that goes to pay the interest on the debt.

State bodies such as NAMA and the IBRC, and even semi-states like the Dublin Airport Authority and the ESB, have huge debt levels. However, because they have their own assets, the interest payments they make do not come out of general government revenue. In fact, most of these bodies have sufficient assets to allow them to not pay the interest but also to fully repay the debts they have accumulated.

These debts could appear on the government's balance sheet and give the impression that the state is going to be utterly overwhelmed by debt. However, it is not the liabilities of these bodies that have to be covered by the state but the losses. And even then it is the interest burden that covering these losses would generate rather than the size of the losses that matters. If NAMA and the IBRC have €20 billion of losses to be covered by the state, then borrowing at 5 per cent would put an interest burden of €1 billion on the state. This is a huge sum of money but is not one that will result in national bankruptcy. There is no suggestion that these bodies will generate additional losses of more than a small fraction of this amount.

While there is uncertainty about these losses, there is no uncertainty about the ongoing need to fund the annual budget deficit. Taking the end-2011 debt of €166 billion, and adding the €40 billion needed for the deficits, means that by the end of 2015 the GGD will be in the region of €206 billion. This is the Department of Finance's forecast, the European Commission's forecast, will be the IMF's forecast, and, for what it is worth, it is my forecast.

Servicing the €206 billion debt mountain we have created will cost about €8 billion a year in cash interest payments. This is the total amount of cash interest the state will have to pay on its debt. Different aggregate debt levels can be obtained whether one includes or excludes a whole range of items. The cash interest to be paid is not open to such interpretation. There are huge government debts in NAMA, the IBRC and other bodies but because they have their own resources the interest on these debts will not be a drain on the government's resources.

A cash interest bill of €8 billion is a huge burden to carry. It will be about 4.5 per cent of GDP and most of this will be paid to external creditors. By 2015 general government revenue is forecast to be around €62 billion with tax revenue of €43 billion. This cash interest will consume close to one-eighth of total government revenue (or one-fifth of tax revenue). The actual servicing cost will depend on the average interest rate, which is estimated to be 5.2 per cent.

Of course if the 5.2 per cent was applied to the €206 billion debt then it suggests that the interest payments should be over €10 billion. The €206 billion will include about €20 billion of promissory notes and there will be nearly €2 billion of interest added to them in 2015. This interest is paid to the state-owned IBRC which in turn will be paying interest to the Central Bank of Ireland for emergency liquidity. The interest due on the promissory notes is not paid to the IBRC but is rolled up into the capital amount. The IBRC will receive a fixed payment of €3.1 billion per year from the Exchequer until the promissory notes plus interest have been paid off. The presence of the promissory notes increases the government debt but does not affect the cash interest payments to be made.

An €8 billion annual interest payment is a huge burden for the country. However, at this stage, default remains an option to be considered rather than an inevitability to be endured.

We will also have substantial assets that would allow us to reduce the debt. In the above analysis we will also still have €13 billion of cash reserves intact. If we exhaust our cash reserves the debt would be €193 billion, but such an action would not be prudent. Although much of the National Pension Reserve Fund has been liquidated to recapitalise the banks there is still around €5 billion remaining in the fund. The banks have also been provided with €3 billion of 'contingent capital' which is due to be returned to the Exchequer in 2014.

The debt will also be lower once, hopefully, a sale for the banks can be undertaken. We have complete ownership of AIB and Permanent TSB and a 15 per cent stake in Bank of Ireland. Although it seems unlikely at present there may yet come a time where we will be able to offload the banks and use the money generated to repay the debt. The amount raised will be nowhere near the €63 billion we have poured into the banks but it will usefully reduce the debt.

It is hard to put a value on the banks but it will be some non-trivial sum. It is easy to suggest that the cash reserves, National Pension Reserve Fund and contingent capital would reduce Ireland's net debt to GDP ratio to around 100 per cent. If 10 per cent of GDP could be obtained for the banks the net debt position would be 90 per cent of GDP. If you prefer GNP as the appropriate measure of the Irish economy we are probably looking at a net debt in 2015 that will be around 115 per cent of GNP: large but by no means terminal.

Table 4.1 shows the breakdown of Ireland's €166 billion GGD at the end of December 2011. In November 2011 a Greek 'default' of 50 per cent on sovereign bonds held by private investors was agreed with the EU. There were many calls that Ireland should seek a similar write-down on its debt. As the table shows, Ireland has €85 billion of outstanding sovereign bonds with another €5 billion to be repaid in March 2012.

The covered banks have around €12 billion of Irish government bonds on their balance sheet. Any write-downs here will have to be made good by capital injections from the state so the net benefit of a default on these bonds would be reduced by the money we would have to put into the banks. The ECB holds an estimated €22 billion of Irish government bonds as a result of the bond buying programme that it has been undertaking since the middle of 2011. The ECB has declared itself not to be a private creditor. This means the 50 per cent write-down would apply to about €50 billion of government bonds which would generate a total debt reduction of around €25 billion. If the Greek 'default' was applied to Irish debt it would reduce the debt total by 15 per cent and bring it down to 90 per cent of GDP. The ongoing deficit and the likely increased interest cost of the remaining debt would quickly see it rise back above 100 per cent of GDP.

As was pointed out above it is not necessarily the size of the debt that matters but the interest burden it places on the government. If a 50 per cent haircut was applied to privately held Irish government bonds it would reduce our interest bill by €1.25 billion per annum, assuming that the average rate on the debt written off was 5 per cent. It is forecast that the general government deficit for 2012 will be €13.6 billion. It would still be above €12 billion if the 50 per cent debt write-down was applied. Even an 80 per cent write-down would only knock €2 billion off the annual interest bill.

It should also be noted that this is only on the assumption that the interest rate on our remaining debt remains unchanged. It would take an increase of only 1 percentage point on the remaining €124 billion of debt to fully offset the interest savings from the initial write-down. It is highly probable that such a rise would occur.

Any Irish default would have to focus on sovereign bonds but these are not held in sufficient quantity by private investors to generate sufficient benefits to offset the undoubted costs that would follow such an action. A default worthy of the name would require losses to be forced on official creditors. Much as it might seem desirable or attractive, it is not possible to unilaterally default on the ECB, EU or the IMF.

By going through the debt numbers, we see that we brought €47 billion of debt with us into this crisis in 2008. Bailing out the banks will have generated around €47 billion of debt by 2015. The annual Budget deficits between 2008 and 2015 will have generated €99 billion of borrowings and we have borrowed €13 billion to build up a cash buffer.

If the country had avoided assuming the bad debt losses of the banking sector, the debt ratio in 2015 would still be around 90 per cent of GDP, which is better than 115 per cent but would not eliminate the fear of default because of the ongoing annual deficits. Of course, without the bank bailout we would also have a €20 billion sovereign wealth fund.

A negative outcome on any of the unknowns described earlier will increase the fear of default, but just because there is a lot of noise suggesting default is inevitable is not enough to mean it will happen. If the necessary steps are taken we can carry the interest burden of a debt of 115 per cent from 2015 and, in time, the debt ratio will fall. It will be painful but it can be done.

We don't need to default on our debt but we may need some further assistance from the EU/IMF. To get through the end of 2015 the government needs to borrow €40 billion to fund its expenditure. The government also needs around €36 billion to roll over existing debt and pay the promissory notes. We need close to €76 billion of funding to see us from 2012 through to the end of 2015.

The EU/IMF deal will provide €34 billion of this. We need to raise an additional €42 billion, or around €30 billion if we use up our cash reserves. The official view is that we will return to the bond markets in late 2013 and begin raising this money then. With current yields on Irish bonds in the secondary market above 7 per cent it is still hard to see how we can raise this money sustainably from private sources. Market sentiment may improve as uncertainty about our situation dissipates, which would allow us to raise the money, but if that does not happen soon enough we will need additional support from the EU/IMF. We could achieve the funding target but if not I believe that this support will be provided because the programme can work.

If the option to default is to be taken, or default occurs because we have not arranged to have the required funding in place, those to suffer will be holders of Irish government bonds. It is more than a little incongruous that senior bondholders who invested in our delinquent banks are getting their money back while those who invested in our country may be forced to carry losses. As with a lot of things in this crisis, including unsupported claims of a €250 billion public debt, this just does not add up. I believe we can avoid that outcome and that we can stabilise our public debt. So this is my default story.

5

A very Irish Default, or
When Is a Default Not a Default?

Stephen Kinsella

*Stephen is a lecturer in Economics at the Kemmy Business School, University of
Limerick, Director of the Centre for Organisation Science and Public Policy, and a
research associate of the Geary Institute, University College Dublin. His website is
www.stephenkinsella.net.*

Default can be defined simply as not paying interest or the principal on debt owed when it falls due. At the time of writing,
November 2011, international bond markets are highly volatile,
expecting a Greek default and clearly worried about an Irish
default. The stability of the global economic system and the Euro
as a currency, and the credibility of the crisis resolution institutions of the European Union, are at stake.

The goal of this chapter is to examine the possible effects of an
Irish default on the European economy as a whole. We will look
at the past performance of the Irish economy, examine the types
of debt Ireland holds at the moment in some detail, and discuss
what *type* of default Ireland might engage in. We will finish by
sketching out the possible consequences for the European economy and the Eurozone of such a default.

Recent history ensures that there are several complicating
factors in the Irish case. It is therefore very important to understand this historical context when examining Ireland's current
difficulties.

The scale of Ireland's funding problem is vast. In 2010, Ireland's domestic economy as measured by its gross national income (GNI) was worth about €131 billion.[1] In 2010 the sum of Ireland's borrowing was about €148 billion. By the end of 2011 it is estimated to be €173 billion, and is expected to peak at around €193 billion by the end of 2014. In ratio terms, the ratio between the output of the domestic economy in a given year and the total level of debt built up over time to be repaid by the sovereign is expected to peak at 140 per cent in 2014 or 2015. By comparison, in 1988, at the nadir of Ireland's last economic crisis, the same ratio was 119 per cent, with a larger funding cost than today, and with a roughly similar unemployment picture to today – approaching 14 per cent of the total workforce.

Karl Whelan[2] argues that a confluence of factors created the preconditions for an economic miracle during the 1980s. In the 1980s the problem was purely fiscal – increasing taxes and cutting expenditure was sufficient to help the economy recover. Other factors contributed, including a series of currency devaluations in 1986 and 1992/1993, our access for the first time to the European single market following the Maastricht Treaty, Ireland's stable labour market, and the demographic dividend Ireland enjoyed as 'the Pope's children' came of age with a high level of freely provided third-level education, just at a time when foreign direct investment was beginning to wash over the nation. Economic growth and prosperity broke out, with Ireland's GNI rising from €49 billion in 1995 to €131 billion in 2009.[3] Ireland's unemployment rate fell from 12.9 per cent in January 1995 to 4.4 per cent in December 2007. Throughout this period, Ireland's inflation rate remained low and relatively stable.

From the end of 2007, things only got worse for Ireland. Ireland's debt levels, only 28 per cent of GNI in 2007, grew in three years to over 114 per cent of GNI by the end of 2011. Unemployment rose from 4.4 per cent in December 2007 to 14.3 per cent in September 2011. Household net worth in Ireland has fallen almost 34 per cent from its peak of €641 billion at the end of 2006.

Ireland had an old-fashioned asset bubble.[4] Over the period 2002–2006, the structure of the Irish economy became increasingly dependent on the construction sector, and by 2006 construction output represented 24 per cent of GNI, as compared with an average ratio of 12 per cent in Western Europe. By the second quarter of 2007, construction accounted for over 13 per cent of all employment (almost 19 per cent when those indirectly employed are included), and generated 18 per cent of tax revenues.[5]

Thus the background for Ireland's current debt problem is a fifteen-year period of robust growth, followed by a four-year period where the gains of the previous fifteen years have been lost to a greater or lesser extent by a large proportion of Irish society. The balance sheets of Ireland's banks were damaged by their exposure to property-related lending. Private bank borrowings on international markets to fund property lending grew from less than €15 billion in 2003 to close to €100 billion in 2007. When the bubble burst, these banks were highly exposed.

The Irish government in September 2008 agreed to guarantee the liabilities of six of Ireland's banks. A series of policies implemented to nationalise, recapitalise and reformat the banks have taken place since 2008, including the setting up of the National Asset Management Agency (NAMA) to oversee the management of good and bad loans taken on by Ireland's wayward banks on behalf of the taxpayer, while issuing government-backed bonds to help shore up banks' balance sheets. As each policy has been implemented the national debt has risen.

The national debt of any country is the sum of all the previous issuances of debt, usually (but not always) in the form of government bonds that have not been repaid yet. Governments borrow over fairly long time horizons when they can, and must repay the interest (and/or the coupon) on the debt until the time comes to repay the principal. Once that time comes, the debt can also be 'rolled over', refinanced or bought back with another debt issuance at higher or lower rates, depending on the conditions in the market at the time. Sometimes the debt is even repaid.

All government debt carries a risk of default. Ireland's national debt profile is composed of several categories, each of which must be considered when thinking about default. We will go through them one by one, but they are government bonds, which includes the pre-crisis government debt; other medium and long term debt; state savings schemes; short-term debt issued for liquidity purposes; promissory notes; debts of central and local government; and sundries.

We will focus mostly on the increasing government deficit financed through international borrowing. We will also look at the emergency liquidity assistance afforded to Ireland's banks, which are being paid off using the promissory notes written to cover some of the cost of bailing out Ireland's banks in addition to the ministerial comforts given for several types of asset classes. We will examine the loans from the European Central Bank (ECB), the European Commission and the International Monetary Fund (IMF), as well as from Denmark, Sweden and the United Kingdom. In addition, the €30.7 billion of state borrowing to fund NAMA must be paid back at some stage, though it is not appropriate to treat this as part of the national debt as yet. Interest must also be paid on all of this debt at varying rates. The

Table 5.1: Composition and Categorisation of Irish Government Debt in Billions of Euro at the End of 2010

Composition of Government Debt	€ (billions)
Government bonds	90.1
Other medium- and long-term debt	0.7
State savings schemes	12.7
Short-term debt	6.2
Promissory notes to financial institutions	30.9
Debt of other central government bodies	5.8
Local government debt	0.8
Other adjustments	1.0
Total	*148.1*

Source: National Treasury Management Agency, *Annual Report*, 2010, p. 14, and author's calculations

total cash cost of debt servicing in Ireland is estimated to be €5.2 billion in 2011, rising to €9.2 billion in 2015.

Table 5.1 shows the various categories and magnitudes of Irish debt as they existed at the end of 2010, and we will go through them one by one in the next section.

Government Bonds

The boom years of the Celtic Tiger are often portrayed as years when the national debt was paid off. In ratio terms, the national debt as a percentage of Ireland's GNI did fall from 89 per cent in 1995 to 28 per cent in 2007. However, the reason for this fall is not that the level of indebtedness fell (the numerator in the fraction), but that total economic output as measured by GNI increased (the denominator). In absolute terms, the Irish state owed €43.6 billion in 1995. The Irish state owed €47.4 billion just as the economy began to collapse in 2007.

Since 2007 the Irish state has added €43.1 billion in state-issued government debt raised on the international bond markets. The cost of funding the state grew at an increasing rate as confidence in the solvency of the state diminished in 2009 and 2010. Because of the erosion of market confidence in Europe's peripheral nations, as well as its own internal problems, Ireland was forced to apply for a loan facility to the International Monetary Fund (IMF) on 21 November 2010.

The EU/IMF loan facility will add to the national debt. The loan facility is worth €85 billion over a three- to four-year period. The facility takes €22.5 billion from the IMF, €17.7 billion from the European Financial Stability Facility (EFSF), controlled by the ECB, and €22.5 billion from the European Financial Stability Mechanism (EFSM), controlled by the European Commission, with €17.5 billion from Ireland's cash reserves (€5 billion) and National Pension Reserve Fund (€12.5 billion).

In addition, the United Kingdom has pledged €3.8 billion, and Denmark and Sweden have pledged €400 million and €600 million respectively. Each of these different 'pots' of loanable funds comes through the IMF with an interest rate. The rates of interest applied by the EFSF and EFSM, on average 3.9 per cent, in each quarterly tranche have been substantially higher than the IMF rates of 3.1 per cent. The EFSF and EFSM rates have come down from an initial average interest rate of 5.82 per cent.

The EU/IMF loan facility attaches stringent 'conditionality' measures to be implemented to receive further tranches of capital. The current set of measures include bringing the budget deficit to within 3 per cent of a primary balance by 2015, various supply side measures, and a privatisation programme of state assets.

State Savings Schemes and Central Government Bodies

A full €12.7 billion of state borrowing exists as state savings schemes, where the lender in this case is the Irish citizen through the national postal service An Post, for example. Another €6.6 billion (€5.8 and €0.8 billion, respectively) exists as borrowing from state agencies and for the purpose of financing local authorities. For obvious reasons, no default can occur for these categories of government debt.

Short-Term Debt

Since 2007, mainly due to a fall in taxation revenues from construction-related activities as the construction bubble burst, the Irish government's expenditures have been much greater than its receipts, and so it has had to run a large primary deficit. The deficit is financed through borrowing at different maturities. The short-term borrowing came in the form of treasury bills to the value of €6.2 billion. The long-term borrowing came from the international bond markets initially, and from 2011 until 2014 at least will come from a consortium of funding bodies led by the IMF, the ECB and the European Commission, though the Irish government has stated its intention to return to the markets in a small way in 2012.

Promissory Notes

Ireland's banks required taxpayer funds to help fund their losses. In particular, Anglo Irish Bank, Irish Nationwide Building Society (INBS) and the Educational Building Society (EBS) have required €30.9 billion in 'promissory notes' just to balance their books, such was the scale of their losses.

A promissory note is an unsecured 'promise to pay' the sum agreed at a later date. The capital injections required were funded by promissory notes issued by the state to Anglo and INBS in lieu of cash, because normal funding channels were not available to these banks.

Promissory notes are not, strictly speaking, government debt, though for accounting purposes by the European statistical agency Eurostat they are treated as such.

Promissory notes are debt vehicles issued by the Central Bank of Ireland, rather than the European Central Bank. They are not, strictly speaking, backed by the ECB, as these notes are not eligible for refinancing operations by the ECB. The liability for these notes falls on the individual issuing state.

The promissory note repayment structure calls for government borrowing of €3.1 billion plus interest and other capital payments each year to repay these notes over a 10 to 15 year period at varying interest rates. These interest rates are pegged to the interest rates on an Irish ten-year bond at the moment.

In summary, Ireland's debt levels and debt servicing will increase over the next few years as the repayment of our EU/IMF loans begin, the repayment of the €90.1 billion of bond financing takes place, and the promissory note repayment takes place. All of this must be funded from Exchequer receipts at some point, imposing a large opportunity cost on Irish society in terms of the provision of state services.

Having looked briefly at the recent economic history of Ireland, and in some depth at the current and future debt profile of the nation, then this is the picture we must have in our minds when thinking about an Irish default. There is not one single 'pot' of cash to be defaulted upon, but rather selective categories of national debt. Two elements of the picture remain: the role of the ECB and the outstanding liabilities of the covered banking institutions.

Central banks exist to dampen the natural fluctuations within the credit and leverage cycles caused by the movement of capital.[6] The ECB has acted as it saw fit to stabilise the European economy, but not as a textbook central bank might. Central banks can issue bonds to 'cleanse' the balance sheets of wayward banks, transferring assets to the central bank's balance sheets to contain the contagion effects of banks getting into trouble. Central banks can also call for debt write-downs and enforce them.

In the Irish case, no debt write-downs of senior bondholders were considered or allowed, while large amounts of emergency liquidity assistance were given by the ECB to Irish banks via the Central Bank of Ireland to allow private banks to continue their operations.

The risk of the creation of emergency liquidity assistance for a private bank is borne by the national central bank that decides to fund the private bank in that manner. The emergency liquidity assistance being given is equivalent to the promissory notes being written for the damaged Irish banks, discussed above, in that the national government, itself in rough shape economically, must have the appearance of guaranteeing large amounts of capital. The implicit lender of last resort – the ECB – waits to learn whether it will be required, or not. In the event of an Irish default, it certainly would be.

Finally, to get a clear(ish) picture of who might be affected by any default, we have to ask who our creditors are. The Bank for International Settlements[7] publishes annualised data on debt holdings by banks and by country. These statistics are skewed in the case of Ireland by the presence of large banking conglomerates – hence the use of the '(ish)' above – but Table 5.2 gives the debt position as of March 2011 for Ireland's banks.

We can see from Table 5.2 that Ireland's public sector has just over €18 billion held in European and non-European banks, with foreign claims amounting to close to €473 billion outstanding at the end of March 2011. The non-bank private sector in Ireland has €302 billion in European banks and €73 billion in non-European banks. The liabilities of the banking system in Ireland are roughly four times the yearly income of the nation. The liabilities of the banking system matter in the consideration of any Irish default. The reason for this is simple: Ireland's banks are guaranteed by the sovereign, and are inextricably bound to the state via the banking guarantee and by the provision of emergency liquidity assistance. Any change in the terms of debt settlement agreements between a sovereign and its creditors will perforce damage the banking sector.

What default strategies might the Irish economy employ? Let us work under the assumption that Ireland remains within the Euro currency and therefore is not permitted to require senior bondholders to 'burden share' in the losses of the banks they invested in.

It is important to note that the rest of the debt either accrued to this point or locked in via the EU/IMF loan arrangement is either sovereign debt or a mixture of local and savings debt and the promissory notes written to cover the losses some private banks sustained following the collapse of the construction sector.

Remembering that a sovereign default is simply not paying interest or a principal owed to creditors, there are several default strategies a government might employ.

The first default strategy is the 'nuclear' option of reneging on most of the outstanding debt of the nation. There are very few examples of this type of default outside of wartime episodes, where the debtor nation feels it need not pay back the debts accrued to an aggressor. The post-war category includes civil wars, and examples of these defaults would be China in 1949, Czechoslovakia in 1952 and Cuba in 1960. In these cases, the debt reneged upon is characterised as 'odious'.

The second type of default is partial, and occurs following a credit bubble. These are by far the most common, and Russia's default in the 1998 (discussed in Chapter 7 of this book) is the largest recent example.

Table 5.2: Consolidated Foreign Claims and Other Potential Exposures on an Ultimate Risk Basis for Irish Banks in Amounts Outstanding (€ Billions)

	Banks								
	European	Non-European	France	Germany	Italy	Japan	United States	United Kingdom	Total of 24 Countries
Foreign claims	378	95	30	117	13	21	137	59	473
Public sector	15	4	3	3	1	1	5	2	18
Banks	61	18	8	25	2	2	15	15	79
Non-bank private sector	302	73	19	88	11	18	117	43	375
Other potential exposures	142	66	25	39	12	1	48	60	208

Source: Bank for International Settlements (2011) *Quarterly Review, September 2011*, Table 9E, pp. A104–A105.

The third type of default is a 'soft' default, or a restructuring of privately held debt over time. So the debtor agrees to repay the full amount but over a longer time horizon with perhaps a lower interest rate. This is a default in that the interest applied to the restructured loan will typically not yield the same return as the original debt contract. Examples of post-war debt restructuring abound, especially in the 1970s and early 1980s, and include Turkey in 1978, Romania in 1981 and Poland in 1981. Almost every Latin American economy defaulted or restructured their debts in this period as well.

Ireland really has two choices: it can default on its sovereign debt or try to recoup some of the losses on promissory notes. The first option should be resisted until all other options have been exhausted. The second option carries no fiscal or monetary consequence beyond a renegotiation with the ECB over the terms of the repayment of the promissory notes. This is a default, as defined here. But it is also not a default. No credit default swaps will be triggered; no credit ratings will be damaged. The Irish state is agreeing, through a third party, to pay itself less and over a longer time. This would be a very Irish default.

Now, what would the consequences for such a default be in Europe? We must always consider the political economy of each situation Ireland finds herself in. Assuming Ireland remains steadfast in its application of austerity policies, and assuming the stability of the Eurozone was at stake, a renegotiation of Ireland's emergency liquidity assistance, or the promissory note structure, would give precedent to other nations to act in a similar manner.

For the ECB, the creation of assets by national central banks with banking systems in trouble is anathema. Yet the dilution of the promissory note structure would, in all likelihood, have no significant effects on the balance sheet of the ECB, beyond the creation of an expectation that the ECB would move to shore up the balance sheets of its wayward national central banks via emergency liquidity assistance measures.

In summary, then, at the end of 2011 Ireland has few options to default, when considering the political economy of a nation inured to austerity policies, bent under EU and IMF condition-ality, and zealous to remain in the Eurozone. The benefits of a default are not paying back all of one's debts. The costs come when new debt must be raised, and when trade depends upon certainty. Markets are forward looking, but they do remember sovereign defaults – for a while, at least. The Eurozone will not tremble at the restructuring of our debts, owed only to ourselves.

Endnotes

1   In this chapter I use gross national income (GNI) rather than gross domestic product (GDP) or gross national product (GNP). Gross national income is similar to gross national product but also deducts indirect business taxes and EU taxes and subsidies. The difference between gross national and gross domestic product is that while GDP includes the income of the multinational sector, GNP does not.

2   Karl Whelan (2010) 'Policy Lessons from Ireland's Latest Depression', *Economic and Social Review*, Vol. 41, No. 2, pp. 225–254.

3   Colm McCarthy (2010) 'Fiscal Consolidation in Ireland: Lessons from the Last Time' in Stephen Kinsella and Anthon Leddin *Understanding Ireland's Economic Crisis: Prospects for Recovery*, Dublin: Blackhall Publishing, pp. 103–116, and Stephen Kinsella (in press) 'Is Ireland really the Role Model for Austerity?', *Cambridge Journal of Economics*.

4   Stephen Kinsella and Anthony Leddin (2010) *Understanding Ireland's Economic Crisis: Prospects for Recovery*, Dublin: Blackhall Publishing, for an overview of how the crisis came about in the early 2000s.

5   Constantin Gurdgiev, Brian M. Lucey, Ciaran Mac an Bhaird and Lorcan Roche-Kelly (2011) 'The Irish Economy: Three Strikes and You're Out?', working paper available from SSRN: <http://ssrn.com/abstract=1776190>.

6   Hyman P. Minsky (1986) *Stabilizing an Unstable Economy*, New Haven, CT: Yale University Press.

7   Bank for International Settlements (2011) *BIS Quarterly Report*, Q4 2011, available from: <http://www.bis.org/publ/qtrpdf/r_qa1109.pdf>.

6

How to Survive on the *Titanic*: Ireland's Relationship with Europe

Megan Greene

Megan is Head of European Economics at Roubini Global Economics and previously worked as a senior economist with the Economist Intelligence Unit.

The prospects for the Eurozone do not look good. A number of weaker Eurozone countries – Greece, Ireland and Portugal – are being kept on life support by bailout packages with terms and conditionality that may well end up killing the patients. Italy and Spain are increasingly looking insolvent and will probably be forced to seek bailouts as well. Without growth in the region, a negative feedback loop of austerity and recession has already begun. In order to regain competitiveness and return to growth, a number of Eurozone countries are likely to opt to abandon the common currency. However, against this very grim backdrop Ireland has been held up by EU leaders as a bright light. The small, open economy has been a model student in terms of complying with the terms of its bailout agreement and hitting all of its targets. The EU, European Central Bank (ECB) and International Monetary Fund (IMF) (the so-called troika) see Ireland's performance as a vindication of their response to the crisis, with competitiveness gains and economic growth reported in the first half of 2011.

But any good news in Ireland must be set against the enormous costs the country has had to bear. It experienced a depression in 2008–2010, the state has been saddled with the private debt of the banking sector, the public has seen five austerity budgets and counting, and unemployment has remained stubbornly high. For these reasons, since the beginning of the Eurozone crisis in 2008 the public, and more recently members of the Irish political elite, have increasingly questioned whether the benefits of Eurozone membership still outweigh the costs. This question will only increase in relevance if, as is likely, other countries drop out of the common currency in an effort to regain competitiveness. Ireland's calculus in determining whether to stay in the Eurozone or exit is unique because of its reliance for economic growth on the output of multinational corporations (MNCs), many of which use Ireland as a springboard into the single market. To leave the Eurozone would be to risk deterring these MNCs by undermining Ireland's position within Europe. It is in Ireland's best interest to remain in the Eurozone in order to protect the country's relationship with the EU and, therefore, its growth model.

Prospects for the Eurozone Are Grim

Before considering the prospects for Ireland's relationship with Europe, it is necessary first to canvass the likely future of the Eurozone and EU. By the end of 2011, the region's crisis had shown no signs of stabilising and had spread beyond weaker Portugal, Italy, Ireland, Greece and Spain (the PIIGS) and well into the core. Not only were Italian and Spanish bond yields shooting up to clearly unsustainable levels, but Belgian, Austrian and French bond yields had risen sharply as well. Meanwhile the prospect of weaker countries leaving the Eurozone was becoming increasingly likely.

Response a Bust

The crisis response by EU leaders so far has been lacklustre at best. The main component of the response for weaker countries facing unsustainable borrowing costs in the markets has been a bailout package from the EU and IMF accompanied by strict conditionality. The conditionality is meant to ensure measures are implemented to achieve two things: to boost the countries' competitiveness and to rein in their fiscal dynamics. However, if we use these two objectives as our metrics for success, this plan has been a clear bust everywhere in the periphery except arguably in Ireland. Using unit labour costs as an indication of competitiveness, Greece and Portugal have seen their unit labour costs fall only very mildly, while Ireland has had its unit labour costs fall more sharply. Using budget deficits as an indicator of fiscal developments, Greece's primary deficit (the government deficit excluding debt servicing costs) actually increased in 2011 compared with 2010. Portugal reduced its 2011 budget deficit by implementing a number of one-off measures but this will not work in the future, particularly as Portugal's gross domestic product contracts. According to the troika's quarterly assessment, Ireland was ahead of the budget deficit reduction targets in 2011 as stipulated by the bailout programme.

In the case of Greece, EU leaders went beyond providing a bailout programme with strict conditionality, allowing Greece to negotiate a voluntary debt exchange with its creditors, dubbed private sector involvement (PSI). According to the terms of this exchange, banks holding Greek government debt would agree to accept longer-dated bonds, effectively writing down their holdings by at least half. But the effectiveness of this strategy is questionable. While PSI helps to address a country's debt stock problem, it does not address the flows of debt that a country like Greece will continue to accrue in the absence of structural reforms and economic growth.

Greece as a Model

EU leaders have gone out of their way to insist that Greece is a unique case. However, it seems much more likely that Greece will become a model for how to handle weaker countries in the Eurozone. At the time of writing (early 2012), Greece faces a stark choice in terms of how to return to growth. The country can either continue along its current path, implementing harsh austerity measures and savagely cutting wages and prices in an attempt to undergo an internal devaluation and regain competitiveness. This would involve tolerating up to a decade of recession or depression. Alternatively, Greece could abandon the Euro, reissue the drachma and see it devalue massively. The result would be a much faster boost in competitiveness and return to growth.

Leaving the Eurozone would certainly be painful and messy for Greece. However, some of the deterrents against leaving, such as the prospect of sovereign and bank default, seem increasingly likely even within the Eurozone, which impacts the cost–benefit analysis of Eurozone membership. Furthermore, it would be in everyone's best interests – the core countries, the peripheral countries, the ECB, the IMF and Greece – for a Greek Eurozone exit to be as managed and negotiated as possible. It therefore seems likely that it will be handled much like a divorce. Greece and the EU would decide that they simply do not belong together, and the EU would offer bridge financing and take efforts to protect its own banking system as it facilitates Greece's exit from the common currency.

Any managed exit by Greece wouldn't take place in a vacuum. Once Greece exits, Portugal would likely face the same choice about competitiveness and growth. It too would choose to exit the Eurozone. Ireland would face the same decision, and while it may choose to follow suit it would be misguided to do so. This rippling wave of potential exits from the Eurozone would not stop with the three countries currently in receipt of bailout funding. Ongoing efforts to provide a backstop for the huge financing needs of Italy and Spain look insufficient to do anything more than buy some time. Eventually, these two countries will also face the same question as Greece: they can either return to growth via a decade of austerity and recession/depression or they can choose to leave the Eurozone in as managed a fashion as possible.

Changing the Rules of the Game

A break-up of the Eurozone as outlined above is very likely, but it is not inevitable. If a number of conditions are met, the common currency can stick together. First and foremost, the Eurozone must return to growth. For this to happen, the ECB must provide massive amounts of quantitative and credit easing. Second, the ECB must talk down the Euro aggressively so that it is at parity with the US dollar. However, given that the Eurozone is one of China and the US's biggest export markets, it is questionable whether China or the US would tolerate such a weak Euro. Third, core countries would need to provide fiscal stimulus measures to trickle into the periphery. The chances of all three of these measures occurring simultaneously are extremely low.

Beyond these measures to stimulate growth in the Eurozone, EU leaders would need to fundamentally change the structure of the Eurozone so that it includes either fiscal transfers or joint assets and liabilities (in the form of Eurobonds). In late 2011, EU leaders (except for UK Prime Minister David Cameron) agreed in theory to treaty changes (dubbed the 'fiscal compact') that were touted as the first step towards fiscal union. At the heart of these changes is more fiscal discipline, with more automatic sanctions imposed on countries that miss fiscal targets. These are not steps towards fiscal union. Rather, the treaty changes proposed institutionalise the asymmetric adjustment occurring in the Eurozone, whereby the peripheral countries are forced to make all of the adjustment while the core countries do not adjust at all. Not only is this a surefire recipe for recession in the peripheral countries, but it also indicates how far EU leaders are from accepting fiscal transfers or Eurobonds.

Eurozone Break-Up the Death Knell for the EU?

According to the Treaty on European Union, a country cannot exit the Eurozone without also exiting the EU. But this is a legal technicality, not a practical, moral or ideological necessity. Legal impediments can easily be overcome by agreeing and writing new rules. The EU existed without a common currency before the introduction of the Euro. Those countries that are currently in the EU but do not use the Euro benefit significantly from the single market. It is in all EU member states' best interests to keep the common market together, and consequently it seems likely new legislation to allow for this will be agreed.

Ireland's EU Relationship: It's Complicated

The Irish public has been increasingly ambivalent about EU membership for more than a decade. Previously, sentiment towards the EU was overwhelmingly positive, reflecting a wide range of benefits that were associated with membership. There were direct economic gains, both in terms of structural funds received from the EU as well as, crucially, the massive expansion of the market into which companies based in Ireland could sell. More generally, EU membership contributed to a national feel-good factor. It was seen as a way of emerging from the UK's shadow to act on an equal footing with Europe's major powers in the numerous EU policy areas requiring unanimous decisions.

However, Ireland is deeply protective of its sovereignty and anti-European sentiment emerged and hardened in response to EU treaty revisions that were perceived by many to encroach too far on Ireland's right to make decisions for itself. This was highlighted in 2001 and 2008 when Ireland rejected the Nice and Lisbon treaties, respectively. Both treaties were subsequently approved at the second time of asking, but for critics of the EU these second votes were simply further evidence that Brussels was contemptuous of democracy at the national level.

Anger directed at the EU has intensified and widened since the eruption of the Eurozone crisis, largely in response to key terms of Ireland's EU/IMF bailout, such as the ECB's insistence that senior bondholders in Ireland's zombie banks be made whole (repaid in full) by the taxpayer. There is now a clear dichotomy in Irish society and politics between those who argue that Ireland's national interest lies in unilaterally breaking with the terms of the bailout, and those who argue that Ireland's core interests lie in being anchored within European political and economic structures, even if the price is compliance with bailout rules that are perceived to be unjust.

The European question is an increasingly important driver of the country's domestic politics. While the current coalition government of Fine Gael and Labour has not rocked the boat with Europe since taking office, on the campaign trail both parties sought to woo voters by adopting a more confrontational stance than usual. Moreover, the government's relative meekness in office (the Minister for Finance, Michael Noonan, has repeatedly called for debt relief from the troika only to back down immediately when rebuffed) has seen it lose support to the populist left-wing nationalism of Sinn Féin, previously a fringe party with its roots in the Northern Ireland conflict, but now the second most popular party in Ireland according to one opinion poll in late 2011.

In order to lessen the attraction of Sinn Féin's message of easy unilateralism, the government has sought to up the stakes by highlighting the risk that Ireland might end up outside the Eurozone. After EU leaders agreed in principle the terms of their 'fiscal compact' in late 2011, Minister Noonan announced that any Irish referendum on the changes would amount to a vote on whether the country would remain in the Eurozone.

Ireland's Growth Model Tied to the EU

If even the finance minister is openly acknowledging the possibility of Ireland leaving the Eurozone, is that the best course of action for the country? The answer is no for two main reasons: an Irish exit is more likely than others to be disorderly and the risk to Ireland's growth model from exiting is likely to be even greater than for other countries.

The longer Ireland continues to comply with its bailout agreement, the greater its debt burden becomes. If the Eurozone is going to fall apart anyhow, some would argue the Irish government should stop saddling itself with ever higher debts from making bondholders of zombie banks whole or repaying the promissory notes that were used to pour cash into those banks as the crisis was unfolding. This argument holds even more weight if Greece and Portugal default on their sovereign debt and choose to exit the Eurozone. If other countries are not repaying their bondholders, why should Ireland?

The answer to this depends in part on how the exit process is handled. I have argued that Greece and Portugal will agree with the troika that they are not meant to be in the common currency, and their exit will be managed and orderly. However, it is doubtful that the troika will agree Ireland should follow suit and leave the Eurozone. Ireland stands apart from the other bailout countries in that it has not only hit all of its bailout targets, but it shown some signs of a return to growth as well (albeit followed by further contraction). The EU has gone out of its way to praise Ireland for being a model student, complying with all the bailout rules and vindicating the troika in its insistence that austerity is the best path towards competitiveness and growth. It is unlikely the troika will turn around and accept that its plan for handling the crisis is misguided and that Ireland could potentially be insolvent.

It seems more likely therefore that an Irish exit from the common currency would have to be unilateral, without any transitional support from the troika. This would be messy and painful for any country. Eurozone exit would result in immediate sovereign and bank default, and bank runs would necessitate capital controls. Ireland would be frozen out of the markets at a time when it is running a primary deficit and needs immediate and ongoing funding for the government to continue offering regular services.

Because of the structure of Ireland's economy, a unilateral Eurozone exit would be particularly disastrous. Ireland's economy during the boom period in the 1990s and especially since the collapse of the property market in 2007–2008 has been heavily reliant on exports as a driver of growth. Ireland's export sector is comprised primarily of multinational corporations (MNCs) that have established their European headquarters in Ireland. The most successful industries, which were relatively resilient even during the depression Ireland experienced in 2008–2010, are the computer services and the pharmachemical goods industries. MNCs are attracted to Ireland for a number of reasons: Ireland boasts a highly educated, English-speaking workforce; the corporate tax rate is only 12.5 per cent and Ireland can offer MNCs rock-solid access to the greater EU market.

This last factor is absolutely key. If Ireland were to unilaterally defy the terms of the EU/IMF bailout agreement and walk away from Eurozone membership it would inevitably raise questions in the minds of MNCs as to Ireland's long-term position in a changing European order. Ireland would risk appearing to be a semi-detached member of a club in turmoil. This is not the ideal foundation on which to build a pitch selling the country as an ideal place to set up shop. Moreover, a unilateral Irish exit would lead to tensions with and resentment from other EU member states, which could manifest itself in a number of ways, including increased pressure to force up Ireland's low rate of corporation tax.

The cost of repaying bank bondholders and official sector loans while undergoing harsh austerity is extremely high. But the cost of unilaterally deciding to exit the Eurozone would undoubtedly be even higher. Ireland would be frozen out of the markets with a primary deficit and without a prayer of getting continued funding from the other EU member states it had just burned. Against this backdrop, the country would then have to develop a new growth model that is less reliant on MNCs for growth. The Irish government would hardly be in a position to provide support for domestic demand, nor would banks be able to offer financing to small, indigenous companies that might fill any vacuum left by MNCs.

Stay the Course

The prospects for the Eurozone staying together are very grim, but this does not necessarily bode poorly for Ireland. Much more important for Ireland than its relationship with the Eurozone is the country's integration in the wider EU market. The repayment of bank and official loans and continued austerity will weigh on Irish public finances and economic growth for years to come. This is indeed a heavy burden that might have been avoided – the Irish government had a number of chances to force a change in the terms of its bailout agreement. Having accepted the bailout terms thus far, however, it is in the country's best interest to continue to comply with the rules set out by the troika. Claims that Ireland's national interest lies in unilaterally leaving the Eurozone are woefully misguided. It is in Ireland's best interest to stay the course and continue to protect its relationship with the EU by maintaining its relationship with the Eurozone.

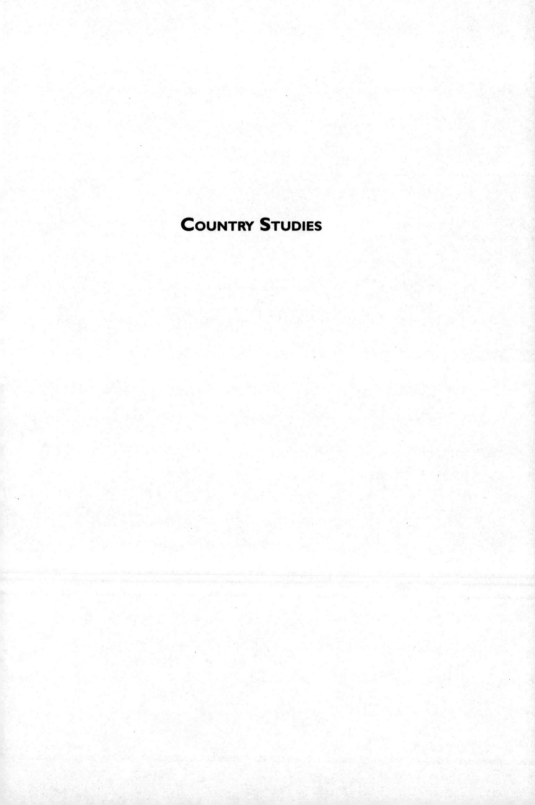

COUNTRY STUDIES

7

The Russian Crisis and the Crisis of Russia

Constantin Gurdgiev

Constantin is adjunct professor at the School of Business, Trinity College Dublin, and a director of St Columbanus AG, a Swiss asset management company. An internationally syndicated newspaper columnist, he blogs at trueeconomics.blogspot.com.

Introduction

In 1998, following some ten years of structural reforms that began during the late Soviet era under the *perestroika* process and continued after the collapse of the USSR, Russia recorded its first year of economic growth. The nascent middle class, starting to emerge in the country after the tumultuous years of early transition from the Soviet era, was enjoying what appeared to be the second year of rising disposable real incomes.

Then, with virtually no warning, by the end of August 1998, Russia found itself in a financial pariah state position, having defaulted on foreign-held sovereign debt, devalued its currency, imposed strict capital controls and bankrupted a large number of domestic firms and banks. A long-evolving sovereign crisis, having morphed into a fast-moving currency and banking crisis, had left deep scars on the socio-economic environment with middle-class savings either frozen in quasi-solvent banks or destroyed in their totality in dozens of fully insolvent smaller banks and investment funds. Foreign creditors – the lifeblood of an imports-dependent economy – were forced to write down their Russian assets as domestic banks suspended repayments of all external loans.

Despite the dramatic disruption caused by the crisis, the Russian economy staged an impressively swift comeback. The pain of the immediate crisis aftermath lasted a relatively brief period of time –approximately six to eight months – and the economy was able to rebound quickly and sharply. A decade-long economic boom followed the painful adjustments. During this time, the dollar value of Russian economic output increased ten-fold and the stock market rose more than twenty-fold to mid-2008. Devaluation triggered rapid structural rebalancing of the Russian economy and – helped by increases in oil and gas prices and general commodities inflation – by 2000, as shown in Figure 7.1, the economy not only recovered the losses triggered by the default, but also regained all of the ground lost since 1987–1988 reforms.

Figure 7.1: Gross Domestic Product per Capita, Current Prices, US Dollars

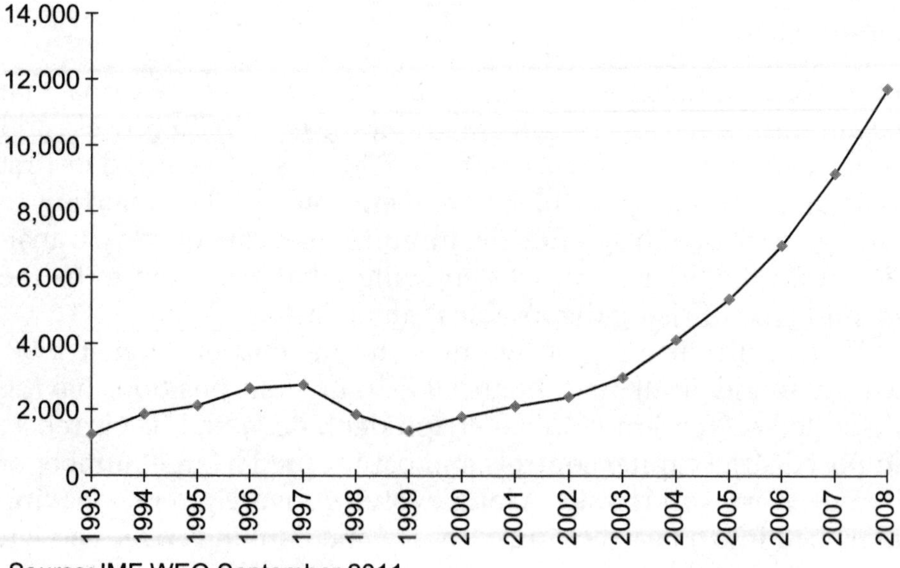

Source: IMF WEO September 2011

This process of recovery took a remarkably short period of time, with signs of emergent strengthening of the economy appearing in late 1999 and full macroeconomic recovery firmly established in 2000, less than one and a half years after the default. Russia returned to borrowing from the global markets within twelve months of its default, and booming exports-related revenues, along with prudent fiscal management and reformed tax policies, have resulted in the government repaying most of its debts in full, often ahead of schedule and in some cases even at a premium.

This historically unprecedented experience offers interesting insights and important lessons for the European crisis, and in particular for Ireland, as it highlights the overall importance of growth dynamics in determining the sustainability of a post-default or post-debt restructuring adjustment path. Although in the Russian case growth dynamics were driven by a combination of domestic and foreign factors not open to the Eurozone member states today, from the point of view of the impacted states with strong potential growth fundamentals, such as Ireland, the lessons from the Russian default present a hope for some significant upside potential for swiftly resolving debt overhang problems via a structured default. The Russian experience, however, also shows the importance of tangible and deep reforms in underwriting the process of recovery from the default.

In this context, let us first examine Russia's road to default, and take a brief look at the adjustment and recovery path taken since 1999 through 2008.

The Roots of the Crisis: 1995–1997

The roots of the 1998 Russian crisis can be found in the events that start with the collapse of the USSR, when the Russian economy inherited all of the USSR's debts and crumbling economic institutions and structures. This little known fact, often omitted from the discussion of the role of Russia in the post-Communist economic transition in the broader Central and Eastern Europe and Commonwealth of Independent States (CIS) regions, nonetheless serves as the departure point for the analysis of Russia's fiscal policy dynamics in the 1990s.

In April 1996, Russia began a series of international negotiations aimed at rescheduling the repayment of foreign debts inherited from the USSR. Until then, the Russian economy was saddled with the massive burden of covering $100 billion of debt that it assumed following the collapse of the Soviet Union. Overall, upon dissolution of the USSR, Russia assumed the entire foreign external debt of the Soviet Union despite the fact that Russia accounted for less than half of the total population of the USSR and for approximately 50 per cent of its national income. The level of debt carried by Russia from the USSR was equivalent to 117 per cent of the country's gross domestic product (GDP) in 1992. According to Nadmitov:[1]

> This level of debt was too heavy for a transitional Russian economy that needed further financial injections [in order to finance investment and transition]. The combination of a fall in output coupled with the fiscal costs associated with the transition made the scheduled debt service a significant burden. For ten years between 1991 and 2001 Russia reached six multilateral debt rescheduling agreements with official creditors, [and] held five formal debt relief and principal deferment negotiations with commercial creditors ....

Thus, from the Russian perspective, the 1996 re-negotiations of sovereign debt were a major move in the direction of stabilising the economy.

At the same time, late 1995 and 1996 were marked by improvements in the trade balance. Although the rate of growth in exports of goods and services declined slightly from 7.7 per cent in 1995 to 6.8 per cent in 1996, both years posted well above average increases in export volumes for the entire post-USSR period. At the same time, the rate of growth in imports of goods and services had fallen from 17.7 per cent in 1995 to 6.2 per cent in 1996, marking the first year since the transition began when the growth in exports was exceeding the growth in imports. At the same time, exports of oil rose from $14.6 billion in 1994 to $18.3 billion in 1995 and $23.4 billion in 1996. The heavy dependency of Russia on imports was itself the legacy of the Soviet Union economic organisation, which favoured specialisation across individual republics and between the member states of the COMECON (the common trade area of the former Warsaw Pact) block. Restructuring of this specialisation was always envisioned as a painful and long-term process, which was further disrupted by the mismanagement of trade flows upon the dissolution of the USSR.

Russian GDP in nominal terms rose from $276.9 billion in 1994 to $313.5 billion in 1995 and $391.8 billion in 1996. With slowing inflation (down from 215 per cent in 1994 to 21 per cent in 1996), real economic growth improved from -12.7 per cent in 1994 to -3.6 per cent in 1996. 1997 became the first year in the post-Soviet period when Russian real GDP actually expanded, achieving 1.38 per cent growth year on year. Inflation came under much stricter control at 11 per cent and by the end of 1997 Russian nominal GDP rose to $405 billion.

To a large extent, this effect was driven by improved volumes of exports of energy (oil and gas) and other primary materials. As illustrated in Figure 7.2 (index of prices for natural gas), Russian deliveries to Europe firmed up from 39.1 in 1994 to 46.5 in 1996 – the highest level since 1991. Average crude oil prices, which had stood at $15.95 per barrel in 1994, rose to $20.37 per barrel in 1996, also the highest price achieved in five years. Wheat, barley and cereal prices also posted decade highs in terms of prices in 1996, as did tin and nickel. Although energy accounted for 45 per cent of Russian exports by 1997, the overall exports of goods and services were on an improving trend in 1994–1996 and through the first half of 1997. While the legacy debt of the USSR was now close to the sustainable levels, the financing costs required to maintain the government debt remained high.

Russia entered the April 1996 negotiations on debt reduction with the Paris and London Clubs of borrowers – two international arrangements representing large groups of sovereign and private lenders – with its economic performance finally starting to show some signs of life after six years of rapid decline. These transitional years followed two decades of Soviet-era stagnation and economic decay. The analysts' consensus on the Russian

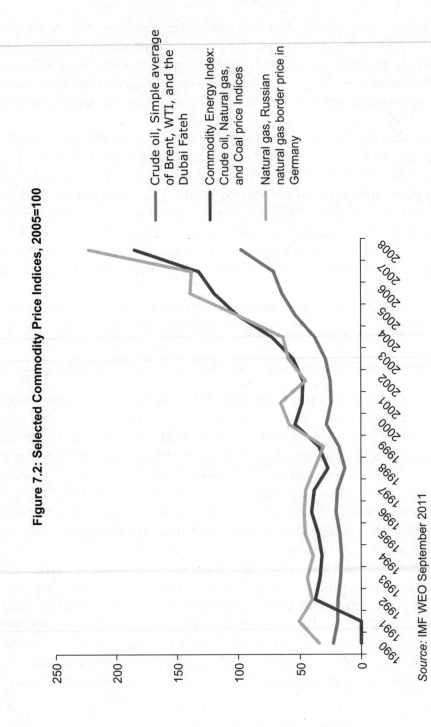

Figure 7.2: Selected Commodity Price Indices, 2005=100

Crude oil, Simple average of Brent, WTI, and the Dubai Fateh

Commodity Energy Index: Crude oil, Natural gas, and Coal price Indices

Natural gas, Russian natural gas border price in Germany

Source: IMF WEO September 2011

economy and fiscal conditions between 1996 and 1997 was, thus, favourable. This change in the outlook was a marked departure from the preceding decades. At the conclusion of these debt talks in September 1997 Russia agreed rescheduling the repayment of some $60 billion worth of ex-Soviet debt with the Paris Club. In October 1997, Russia rescheduled repayments on $33 billion of debts to the London Club. As a part of these agreements, Russia lifted the restrictions on foreign holdings of its sovereign bonds. By the end of 1997, foreign residents held almost one third of all state-issued short-term bills (GKOs).

The Blow Up: 1997–1998

Improved international ratings and subsequent gains in access to international lending markets, however, were not reflected in a matching improvement in the federal government's fiscal performance. Tax collection remained endemically mired in corruption, and harmful regional and federal competition; and the black markets continued to expand.

In addition, based on improving credit ratings, Russian banks aggressively courted foreign funding, with the ratio of foreign liabilities to assets rising from 7 per cent in 1994 to 17 per cent by the end of 1997. Exacerbating this growing risk exposure, the majority of investment contracts held by foreign investors in Russian banks (some $6 billion in total) were short term and held off balance sheet.

This meant that while on the surface the Russian economy was at the starting line for economic recovery, by late 1997/early 1998 a number of structural weaknesses were present behind the scenes. Improved access to external funding coincided with continued declines in private investment: between 1994 and 1997 total investment in Russian economy dropped from 26 per cent to 22 per cent of GDP. Increases in official and banks inflows masked even more pronounced declines in private foreign direct investment (FDI). In addition to endemic tax collection problems, rising unemployment (up to 10.8 per cent in 1997 from 7.2 per cent in 1994) contributed to shortfalls in government revenues. By the end of 1998 general government net borrowing was running at 8 per cent of GDP, the structural deficit widened in 1997 to a massive 16.3 per cent of GDP, and general government debt was on track to hit 100 per cent of GDP in 1997–1998. Wages backlogs exceeded 40 per cent of payrolls by 1997 and tax evasion, including by ordinary workers, was rampant.

Much of the economy remained captured by extraction sectors, with imports of goods rising 11.6 per cent year on year in 1997, while exports of goods were shrinking 1.05 per cent. Agriculture and food, and consumer goods remained particularly weak domestic sectors. By 1997, virtually every shelf in the average Russian supermarket was occupied by imported foodstuffs. Where domestic producers attempted to compete with branded foreign consumer goods, this competition almost invariably took place at the lower end of the value-added spectrum.

The lack of diversification in the Russian economy was caused by a combination of two factors. Firstly, the break-up of the Soviet Union and, equally importantly, the COMECON trading block exposed the Russian economy to a simultaneous loss of some markets for its output and a tightening of supply of consumer goods. Russia's energy, chemicals and heavy industry specialisation within the USSR has led to a de facto de-diversification of its economic activities. There were significant supply disruptions to Russian industry from the former COMECON member states, in effect shutting down production of internationally marketable heavy industrial equipment, aircraft and other goods traditionally specialised in by the Russian economy. Secondly, Russia's development since its 1991 independence from the USSR saw an increasing domestic and foreign capital push toward investment in oil and gas, as well as other extraction industries. Much of the economic policy at federal level reflected this development, especially since tax competition between federal authorities and local governments in the area of corporate tax revenues left the federal state budget more exposed to dependency on exports revenues from oil and gas sales. This further incentivised significant policy biases in favour of extraction sectors between 1993 and 1997.

The economic unravelling began in the foreign exchange markets in the last quarter of 1997 when, following the Asia Pacific currency crisis, the Russian ruble came under sustained devaluation pressures. By late November, the ruble was sustaining a deep speculative attack, just as the oil and gas prices began to moderate, signalling a twin currency valuation and currency demand crunch. Ruble overvaluation was sustained on the basis of the core government objective to keep inflation under control. Within just one month – in December 1997 – the Central Bank of Russia was forced to incur foreign exchange reserve losses of some $6 billion trying to defend the ruble. The problem was further exacerbated by the structure of the short-term bills (GKOs) issued by the Russian government, which contained an explicit hedge against ruble–dollar devaluation. This proviso was a direct outcome of the poor quality of expert advice Russia received from the international lending bodies, such as the International Monetary Fund (IMF) and the World Bank.

Inflationary control measures coincided with a defence of the overvalued ruble throughout most of 1998. The Central Bank of Russia attempted not only to deploy open market operations to sustain ruble valuations, but also increased the lending rate – the rate at which the Central Bank lends short-term funds to registered banks – from 2 per cent to 50 per cent in early 1998. With the developments in the Asian currency crisis in the background, in December 1997 the IMF re-launched loans disbursement to Russia, with a loan of $700 million. At the same time, the IMF urged Russian authorities to close the fiscal deficit gap in part by improving tax revenue collection.

Sustained pressure on the ruble accelerated into 1998 as it became increasingly apparent that economic growth would not reach the 2 per cent budgetary assumption. Tax reforms in February 1998, aimed at streamlining tax codes and improving tax collection, came in too late to reassure foreign investors that the Russian government's deficits were on a sustainable path. According to analysts, the Russian federal tax system of 1992–1999 was:

> ... characterized by extreme instability, complexity, and uneven distribution of tax burden, weak administration, low competitiveness and poor transparency. High rates of income and profit taxes were ones of the biggest business development disadvantages and because of weak administration of these taxes; they created the background for the shadow economy.[2]

The February 1998 reforms proposals were put in place primarily to alleviate IMF concerns regarding fiscal sustainability and to allow the IMF to extend its loans to Russia by one year. But the reforms, favoured by the Yeltsin administration, were not supported by the broader political establishment. The reforms did run into trouble in the State Duma (the lower house of the Russian Parliament), which briefly suspended hearings on their adoption in July 1998. The version of tax reforms that was finally approved on 16 July failed to commit to implementing the full $16 billion in tax revenue measures, as the State Duma scaled back President Yeltsin's proposals for higher sales taxes and land value taxes. In line with Duma approval, the IMF announced $23 billion worth of emergency loans to the Kremlin on 13 July 1998, well in excess of the normal special drawing rights (the unit of IMF capital-determining currency) allocations allowed.

Even before this disbursement took place, the Russian government had repeatedly tried to secure IMF funding since late March 1998. As financial conditions continued to deteriorate through the end of the first quarter of 1998, President Boris Yeltsin took a series of steps attempting to bring under control the twin economic and political crises. On 23 March 1998 he unexpectedly dismissed the entire Cabinet, sacked Prime Minister Viktor Chernomyrdin, and appointed the heretofore unknown 35-year-old Sergei Kiriyenko as the head of government. Kiriyenko's inexperience in the federal political structures proved a fatal error. The new prime minister's first political appointment took place in

1997 when he was given the portfolio of the First Deputy Minister for the Fuel and Energy Sector. Thus, prior to his appointment
as Prime Minister, Kiriyenko had less than twelve months' experience in government and no direct experience in federal politics,
and came from a corporate background.

The appointment of Kiriyenko as the country's prime minister
acted to further destabilise the already fragile political balance
between Yeltsin and the State Duma, as well as between the
federal state and regional authorities. It took Yeltsin until 24
April to finally secure Duma approval of the new prime minister
and even that required forceful threats from the President to the
parliament, including the threat of dismissal.

Kiriyenko showed his lack of experience when in a public interview he stated that Russian federal tax revenues were running
26 per cent behind targets. Instead of directly and transparently
promoting government budgetary plans for reduced deficits,
Kiriyenko made a bizarre statement that the federal government
was, at that point in time, 'quite poor'. Kiriyenko's public gaffe
reinforced an already growing public perception that the ruble
was to be devalued against the US dollar – the preferred store-
of-wealth currency in Russia in the 1990s. In May 1998, Sergei
Dubinin, chairman of the Central Bank of Russia, made another
public statement that referenced the possibility of the Russian
government facing a full-blown debt crisis between 1998 and 2000.
Both Kiriyenko's and Dubinin's statements added fuel to the fire
of speculative attacks betting on a ruble devaluation and rapid
withdrawals of funds from Russian banks. Both represented the
degree of policy incoherence that characterised the later period of
Yeltsin's administration. Both were newsworthy items in markets
already stressed by the continued Asian currency crises.

Selling pressures on Russian GKOs accelerated. It is worth
noting that GKOs were accumulating in the hands of large institutional investors with a significant appetite for risk. In addition,
these instruments were also held on banks' balance sheets. With
GKO prices collapsing, foreign investors began aggressively
deleveraging out of the GKOs. However, the same did not take

place in the Russian banking sector, with Russian banks continuing to accumulate GKOs in a speculative bid to boost profits,
while simultaneously relying on the sovereign nature of these
bonds as a 'guarantor' of their safety. Deleveraging by foreign
investors was met by the Russian treasury with increases in the
short-term yields on reissued GKOs and by May 1998 government
bond yields had reached 47 per cent. Only then did the Russian
banks enter the process of gradually reducing their exposures to
the new debt issuance and even then the Russian banks' deleveraging out of GKOs was slow and mostly concentrated among a
handful of medium to large banks exposed to international banking services competition.

Meanwhile, retail deposits started to dry out as domestic savers
switched into hoarding cash. Demand for dollars rose both exter-
nally and internally, since the US currency served as the main
store of value since the late Soviet era. Capital expatriation rose
dramatically. Between 1997 and 1998, growth in ruble deposits
by Russian residents fell from 30 billion rubles per annum to 1.3
billion rubles per annum, despite the fact that the money base
continued to expand as shown in Figure 7.3.

Figure 7.3: Total Deposits in Russian Credit Institutions, millions of rubles

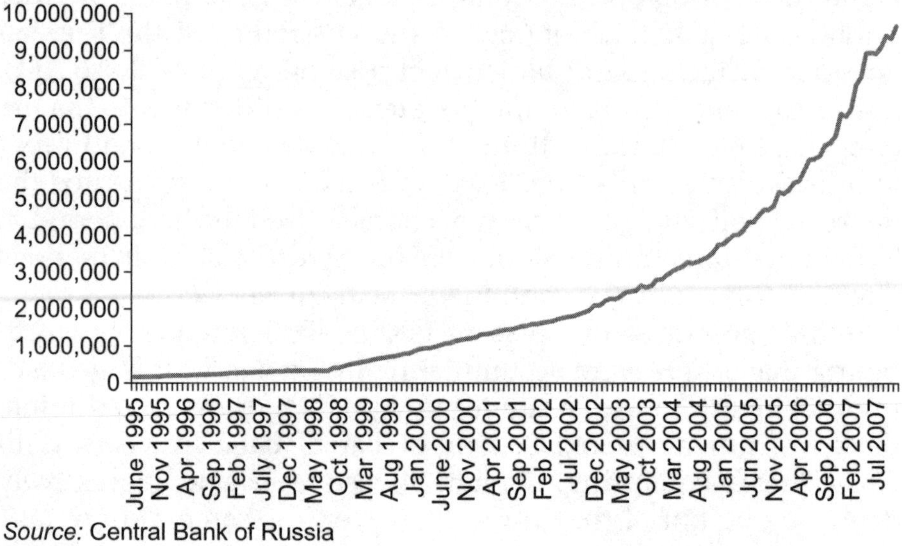

Source: Central Bank of Russia

The deleveraging was amplified by the aggressive drive by the Russian authorities to improve tax revenue collection. As part of the tax reforms back in 1997 Russia had created a much more effective and less corrupt treasury system which was modelled on a similar system already in operation in the city of Moscow. The agency concentrated its efforts on the extraction industries with access to foreign currencies. Unfortunately, these sectors were also heavily reliant on imports of capital equipment to sustain their production growth. Many exporting firms, pushed to the limit by federal tax collectors, were suspending payments on equipment purchasing contracts. As the price of oil, and to a lesser extent natural gas, continued to trend downward, reaching $11 per barrel in May 1998, many voices within the corridors of power were speculating about the need for drastic devaluation of the ruble. These rumours helped to push up the risk premiums on Russian GKOs in the international markets and precipitated rounds of foreign exchange hoarding by exporters and Russian banks. As the result, the domestic banking system was effectively split into two, with foreign-trade-engaged larger and state-owned banks running hard currency balance sheet operations to hold increasing reserves of foreign liquidity, and smaller domestic savings banks becoming completely exposed to ruble valuations. As the Central Bank of Russia continued to pump billions of dollars into foreign exchange markets in a futile attempt to defend the ruble, the former group of banks became extremely important to the Russian federal authorities, in part ensuring that following the default these banks will be taken into state ownership and preserved. Meanwhile, purely domestic banks in the second group were clearly falling out of the market operations and becoming less important to the Central Bank in its crisis management mode, thus ensuring their eventual bankruptcy post-default.

The structure of taxation was decisively shifting away from supporting capital investment and in the direction of reducing tax credits available to businesses and banks. For example, 1998 tax reforms included a cancellation of the practice whereby government departments and ministries, as well as state-owned enterprises, issued tax credits in payment for private sector supplies of goods and services.

Even with these draconian changes, the federal government was able to increase tax collection only marginally to approximately 10 per cent of GDP. Meanwhile, the budgetary performance was going from bad to worse. In 1997 the deficit reached 6.1 per cent of GDP and the government hoped to reduce it to 5 per cent in 1998. However, two factors underpinning these plans never materialised. Firstly, the deficit target for 1998 was based on assumed growth of 2 per cent in real GDP, while real growth came in at a contractionary -5.35 per cent instead. Secondly, Budget 1998 was computed on the basis of the highest interest rates on government debt of 25 per cent. By mid-1998, interest rates stood at six times that, implying that debt servicing consumed over half of government revenues. The end result was a fiscal deficit that reached 7.95 per cent of GDP in 1998.

By the end of May 1998, demand for GKOs began to collapse with yields rising to over 50 per cent and weekly bond auctions failing to attract sufficient numbers of bidders to allow for the full allocation of bonds in the market. This put pressure on the government that required an ever-increasing frequency of issuing new bonds to roll over the existent debt. Shrinking demand for GKOs was thus met by dramatically growing supply of these bonds. The Central Bank of Russia continued to hike lending rates, reaching 150 per cent. Dubinin attempted to calm devaluation fears by saying, 'When you hear talk of devaluation, spit in the eye of whoever is talking about it.' Russian asset markets reflected the fate of the GKOs with markets experiencing massive sell-offs. On 18 May the Russian stock market registered a 12 per cent drop, and in the first six months of 1998 stocks were down 40 per cent on 1997 levels. These developments prompted James Wolfensohn, the head of the World Bank, to declare the Russian market to be in crisis and the Chairman of the Russian Securities

Commission to respond with a statement that the market's situation was 'nothing other than a crisis'.

By June 1998, Central Bank interventions in the currency markets were draining $5 billion of reserves as Russia headed toward a September deadline for the redemption of billions of dollars' worth of ruble- and dollar-denominated corporate and government debts. A July 1998 IMF assistance programme injected $4.8 billion in funds designed to shore up the collapsing GKO markets, with an additional $6.3 billion committed for later months. Yet, in the very same month, capital outflows from Russia, Central Bank interventions and declines in oil and gas revenues due to falling prices shrunk the money supply by approximately $13 billion. Even with that, IMF funding was clearly not going to come at the rates required to buy significant time. Overstretched by the funding requirements of the Asian currency crises of 1997–1998, the IMF had to dip into emergency credit lines itself – something it has not done since 1978 – to find money to finance the first tranche disbursal to Russia. This did not go unnoticed by foreign investors who accelerated their selling of GKOs and other Russian assets following the IMF announcement.

The 13 August stock market crash of 65 per cent precipitated the end of the Russian government's efforts to defend the ruble. Following the stock market crash, GKOs yields rose to over 200 per cent. On 17 August 1998, the Russian government enacted drastic devaluation, froze domestic bank accounts and declared a moratorium on debt repayments to foreign GKO holders, while fully defaulting on domestically held debt. Commercial accounts in the banks were frozen for 90 days and many companies ended up losing all their deposits and payment streams as dozens of banks went bust virtually overnight. On 24 August the government fell with Prime Minister Kiriyenko dismissed by Yeltsin, and on 2 September 1998 the Central Bank abandoned interventions in the foreign exchange markets, allowing the ruble to float against all currencies.

Post-Crisis Recovery

According to Moody's research,[3] the Russian default – $72.71 billion – accounted for over 96 per cent of the total worldwide default volume of $76 billion in 1998. The event constituted the second largest default (after Argentina's $82.27 billion default in November 2001) over the entire period of 1998–2006. Furthermore, according to Moody's, the Russian default was associated with the lowest recovery rate (18 per cent) of all defaults over this period. Following the August 1999 and February 2000 restructurings debt burdens overall fell to a more sustainable level of 59.9 per cent of GDP in 2000, down from 99 per cent in 1999. The appointment of a new government, with Viktor Chernomyrdin returning as Prime Minister, was the first stage of the stabilisation. Chernomyrdin had served as Prime Minister in 1992–1998, a period that taught him some core lessons. Firstly, that ruble devaluation was inevitable and losses of foreign reserves cannot be sustained without destroying the economy. Secondly, the political balance between the Duma and the presidential administration was a precondition for success of longer term reforms. And thirdly, that the state finances had to be scaled back on the expenditure side in order to unwind accumulated internal debts.

However, Chernomyrdin's second tenure did not have the full backing of Yeltsin, who was battling for his own political survival. The Russian economy ended 1998 with GDP down 5.345 per cent in constant prices and the country's GDP fell from $404.9 billion in 1997 to $271 billion in current prices in 1998 – a level that threw Russia back to its 1993–1994 average. Devaluation pushed domestic inflation to 84 per cent, primarily impacting imported goods. Crucially, Chernomyrdin failed to win over the Duma and enact any significant reforms.

At the same time, a 75 per cent devaluation of the ruble helped push Russian exports. The Russian current account posted a deficit of 0.02 per cent of GDP in 1997 and by the end of 1998 was running at a surplus of 0.08 per cent. In 1999 the external balance of the Russian economy rose to a massive 12.6 per cent surplus, and thereafter, in 1999–2008, current account surpluses averaged 10.1 per cent of GDP per annum. If in 1998 Russian economy's trade balance contributed roughly $219 million, by the end of 1999 the same figure stood at $24.6 billion and by 2008 it rose to $103.7 billion. In the early post default years much of the economic recovery was attributable to a decline in consumer imports and the subsequent rapid substitution of domestically produced goods for foreign imported goods. After 2002, rapid increases in oil and gas prices helped to accelerate current account growth momentum. However, monetary and fiscal policies also helped. The transition of power from Boris Yeltsin to Vladimir Putin on 31 December 1999 ushered in a completely new era of political stabilisation (although this was achieved at the expense of rolling back some of the reforms established under previous rounds of democratisation in 1991–1997) and a focus on some core structural reforms.

In particular, the new administration moved swiftly to address Russian fiscal deficits, as illustrated in Figure 7.4.

This was achieved in three core steps. Firstly, the Russian state implicitly recognised the inability, at least during the recovery stage, to finance a significant extension of the welfare state beyond its core functions of supporting education, basic health and limited social welfare. This led to the renewed push toward a reduction in public spending and rationalisation of budgetary allocations.

Secondly, the government dramatically improved its enforcement of tax collection and set rapidly on course to restrict tax competition from the regions. Rolling back excessive autonomy granted to the regions by Boris Yeltsin, Vladimir Putin managed to dramatically lower federal tax revenue slippages due to regional authorities' corruption and collusion with private enterprises.

Thirdly, in 2001 the government launched ambitious tax reforms which saw a reduction in the overall tax burden on individual incomes, streamlining compliance and, once again, beefing up enforcement. A progressive personal income tax system that imposed a range of tax rates between 12 per cent and 35 per cent

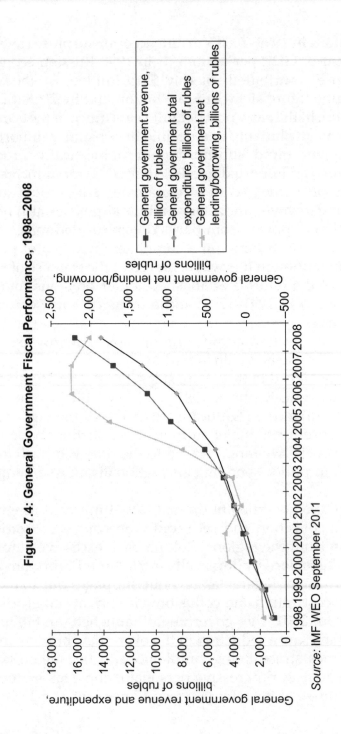

Figure 7.4: General Government Fiscal Performance, 1998–2008

Source: IMF WEO September 2011

was reformed into a flat tax system with single rate of 13 per cent. Between 2000 and 2001 income tax revenues increased from 175 billion rubles to 256 billion rubles, a rise of 46 per cent in just one year. The annual rate of growth in income tax revenues for 2000–2004 hit almost 35 per cent and the overall share of income tax revenues in the overall government revenues rose from 8.3 per cent in 2000 to 10.6 per cent in 2004. In addition to reforming personal income tax rates, the Putin administration also reduced the headline corporate tax rate from 35 per cent to 24 per cent in 2002. The initial impact of this change was to reduce corporation tax revenues in 2002 from 514 billion rubles in 2001 to 463 billion rubles in 2002. Boosted by economic growth and the reduced burden of compliance, as well as by the improved enforcement of tax codes, corporation tax revenues rose to 868 billion rubles in 2004. Reforms of tax codes and the lowering of the corporation tax rate also explain the rapid expansion of investment in the economy. In 2002 the inflow of FDI into Russia amounted to $4.0 billion. This increased to $9.4 billion in 2004.

Russia was able to access funding markets relatively quickly post-default, as was the general experience with defaults in the 1990s. Gelos et al.[4] found that for defaults that took place in the 1990s the average return to funding markets took 3.5 months, as opposed to 4.5 years for defaults during the 1980s. However, in the case of Russia the return to the markets initially was a costly one with 2003–2005 bond spreads remaining above 200 basis points, despite the fact that the country was showing very robust rates of economic growth and double digit surpluses on its current account. This is most likely related to three factors. The Russian default, as noted above, was characterised by extremely low rates of recovery on government bonds. In addition, most of the Russian government debt pre-default was held by foreign investors, implying a much more significant impact on foreign bondholders. Lastly, the Russian economic recovery was perceived to be primarily driven by rising oil prices – a perception that is well grounded in reality.

The immediate disruption caused by the default and the currency crisis was painful. Unemployment rose from 10.8 per cent in 1997 to 13.0 per cent in 1999 – the peak of official unemployment for the 1990s. In some areas, especially in industrialised central Russia, the collapse in investment led to the effective shutting down of industrial production. In many regions unemployment reached 18–20 per cent, and these numbers concealed the fact that, in addition to massive jobs losses, many in employment saw their wages delayed. Payments arrears and a stalled banking system meant that backlogs of wages rose to 50–60 per cent in cities such as Nizhny, Novgorod and Penza. Moscow itself weathered the storm much better due to more efficient payments systems and the city's government's more proactive stance on payments to its employees.

The crisis materialised at the time when many Russian industries were at the tail end of the process of realisation that state orders and older patterns of production, reliant on government and military orders, were coming to an end. This meant that many impacted enterprises, especially the larger ones, were already on the cusp of transitioning to more market-driven economy. The crisis accelerated this process. The collapse of the ruble in 1998 improved the competitiveness of domestic products and services. As imports prices quadrupled virtually overnight, domestic industrial and agricultural output increased. For example, within two years of the crisis, unemployment in one of the core industrial regions – the region of Penza – fell from 18 per cent to 1.5 per cent and industrial output grew by 141 per cent. Remonetisation of the economy following the ruble devaluation provided the necessary liquidity to pay down salaries and wages arrears and consumer spending rose by late 1999. The government policy of centralisation of authority away from a regional distribution of power – the default option pursued by the Yeltsin administration – also helped. The Kremlin forcefully re-asserted central control over the regions and this political move was backed by Moscow's efforts to repay regional governments' debts to state employees. Within three years of default, the demand for skilled workers rose and the Russian middle class regained all income and savings losses sustained in the crisis.

One feature of the Russian crisis was the collapse of the banking system. The banking crisis in the Russian case was driven by a number of factors related to the broader problems in the Russian economy. During the early 1990s, Russian industrial enterprises set up a number of their own banks for the purpose of enhancing internal control of their capital and using industrial funds to earn additional income from lending. By 1996–1997, however, the system of credit in the country had firmly shifted away from lending to enterprises and was more geared toward booming domestic credit and government securities. According to the Organisation for Economic Co-Operation and Development (OECD),[5] by the end of 1997 the commercial banking sector held almost 75 per cent of ruble-denominated deposits in form of federal government debt. At the same time, OECD data suggested that private sector credit fell from 12 per cent of GDP in 1994 to 8 per cent in 1997. High interest rates and banking sector inefficiencies have meant that large segments of the Russian economy were operating on informal credit and barter.

Following the default, remonetisation of the economy has meant that black market credit and payments transactions, especially those involving barter, have declined. This decline was almost immediate, as noted in Huang et al.,[6] who show that barter and non-cash payments fell 20 per cent in 1999 and continued to decline in importance in 2000 and 2001. Subsequent tax reforms streamlining personal and corporate income taxation measures and compliance added further strength to the process of normalisation of the Russian payments systems.

The consolidation of the banking crisis post-default and the collapse of overall government asset markets meant that the banks were incentivised to start lending to the real economy. Between 1998 and 1999, the volume of ruble loans rose from 123 billion rubles to 293 billion rubles. The volume of total loans rose from 310 billion rubles in 1997 to 597 billion in 1999 and 1,418 billion in 2001.

The consolidation of the banking sector saw three core state-owned banks capturing some 80 per cent of the liquid banking assets in the country – a move that instilled more confidence in the banking system's stability within a population that lost all trust in private banks during the default. According to Huang et al., the collapse of the assets acquisition conduit via government securities meant that surviving banks were forced to seek new assets in the commercial lending markets. The cost of credit therefore declined and many enterprises were able to access new credit. The virtuous cycle of improving credit ratings for many enterprises, spurred on by robust economic growth in 2000–2002, was reinforced by these developments in the banking sector. Reversal of the capital flight out of Russia, in part largely predicated on capital controls imposed during the crisis, also helped.

The banking sector collapse and ruble devaluation have significantly reduced the overall dollar equivalent volumes of household deposits. In June 1998, total household deposits stood at around $40 billion. This number fell to $12.1 billion by December 1999. Likewise, capital controls have meant that many commercial creditors were made insolvent almost overnight. As reported by Euromoney,[7] a World Bank study found that in 1999 the majority of losses within the banking system in Russia were driven by commercial loans, not the government assets bust. Specifically, loan loss provisions amounted to $64.3 billion in 1999 and 34 per cent of net charges to banks' capital. Losses on government assets were only 13 per cent.

These processes crystallised losses on banks' balance sheets and forced significant reforms of the banking sector, including much tighter supervision and stricter lending rules. But the main thrust of reforms was the significant reduction in cross-ownership of banks by industrial companies in the private sector. In the early 1990s, large number of banks was created within the industrial groups that were privatised during the Yeltsin era, and especially during loans-for-shares schemes. These banks acted as conduits for industrial oligarchs' access to government lending arbitrage. The banks borrowed cheaply from the Central Bank of Russia and rolled borrowed funds into GKOs. Some of these loans were used to further increase industrial companies' access to capital that was used to finance purchases of state-owned assets in extraction sectors and finance bidding for lucrative licenses. Post default, a large number of these banks went bust and the remaining ones were consolidated in super-sized commercial banking entities, such as Gazprombank. This consolidation, and state backing for the larger banks, has meant that domestic depositors, including retail savers, improved their perceptions of the banking sector in general. A deposit insurance scheme also backed by the state that was put in place in December 2003 further reinforced this build-up of confidence. The result was an increase in deposits that continued unabated from 1999 through the period of post-crisis shock.

Conclusions

Overall, Russian experiences in the post default adjustment reveal a number of important lessons for the peripheral countries of the Eurozone that are witnessing a similar crisis today.

Rapid recovery from the default is possible, even when such a default takes place without proper planning and contingent hedging, under favourable external conditions. Reforms, especially structural reforms of market institutions related to the underlying causes of the crisis, promote long-term growth and recovery and do contribute positively to the defaulter's ability to return to funding markets within a short period of time. Furthermore, these positive aspects of post-default recovery are reinforced for countries with no past history of defaults. Disruptions to normal functioning of the banking system and economic transactions in the short run represent one of the two core downside factors in the default scenario. The other is the significant reduction of real savings levels due to bankruptcies and devaluations of banks. Both of these factors require serious contingency planning and the creation of systemic responses that can help mitigate their adverse impacts on the overall economy. However, as experience in Russia shows, even extremely painful after effects of the default, such as a collapse of private savings, can be effectively mitigated by aligning fiscal reforms with the objectives of helping adversely impacted households to rebuild their savings and wealth. In Russia this was achieved through robust repayment of accumulated government liabilities toward state pensioners and employees, as well as through the creation of a benign personal income tax environment combining low rates of income taxation and a flat tax system of income tax. Lastly, in the case of Russia, the default on sovereign debt can be seen as a catalyst for real and sustainable long-term reforms of the economic institutions. While this process is far from complete, the Russian economy performance since 1998–1999 has been impressive.

Endnotes

1   Nadmitov, A. (2004) 'Russian Debt Restructuring: Overview, Structure of Debt, Lessons of Default, Seizure Problems and the IMF SDRM Proposal', paper presented at the International Finance Seminar, Harvard Law School , available from: <www.law.harvard.edu/programs/about/pifs/llm/sp26.pdf>, pp. 5–6.
2   Krivka, A. (2006) 'The Experience of Russia in Reforming Tax System: Achievements, Problems and Perspectives', *Vaduba Management*, Vol. 2, No. 11, pp. 73–74.
3   Moody's Investors Services (2007) 'Sovereign Default and Recovery Rates, 1983–2006', Global Credit Research Note, June.
4   R.G. Gelos, R. Sahay and G. Sandleris (2004) 'Sovereign Borrowing by Developing Countries: What Determines Market Access?' IMF working paper no 221, November 2004.
5   Organisation for Economic Co-Operation and Development (1997) *OECD Economic Surveys: Russian Federation 1997*, OECD: Paris, 1997-19.
6   H. Huang, D. Marin and C. Xu (2003) 'Financial Crisis, Economic Recovery and Banking Development in Former Soviet Union Economies', CESifo working paper no. 860, February 2003, available from: <http://www.ifo.de/portal/pls/portal/docs/1/1189878.PDF>.
7   *Euromoney* (1999) 'Russia, The Newly-Wed and the Nearly Dead', 10 June, available from: <http://www.euromoney.com/Article/1005258/Russia-The-newly-wed-and-the-nearly- dead.html>.

8

Iceland: The Accidental Hero

Elaine Byrne and Huginn F. Þorsteinsson

Elaine is an assistant professor of Politics in Trinity College Dublin and a political columnist. Her website is www.elaine.ie. Huginn is a philosopher and adjunct professor at the University of Akureyri. He was the policy adviser to the Icelandic Minister of Finance (2009–2011) and is currently the adviser to the Minister of Economic Affairs and Minister of Fisheries and Agriculture.

The boom to bust story of Iceland's economy is well documented. After a number of years of sensational economic growth from 2002 to 2007, the economy began to destabilise with dramatic consequences in October 2008. Within a span of less than a week, the entire financial sector, ten times the gross domestic product (GDP) of Iceland, went bust. The stock market was nearly wiped out. The economic outlook was not favourable. Interest rates and inflation were at 18 per cent. Unemployment sharply rose from 1 per cent to 9 per cent. Government revenue was rapidly evaporating but government expenditure had surged. The Icelandic króna (ISK) was in free fall and the reputation of the country was in absolute tatters. The entire financial sector had collapsed lock, stock and barrel.

The three main banks, Glitnir, Kaupthing Bank and Landsbanki, collapsed creating significant turmoil in the financial markets. This in effect shut down the foreign exchange market and caused a dramatic depreciation of the króna. The immediate consequences were the nationalisation of these three banks, which accounted for 85 per cent of the banking system. The

International Monetary Fund (IMF) immediately intervened with a $2.1 billion package in order to avert a further meltdown of the Icelandic economy.

Iceland's situation was so bad that Poul M. Thomsen, the IMF's mission chief for Iceland, described it as 'unprecedented.' Thomsen recalled how 'the sense of fear and shock was palpable — few, if any, countries had ever experienced such a catastrophic economic crash.' Others pointed to Iceland as the canary in the coal mine. Even the word 'Iceland' came to have certain connotations linked to it, such as reckless banking and financial catastrophe. Greek and Irish politicians, overwhelmed by their own growing economic problems, were keen to stress that they were not Iceland.

'Ireland is not an Iceland which has somehow acquired a series of foreign obligations and saddled them on its taxpayers' observed the late Brian Lenihan in his Dáil contribution of 1 April 2010. In his address to the Irish Taxation Institute earlier that year, the Minister for Finance argued that those who advocated for the Icelandic approach – the 100 per cent bank nationalisation – were wrong. Lenihan even felt it necessary to point out the folly of Icelandic policy with the use of an exclamation mark in his presentation to the tax consultants, accountants, barristers, solicitors and other financial professionals in attendance: 'Only one country has followed this approach in this crisis: Iceland!'[1]

Within eighteen months of this address, the IMF/ECB/EU troika had intervened in Ireland and the entire Irish banking sector was nationalised or part nationalised. Ireland experienced the deepest and fastest contraction of any western economy since the Great Depression. The Governor of the Central Bank, Patrick Honohan, described it as 'the most expensive [banking crisis] in history.' By August 2011, the European Central Bank (ECB) and the Irish Central Bank had pumped €150 billion into Ireland's six banks. The gag 'What's the difference between Iceland and Ireland? One letter and six months', first aired in January 2009 on the BBC daily current affairs programme *Europe Today*, was now on Ireland. Even *The Economist* magazine got in on the act, referring to the Irish economy in February 2009 as 'Reykjavik-on-Liffey'.

Yet, in the three years since the 2008 Icelandic collapse, the Nordic country has made a remarkable and noteworthy economic recovery. The IMF approved the final loan tranche in August 2011, marking the end to a 33-month rescue package. The Finance Minister, Steingrímur Sigfússon, subsequently announced that 'All the program objectives have been achieved.' Nemat Shafik, IMF Deputy Managing Director and Acting Chair, likewise stated 'Key objectives have been met: public finances are on a sustainable path, the exchange rate has stabilized, and the financial sector has been restructured.'[2] The economy has stabilised, fiscal adjustment has been successful, economic growth is picking up and the sovereign financed itself successfully in the bond market in May 2011 on what were considered good terms.

Iceland and Ireland – The Difference Is More than a Letter

Ireland and Iceland share remarkable parallels. Both countries enjoyed enormous growth at the beginning of the twenty-first century but by the end of the first decade were clients of the IMF. This growth was, in part, fuelled by a large expansion of Irish and Icelandic financial institutions. A housing bubble, an immense increase in purchasing power and excessive lending to companies and households also occurred. Much of the policy implementation was similar. The regulatory powers of supervisory authorities were relaxed as the market was regarded as adequately self-regulating. Taxes on capital gains, corporate tax and taxes on high income were lowered because they were thought to discourage growth in the economy. The Irish Minister for Finance, Charlie McCreevy, reduced income tax rates to 42 per cent and 20 per cent in Budget 2001, earning a rebuke from the European Commission, which reprimanded Ireland for its expansionary budget policy.

The Icelandic and the Irish governments in the early to mid-2000s were thought to be daring and were lauded for being so. Accordingly, Icelandic entrepreneurs earned the moniker 'Finance Vikings', whilst Ireland became the 'Celtic Tiger'. The two countries served as paradigms of how increasing freedom in the market place served to ensure that everybody would benefit from growth. The neo-liberal economic philosophy – the rising tide lifts all boats – was virtually unquestioned.

Iceland and Ireland have more in common with each other than with the PIG countries facing grave economic difficulties accessing the sovereign debt markets – Portugal, Italy and Greece. Iceland's and Ireland's economic collapses stem from crises within their banking systems. This was not the case in Portugal, Italy and Greece, where a public debt problem has been gradually mounting. Yes, their banks are in trouble but not in the same manner as in Iceland and Ireland. Spain's difficulties may be more akin to Iceland's and Ireland's but there are other issues that explain its weaknesses such as unemployment, which was a reality before the European financial crisis.

Nonetheless, there are important dissimilarities between the Irish and Icelandic cases. Iceland is a very small economy in the sense that the country's population of only 300,000 is just a quarter that of Ireland's capital city, Dublin. An argument can therefore be made that even though Iceland's crash was harder hitting than Ireland's, the difference in the size of the economies has allowed the Icelandic case to be more manageable. It is easier after all to turn a small tugboat around than a large tanker.

Iceland is not a member of the European Union and had the policy option to devalue its own independent currency, unlike Ireland. The devaluation of the króna, by more than half, has been difficult for Icelandic households and companies as many of them had foreign exchange-linked loans. However, it has been helpful in creating a considerable trade surplus by boosting earnings in the export sector. A devaluation of the Irish currency would have served a small, open, trade-dependent economy like Ireland's well. Ireland is particularly vulnerable given its dependence on high levels of foreign direct investment and internationally traded services sectors. Ireland's exports, for instance, accounted for 105 per cent of GDP in the September 2011 Quarterly National Accounts.

Moreover, Ireland is in an IMF programme funded by the 27 EU nations under the watchful eye of the ECB. The United Kingdom made a bilateral loan on favourable interest rates to its closest economic neighbour. Iceland received significant funding from its Nordic neighbours and Poland. That may have contributed to the flexibility within the Icelandic programme, which in many aspects was unorthodox. Iceland imposed, for example, capital controls, something the IMF has traditionally been opposed to. It has also been lauded by the IMF for its commitment to the ideals of the Nordic welfare state.

Bank losses were not absorbed wholesale by the public sector, which was insulated somewhat from vast private sector losses. Poul M. Thomsen noted that the IMF 'had to reach for policy tools that were not part of our mainstream toolkit'.[3] It was private creditors rather than the national Exchequer that ended up bearing most of the losses in the failed banks.

The IMF co-hosted a high-level conference with the Icelandic government in October 2011 to review the conclusion of its programme in the country. The IMF learned three main lessons, Nemat Shafik said:

1. When countries have a clear strategy in mind, as was the case in Iceland, it becomes much easier for the IMF to engage and provide policy support and advice.

2. There are clear advantages to having a heterodox toolkit – more tools are better than fewer.

3. Iceland set an example by managing to preserve, and even strengthen, its welfare state during the crisis.[4]

On the other hand, the Irish government responded to the economic crisis by guaranteeing not only all deposit holders, but also most bank bondholders, in September 2008. This in effect socialised the losses and liabilities of the private sector, thereby exacerbating public debt liability. This in turn limited growth capacity because of severe internal structural problems and the inability to borrow on the markets at viable rates of interest. Irish taxpayers were obliged to undertake arduous austerity with no consequent losses for bondholders. Ajai Chopra, the IMF's mission chief for Ireland, has said that if it wasn't for contagion risks amid turmoil in European financial markets, Ireland would have significantly lower bond spreads. The problems that Ireland faces are not just an Irish problem; they are a shared European problem.[5]

The Icelandic Fairy Tale?

When comparisons between the economic crises of Ireland and Iceland are made, it is often stated that Ireland, unlike Iceland, bailed out its banks. It is also added that the Icelandic authorities were prepared with a blueprint that saved the sovereign from bailing out the banks and made the private creditors suffer by giving them a proper haircut. Only the last part of this story has a grain of truth, but the rest is a fairy tale.

The fact is that when it comes to bank bailouts Iceland is second to Ireland in the post-2008 financial crisis. The Organisation for Economic Co-Operation and Develoment (OECD) reckons that the '[t]otal direct fiscal costs of the recent financial crisis amount to about 20% of GDP, which is higher than in any other country except Ireland'.[6] Ireland's cost is estimated to be 49 per cent of GDP. The development of Ireland's and Iceland's general government debt is almost exactly alike. Both countries lowered their public debt during the boom years. Ireland's debt was about 25 per cent of GDP in 2006 and 2007 and Iceland's stood at 28–29 per cent GDP in 2007. At the end of 2010 both countries' public debt was around 95 per cent.

However, there is an important differences as to how the banks were bailed out which has important consequences for stabilising the debt. If Iceland had followed Ireland's bank bailout example, then presumably Iceland's public debt should have been twice as high as that of Ireland as its financial system was twice the size of Ireland's when measured in terms of GDP.

So what is the crucial difference between the two countries? In essence, Iceland did not have a choice, whereas Ireland did. Iceland had no possibility whatsoever to bail out its banking system whereas Ireland did, or at least believed it had the means to do so. A belief that the European Commissioner for Competition, Joaquin Almunia, described in June 2011 as a mistake because its sweeping scope served to concentrate losses on taxpayers that would have been 'better distributed' in the absence of an unlimited guarantee.[7]

The pre-crash Icelandic government had watched the financial sector expand to well over ten times Iceland's GDP. It did not all of a sudden see the light and stop believing in what it considered as miraculous financial institutions and prepare for a collapse of those banks. On the contrary, the government fought valiantly to the very end to save the banks, and it cost the Icelandic taxpayer dearly.

The Prime Minister of Iceland and the Foreign Secretary went on a roadshow to Copenhagen and New York in March 2008 to assure an increasingly critical business community and the foreign press that the Icelandic banks were sound financial institutions. Despite the looming catastrophe in the banks, the roadshow occurred just seven months before the financial collapse. Extraordinarily, the chair of Iceland's Financial Supervisory Authority gave an interview, published in a prospectus for an Icesave branch which opened in Holland in May 2008. Even in the last days before the collapse the government affirmed that the banks would be backed by the sovereign. Iceland's system of financial management was compromised by regulatory capture, the influence of interest groups and political participants to shape laws and regulations in a way that is beneficial to them.

When the Icelandic banks could no longer finance themselves on international markets they turned to the Central Bank of Iceland (CBI) for financing. Their financing troubles started in 2007 but this was viewed as a temporary problem for the banks and it thought appropriate that the CBI would, as a lender of last resort, assist in financing the banks. This could only go on for a brief period as the banks were so much vastly larger than Iceland's economy. This meant that if the CBI was to keep fuelling the financial institutions external financing would inevitably be necessary.

When it became manifest that this external financing was not forthcoming other measures were required to deal with the inevitable collapse of Iceland's financial system. The country's fortune paradoxically is that in these circumstances the government had zero credibility and the banks were considered to be so toxic that no one was willing to offer financial backing or assurances. It was at this moment that the Icelandic authorities realised that saving the banks was virtually impossible and measures would be needed to minimise the impact of their collapse on the state and on Iceland's economy.

Emergency legislation was rushed through the Althing, Iceland's parliament, which gave the financial services authority and the government unprecedented powers to intervene in the financial markets by, for example, moving domestic deposits, loans and assets into new banks. Most of the foreign loans and assets were left in the old banks and they went into administration. The CBI lost most of the loans it had provided to the old banks, which is an amount equivalent to 13 per cent of Iceland's GDP. Effectively the CBI went into bankruptcy, which is another peculiarity of the Icelandic case. A similar amount of money went into establishing the new banks that took over the deposits, loans and assets of the old banks. The government received a stake in the new banks which since then is estimated to have gained in value. So that does not constitute a loss of taxpayers' money as the bankruptcy of the CBI undoubtedly is. The state could always get some of its money back if it decided to sell its stake in the banks.

The emergency legislation came about because all other routes were closed for Iceland and it is since then an important ingredient in the country's recovery, mainly because of two factors. The first is that the taxpayer was not put at further risk by the financial system. As already explained, the loss of taxpayers' money was considerable but the emergency legislation resulted in the old banks going bust. It meant losses for the creditors of the banks but that is how it should be as they were responsible for lending to the banks. The second is that the country's external debt was minimised. Instead of having a banking sector that was ten times the country's GDP the new banks amounted to twice the value of Iceland's GDP. The difference is vast and is extremely important in the volatile financial climate in the Eurozone.

Ireland's path is considerably different in this respect. The Icelandic banks were too big to save. Although the same ultimately proved true in the Irish case, it took three years to reach this realisation. The Minister for Finance, Brian Lenihan, determined in 2008 that Anglo Irish Bank was of 'systemic importance to Ireland' because of its €100 billion balance sheet. The bank, Lenihan said, 'had grown to half the size of our annual national wealth, so clearly the failure of a bank on that scale would do huge damage to the local economy here in Ireland.' This is a view shared by the Governor of the Central Bank, Patrick Honohan, in his 2010 Banking Report. Honohan argued that if Anglo had been allowed to default it 'would undoubtedly have put funding pressure on the other main Irish banks via contagion .... In this sense, the systemic importance of Anglo Irish Bank at that time cannot seriously be disputed.'[8]

In addition, Ireland received backing to support its banking system from the troika of the ECB, the IMF and the EU. Therefore, unlike in the Icelandic case, the banking system remains oversized and what may even turn out to be worse is that taxpayers' money is what has sustained its size. The question is, of course, whether Ireland should have done something similar to the emergency legislation enacted in Iceland and watched the banks go into administration but rescue assets that were of national interest?

In our opinion such drastic measures may not have been needed but neither was it necessary to back the entire financial system.

Ireland's financial system did not achieve the size of Iceland's when compared in terms of GDP but many of the same factors contributed to its growth, such as extensive borrowing that fuelled a housing bubble, excessive consumption and contributed to an overall growth in the economy in the short term. This means that there are severe inherent weaknesses within the Irish financial sector that the National Asset Management Agency (NAMA) initiative may not be able to isolate and resolve so that the sovereign is adequately protected. The Irish authorities should rather have considered a policy that did defend all of the banks but let the riskier ones go bust, and moved certain assets into other banks that were deemed necessary to rescue from a financial stability point of view. Such a move would have minimised the exposure of the taxpayer and downsized the financial system effectively, which is what Ireland needs.

Iceland initially tried to salvage its oversized banking sector but in the end received no backing for such a move and was forced to use other means to tackle its crisis. These measures have since led the country to become an accidental hero. In retrospect this turned out to be good fortune for Iceland and has helped with the resurrection of its economy. It is, however, important to remember that Iceland incurred severe costs because of the financial crisis. Although Ireland should have not followed Iceland's path completely, one can argue that it would have made sense for Ireland to use a pick and choose policy as to which financial institutions were worth saving. It may seem strange to say this but what seems to be Ireland's misfortune in this regard is just that the Irish banks were not big enough for policy makers to deem it virtually impossible to salvage them. Instead the decision was taken to bail them out because saving them was deemed 'manageable', and that may turn out to be a very difficult route to take. As Professor Morgan Kelly forlornly noted in an *Irish Times* editorial in May 2011, 'While most people would trace our ruin to the bank guarantee of September 2008, the real error was in sticking with the guarantee long after it had become clear that the bank losses were insupportable.'

Public v Private – The Fate of the Sovereign

When countries are faced with the question of whether it is sensible to bail out banks immediate questions are raised about sovereign default. This can be seen in both the Irish and Icelandic cases and in other instances as well. This is one of the peculiarities of the current financial crisis in that financial institutions which are in principle private entities are linked to the sovereign if they are thought to be close to insolvency. During the boom years, when the banks provided handsome dividends to their stock owners and large staff bonuses on top of high wages, little attention was paid to the implications of financial institutions in crisis on public funds. Any critique of big salaries and bonuses was dismissed because the banks as private entities could decide how much of their profits they allocated to meet the demands of their top-level staff.

In the aftermath of the financial crisis it seems, however, that either it was always tacitly assumed that the sovereign backed banks in trouble or few people imagined that they would get into a crisis and difficult questions were never asked. It is clear that the lack of preparation and denial of the severity of the situation within the financial sector in many countries has cost many nation states dearly and also the Eurozone as a whole.

In our view the onus of justification is always on those who want to use public funds to keep a financial institution in business. There are often strong arguments for bailing out banks because it can turn out to be more expensive for an economy not to do so. Nevertheless, those arguments start to lose their appeal in countries with oversized financial institutions that are systematically failing. Then a clear divide needs to be made between private entities and the sovereign. The lesson from Iceland is that if Iceland had been able to continue to finance its banks in 2008 with public funds the sovereign would have probably ended up defaulting, with devastating consequences.

Ireland, like other western democracies, has been captured by big finance but is not cognisant of this reality because moral outrage has been directed towards isolated scandals in the market and unjustified bonuses for individual bankers. It is supposed that the economic collapse is a problem intrinsic to the weaknesses of regulation and the hubris of bankers and property developers. The capture of the state by an oligopolistic financial sector, due to excessive risk taking without consequence, was complemented by the failure of political institutions to anticipate the collapse.

The result from Ireland remains to be seen in the context of a rapidly escalating Euro crisis. The justification for the measures taken in rescuing banks then regarded as of 'systemic importance to Ireland' has become emaciated and unconvincing over time. The fears of contagion amongst financial institutions within other EU member states are understandable and logical. However, if that is the case then the problem ceases to be a problem. The assumption that the Irish taxpayer should exclusively shoulder the burden of private debt is also a problem for those whom they are saving. The weights should be lifted equally by those affected. Otherwise the task becomes too difficult. And *unmanageable*.

Endnotes

[1] Minister for Finance, Mr Brian Lenihan, 'Returning to Economic Growth: The Next Steps', Address to the Irish Taxation Institute Annual Dinner, 26 February 2010, available from: <http://www.finance.gov.ie/documents/speeches2010/spl43irishtax.pdf>.

[2] IMF (2011) 'IMF Completes Sixth and Final Review Under the Stand-By Arrangement for Iceland', Press Release No.11/316, 26 August.

[3] Poul M. Thomsen (2011) 'How Iceland Recovered from its Near-Death Experience', *iMFdirect*, 26 October 2011, available from: <http://blog-imfdirect.imf.org/2011/10/26/how-iceland-recovered-from-its-near-death-experience />.

[4] International Monetary Fund (2011) 'Iceland's Unorthodox Policies Suggest Alternative Way Out of Crisis', *IMF Survey Magazine: Countries & Regions*, 3 November 2011, available from: <http://www.imf.org/external/pubs/ft/survey/so/2011/car110311a.htm>.

5 *iMFdirect* (2011) 'No Country Is an Island: Ireland and the IMF', 14 July, available from: <http://blog-imfdirect.imf.org/2011/07/14/no-country-is-an-island-ireland-and-the-imf/>.

6 Organisation for Economic Co-Operation and Development (2011) *OECD Economic Surveys: Iceland*, Paris: OECD.

7 Arthur Beesley (2011) 'Leading EU Official Says State Bank Guarantee a Mistake', *Irish Times*, 17 June.

8 Patrick Honohan (2010) *The Irish Banking Crisis Regulatory and Financial Stability Policy 2003–2008: A Report to the Minister for Finance by the Governor of the Central Bank*, Dublin: The Stationery Office, p. 131.

9

Irish Public Debt: A View through the Lens of the Argentine Default

Tony Phillips

Tony is a researcher at the University of Buenos Aires and a journalist in political economics. His website is http://projectallende.org/.

Reckless financing in the Irish construction industry combined with a lack of enforcement of national banking regulations with cheap Eurozone credit financed twenty years of Irish economic expansion. An overshoot in loan activity exposed both local and international financiers to speculative loans at the end of a prolonged real estate bubble. When the bubble burst the overextended construction sector collapsed, defaulting on its loans. This destabilised the Irish financial sector, resulting in the insolvency of almost all Irish private banks. Then came the rescue ....

This is the story of how one Irish government reacted to the 2008 financial collapse looking at choices yet to be made that will determine what happens next. The point of view is South American. South American debt initiatives are presented in an effort to determine their applicability to debt accrued in the financial rescue, the legacy of a Fianna Fáil coalition voted out of power in 2011. Here in Buenos Aires just a decade ago the Argentine economy imploded in a sovereign debt crisis. For Argentine economists, hindsight is 20/20. The good news from South America is that a number of non-conventional negotiation tactics can provide legal and tactical armour to a sovereign Irish government willing to defend itself against the debt markets. There is still time for Ireland to incorporate new ideas that can prevent an uncontrolled sovereign default, unnecessary payment of illegitimate debt, or both.

Stepping Up to the Plate

The Irish sovereign debt problems can be solved through hard work. First the new government needs to accept that there is a problem, and then the problem needs to be broken down to its essentials, determining its origin, and, finally, the problem can be dealt with in a proper timeframe.

Translating this to the case in point – any new government needs to admit that Ireland has a sovereign debt problem. This may sound ridiculous but such an admission can be politically difficult, especially when dealing with financial markets. Government denial and cover-up were the unhealthy reactions evident in Argentina in the late 1990s just before the economic collapse. Next up comes financial investigation: positive initiatives like the audit produced in the University of Limerick.[1] Armed with this type of information the new government can determine how the debt came to be and who is responsible for creating it. This helps determine its legitimacy. By separating out illegitimate debt, the nominal debt may be reduced to that which is really essential to pay. Finally, having apportioned blame and begun prosecution of those responsible, one can begin the tough international negotiations to come to a just agreement with creditors. That done, all that remains is to pay off the reduced amount over a reasonable period of time.

During the recovery expert help and solidarity measures from partners can be crucial. The Argentine recovery, which began in 2003, would have been much more difficult were it not for timely solidarity funding from friendly governments.

Last but not least, one has to recognise that sovereign debt is a national sovereignty issue. Any government elected by the Irish people has to be willing to represent the sovereign interests of the nation. Failure to do this questions the sovereignty of the state itself.

Save the Banks!

In 2008 the Irish government scrambled to avoid a national financial collapse of the private banking sector. This involved some extraordinary decisions in the rescue of the insolvent financial system; decisions that were made by the Department of Finance and the Central Bank of Ireland.

A subsequent government enquiry into this rescue led to the production of a report to the Minister for Finance by the Governor of the Central Bank entitled 'The Irish Banking Crisis Regulatory and Financial Stability Policy 2003–2008.'[2] The conclusions of this enquiry are critical of the government rescue. In particular, they argue:

> The inclusion of subordinated[3] debt in the guarantee is not easy to defend against criticism. The arguments that were made in favour of this coverage seem weak: And it lacked precedents in other countries .... Inclusion of this debt limited the range of loss-sharing resolution options in subsequent months, and likely increased the potential share of the total losses borne by the State.

Subordinated debt is debt that a state does not usually pay when rescuing an insolvent banking sector. The handling of the 2008 financial emergency was unnecessarily generous. It resulted in a wholesale conversion of private bad debt (on the books of Ireland's private banks) into government guarantees and public debt obligations for which the Irish taxpayer has ultimately been made responsible. Ireland is not the only nation that faced such a financial collapse; similar financial instability is evident across Europe and elsewhere. The Irish rescue has since been compared with other rescues internationally, notably by Joseph Stiglitz and William K. Black.

Nobel Laureate and former chairman of President Clinton's Council of Economic Advisers Joseph Stiglitz compared some of these financial rescues. He describes the Irish rescue as 'probably the worst model', adding that 'Iceland did the right thing by making sure its payment systems continued to function while creditors, not the taxpayers, shouldered the losses of banks.'

In an Irish radio interview on 15 February 2011, William K. Black, a key regulator and prosecutor in the savings and loans scandal in the United States, was even more emphatic as to the mistakes made in Ireland. Commenting on the parallels between the savings and loans bank rescue and the Irish rescue, he said:

> ... the whole concept of subordinated debt is that it is supposed to serve as risk capital. And so if the bank fails it is supposed to get nothing .... Every regulator knows that ....

Commenting on the Irish rescue, Black derided the generosity of the decisions made:

> We'll pay the subordinated debt holders with the Irish taxpayers paying the money! And of course without asking the Irish taxpayers. It is the most obscene policy. ... We've looked at lots of other countries and nobody has responded to a crisis as stupidly as the Irish government responded. It just gratuitously took billions of Euros from the Irish people to give it to mostly German banks who had no right at all under the laws. They were supposed to lose that money if the bank failed. That was the deal they made.

Feedback on the Rescue

On a visit to Dublin in 2009 I was asked, 'What's the difference between Iceland and Ireland?' 'One letter and six months' was the witty response. Sadly this was not to be the case. In Ireland the banking rescue took much longer than six months to be resolved; in fact it is not over yet. The financial problems have simply been shifted to the public sector. Ireland, unlike Iceland, did not collapse with a bang; it limped on with a whimper. The collapse of the banks in Iceland resulted in vast losses across the world and wholesale bankruptcy of the Icelandic banks. In Iceland the financial problem was so big it could not be solved; so it wasn't solved. Local and international creditors took their losses, licked their wounds and tried to litigate for their money. Iceland is still in the process of recovery. In two national referendums Icelandic citizens said no to payments to foreign creditors, especially those in the UK and the Netherlands, but the cost of trying to rescue its local banking sector is still high and political unrest continues.

Public opinion in Ireland in 2011 is reluctant to make comparisons with Iceland. Maybe it should. The scale of the collapse of the Irish financial sector should not be underestimated. Michael Lewis, in his *Vanity Fair* exposé 'When Irish Eyes Are Crying', cites Theo Phanos, a hedge fund manager working in London at the time, who called Anglo Irish Bank 'probably the world's worst bank; even worse than the Icelandic banks.'

His opinion is supported by the British Independent Commission on Banking Report[4] published in September 2011. In Figure 4.4 of this report, entitled 'Losses suffered by banks in the crisis as a percentage of (RWA) risk-weighted analysis', Anglo Irish Bank was the worst bank in Europe, 'making the greatest cumulative loss over the period 2007/2010' by this measure.

In 2008 Ireland had a largely insolvent financial sector, as did Iceland, but the Irish government's handling of the problem was to shift most of these problems onto the shoulders of its taxpayers and trundle on. This is more akin to Argentina in the 1990s than to Iceland in 2008. In 2011 Iceland began to recover: it issued new sovereign debt at rates of about 5 per cent annually. Argentina had an even harder default in 2001–2002. Argentina is taking longer to recover but it is now on its way. The new Irish government inherited a mountain of sovereign debt; this still lies between Ireland and economic recovery.

Generous to Whom?

The Irish government began a sequence of costly rescue attempts of the private financial sector in 2008. It proved incapable of solving the problems in the Irish banks on its own. A tsunami of private bad debt overwhelmed government finances. The piecemeal nationalisation of the Irish banks was expensive. Irish banks had already sold off many of their best assets in an attempt to avoid nationalisation. The government used off-balance sheet mechanisms to obfuscate the scale of the problem, including the 2009 creation of NAMA (the National Asset Management Agency). NAMA is a 'bad bank' vehicle specialising in property. Since Ireland's principal financial debt problems resulted from property speculation, NAMA represents a big part of Ireland's financial problems. The end result of the rescue was the generation by various mechanisms, including bank guarantees, of what Standard and Poor's (S&P) estimate is €90 billion in new sovereign debt (counting likely future losses in NAMA).

By rescuing Ireland's banks the Irish government also let the Irish banks' creditors off the hook. The money for the property loans loaned out by Irish banks was in turn borrowed from British and European private banks. The European banks insured many of these loans to Irish banks with 'swaps'. A swap is an unregulated insurance policy, a financial product invented by the derivatives financial sector that is concentrated in the US. If the Irish banks had been allowed to default on their creditors, the European banks that loaned them the money could have *called in* the swaps (asking for payment).[5]

The US government salvaged its own financial sector in a similar manner with the 2008 rescue of American International Group (AIG). AIG was a major holder of swaps on debt, including sub-prime mortgages. The buck stopped with AIG, so the US government saved its derivatives sector by saving AIG, which in turn saved its banking sector that had leveraged the ability to generate swaps to 'securitise' debt. The Irish government's wholesale rescue was apparently considered necessary to save the Irish banks but it had the side effect of plugging a hole in the dyke that threatened to drown the swap holders as well. Timothy Geithner answered questions on this matter in the Senate Banking, Housing and Urban Affairs Committee hearings where he discussed the systemic risk that the private European banking sector posed to the US financial sector in question time during the 2011 Annual Report to Congress of the US Financial Stability Oversight Council.

Apart from systemic risk factors, there is the issue of personal responsibility. In Ireland, executives of some major banks failed to declare secret loans that their own banks had made to them personally. For example, the former chairman of Anglo Irish Bank, Sean FitzPatrick, hid an €87 million loan even from his own shareholders. Mr FitzPatrick was arrested but then released. Other individuals absconded from the country without paying back the debt to their own failed banks. Again the apparent attitude of the Irish government is that the Irish taxpayer should take the hit for apparent corruption.

Calling in the Multilaterals

In early 2011 the Irish government rescue effort was finally overcome. The *go it alone* attempts to fix its broken banking sector did not work. The Fianna Fáil government called for help from multilateral lenders, principally the European Central Bank (ECB), the ECB's new rescue fund (part of the European Stability Mechanism – the ESM) and the International Monetary Fund (IMF).

These multilateral banks endorsed the generous Irish rescue and provided short-term liquidity (funding to keep the Irish banks solvent) at a healthy interest rate. This gave the exposed Irish, European, US and other private financial institutions a chance to offload bad Irish debt. Bad loans were converted into loans and liquidity from the multilaterals for which the Irish government provided guarantees. The rescue left the Irish taxpayer with massive debt liabilities and interest to repay as a result of minimal write-downs on the debt. The new debt added further stress to Ireland's economy, now plunged into a deep recession. Ireland became a member of the Highly Indebted Rich Countries club (HIRC) joining four other European members: Greece, Portugal, Italy and Spain. The global financial industry refers to these five European debtors as the 'European Peripherals'. Global bond markets launched a speculative attack on the bonds of all five nations. This compounded their debt problems, raising the ante, and creating a regional sovereign debt crisis.

Passing the Buck

A transfer of political power during an economic crisis – loading the new government with the problems caused by the previous government's financial mismanagement – is all too common in South America. Such a transfer of political power has already happened in Ireland, Portugal, Greece and Italy. Inheriting such a situation is not easy; resolution often implies a break with previous policies.

In the Third World budget deficits and government debt are often very high so sovereign debt carries a perceived default risk. High risk means high sovereign debt costs which adds to the drain on social budgets due to the need to siphon off money paying more interest when rolling over debt. Add corruption or perhaps corrosion to this toxic mix, in the form of a group of political and economic actors who believe they are immune from prosecution, and there you have it: your basic Banana Republic.

Loans to high-risk governments are considered of 'sub-investment' standard, which means the speculative bond markets view them with a mix of trepidation and avarice. Participating governments pay through the nose for bond issuance due to the perceived risk of default. As an Argentine default was becoming obvious to the markets, the *Financial Times* wrote in an editorial on 20 August 2001:

> Investors in government debt would take losses. But they have been happy to receive the fat yields offered by Argentine paper: they must now be prepared to accept that rewards of this kind entail some element of risk.

In other words, investment risk is par for the course; the risk of default is already priced in with the high interest rates, analogous to sub-prime mortgage interest rates on high-risk personal mortgages.

Argentina was not always a third world nation. At the turn of the twentieth century it had a gross domestic product (GDP) similar to that of the US; not any more. If you fall out of the protected rich nations club then your cheap debt privileges are revoked; credit becomes expensive whether you default or not. It is better not to lose one's membership as becoming a member is a difficult process. The European peripheral bond markets in 2011 are starting to look decidedly South American in nature; especially those of Ireland, Greece and Portugal. All three nations are hovering dangerously close to a debt spiral. Their new governments face tough choices.

Latin America has a sad history of sovereign debt and regional debt contagion. In Argentina's case the government has been struggling with the issue of sovereign debt burdens since the first million pound loan by Baring Brothers to President Rivadavia in 1822. Experience has led to some Latin American governments developing useful techniques for dealing with the sovereign debt markets and the IMF. Some of these are less well known outside the region. Applying these techniques to the Irish situation might help avoid an uncontrolled sovereign default.

Tequila Effect, Ouzo Effect

Some sovereign debt crises are not about national economic problems; instead they are spread throughout a region by contagion. One example was the tequila effect that precipitated the Argentine economic collapse in 2001–2002. There are some parallels with the current contagion among the European peripherals.

Latin America's most recent regional sovereign debt crisis was sparked off by the sharp devaluation of the Mexican peso in 1994. A tidal wave of financial damage spread across Latin America in the next few years. The national economies embroiled in the crisis had little in common except a high debt to GDP ratio. The sovereign bond markets meted out similar treatment to all. This sudden change of market confidence was referred to as the 'tequila effect'. It hit Argentina in 1995, so Argentina turned to the IMF for help. After six painful years of slow collapse the

Argentine economy finally succumbed, despite, and in some ways because of, advice from the IMF. The default lasted three more years until the Minister for Economics, Roberto Lavagna, finally reached a substantial agreement, partially restructuring the debt with creditors in 2005. This experience makes Argentine economists only too familiar with the relentless silent panic of a sovereign debt spiral. The longer it is drawn out, the greater the exit of capital and the harder the fall.

Ireland now finds itself enmeshed in a new regional sovereign debt crisis. The crisis began in Athens not Mexico City; might we call it the 'ouzo effect'? Some characteristics are similar. A speculative attack is launched against various regional governments with high debt to GDP ratios. In a debt spiral, interest payments become unbearable leading to more debt and pushing governments toward default. The problem cannot be solved without international intervention so the IMF is called in (with the ECB in Europe). Speculators enter the market exchanging the risk of taking a nominal loss on bond investments for higher interest rates or cut-price bonds. Their strategy is clear: the longer the payments are drawn out, the less likely they are to lose money. The only hope for the bond buyers to walk away whole is a state rescue with minimal haircuts. As luck would have it, that is what they got from the Irish government.

Before we push this analogy too far it is important to note that Ireland (whose S&P bond rating in September 2011 was BBB+) does not yet pay the interest premium on new debt that Argentina does (S&P rating 'stable' B), but the quantity of Irish sovereign debt and the relatively small population (one-tenth that of Argentina) puts Ireland in 2011 in a similar position to Argentina in the late 1990s. Buenos Aires had different problems to Mexico City, and Dublin has more in common with Reykjavik (in terms of the source of its new debt) than Athens, but traders in sovereign debt derivatives differentiate little. A speculative attack means there is lots of money to be made (or lost) in risky sovereign debt in the European peripherals.

What can Ireland Learn from South America?

Conventional options available to the Irish Department of Finance to reduce sovereign debt obligations are few and far between. Growing the economy is currently not an option. It becomes less likely the harder the IMF-recommended austerity measures bite. The fact that Irish sovereign debt is denominated in Euro (a currency whose exchange rate the Irish Central Bank does not control) means that the common strategy of devaluing one's way out of debt – 'quantitative easing' (or printing money) – is also out of the question.

A large increase in taxation is possible but this can also lead to economic contraction. The Irish government raised various taxes in 2010 and 2011. This unpopular option does help Ireland reduce budget deficits but there is too much debt to be paid off. Also, in Ireland's case, the source of national debt is not chronic budgetary problems. Instead this debt is the result of a financial rescue gone awry. Ireland's focus on austerity measures and interest rates is misplaced. Restructuring the rescue debt might be a more appropriate option.

When in 2011 Ireland called in the multilaterals, Dublin five-star hotels were filled with financial consultants. Local commentators described their visitors as 'the carpetbaggers' or simply 'the Germans'. There were formulaic calls for austerity from the luxury suites. Investors were on the look-out for possible bargains in future privatisations. The IMF/ECB advisors mandated austerity, despite the advice of Nobel Laureates such as Joseph Stiglitz and Paul Krugman. Both argue that cutting national expenditure causes the national economy to contract, thus making the option of growing your way out of the debt spiral even less likely.

In the late 1990s in Argentina austerity measures were also an intrinsic part of the IMF's 'structural adjustments.' Just as Stiglitz and Krugman now suggest, Argentine belt tightening pushed the economy deeper into recession. It delayed the default by about five years. This provided time to pressurise the government to a fire sale of state assets (as now advocated in Greece, Portugal and Ireland). A lack of capital controls also gave more time for outflows of capital that further aggravated the financial problems. Again we see parallels in the European peripherals.

In Argentina the IMF advocated privatisations of pension and energy assets. Removing access to pension funds proved especially egregious to public finances. The fire sale of public assets to private companies was unpopular but was managed with the assistance of corrupt representatives in the national parliament and senate. The largest sale was that of state oil company YPF to the Spanish multinational Repsol. Similar fire sales occurred all across Latin America. For example, in Brazil the state-owned Vale steel company was also sold off for an anomalously low price. It is now part of the world's largest private steel company.

Argentine state finances were further weakened by the privatisations, resulting in the loss of public income. The government had even less economic control over critical infrastructure, especially in the energy sector. The privatisations occurred and then the default happened anyway in 2001–2002.

Given the lack of conventional economic options available to the Irish government in 2011 the consequences of Ireland's debt spiral are quite predictable. Unless Ireland negotiates a reduction in sovereign debt, unless it employs other successful unconventional alternatives, or unless there is a miraculous improvement in economic conditions, the best case scenario is that the Irish taxpayers will pay more debt than they should, and in the worst case scenario Ireland will default sooner or later. If a default is inevitable it is better to do it sooner rather than later, employing tough negotiating practices, and in a controlled manner.

Lessons from the Argentine Default

If anything can be learned from the Argentine default it is that an *uncontrolled* hard default (such as that which occurs after a prolonged debt spiral) should be avoided at all cost. The Argentine economy resisted the pressures of the tequila effect for a few years but by the second quarter of 1998 the Argentine economy fell into steep decline. The GDP dropped 19 per cent and foreign direct investment fell by 60 per cent in five years. Many businesses failed and factories closed, primarily because of the artificially high peg of the peso exchange rate with the US dollar (1:1). This exchange rate affected the competitiveness of Argentine exports so local manufacturers could not compete with cheaper imports in a shrinking local market. Unemployment increased to 24 per cent, slightly above 2011 levels in Spain.

In 2001 the Minister for Finance, Domingo Cavallo, tried to prevent a run on the banks. He limited ATM withdrawals to 250 pesos per week. The 'smart money' had already left the country in dollars. The middle classes came into the streets demanding access to their accounts in marches (called 'cacerolazos') men, women and children marched beating pots and pans like drums. The political crisis escalated, each new government played ball with the IMF. The streets became more violent and police reacted with more violence: 34 people were killed. Many thousands more were to die in the next three years from suicide, health problems and malnutrition. Eventually, starvation occurred in remote regions of the country. The middle classes were decimated. The government collapsed again and again. In January 2002 the Argentine peso was devalued by 75 per cent. A peso was then worth between 25 and 30 US cents. Ordinary citizens lost much of their savings. There were more suicides.

Subsequent governments declared a unilateral cessation of debt payments including a cessation of interest payments (a default). The default continued for 38 months while the government used their taxes for national recovery instead of interest payments. Finally, just over 50 per cent of the debt was renegotiated (the technical term is 'restructured') with about 70 per cent of the creditors accepting just less than 40 cents on the dollar with no interest.

Sovereign debt was reduced but the financial problems did not end there. Argentina is still on a fragile road to recovery. One of the most obvious legacies is a more regressive distribution of wealth. The rich got richer and the middle classes got poorer. The poor, as ever, bore the brunt, and some of them starved.

In 2012 Argentina has about the same nominal sovereign debt as in early 2002. An average GDP growth rate of 8 per cent for a decade means this represents very much less as a percentage of GDP, which has almost doubled since 2003. A higher proportion of Argentine debt is now denominated in pesos. This is easier to pay as Argentina can print pesos.

Argentina is now a member of the G20. Though still shut out of the private debt markets for government bonds, it is currently renegotiating its debt with the 'Paris Club' (an international arrangement representing large groups of sovereign and private lenders which is the final arbiter in default negotiations, with offices in Paris),[6] and is under extreme pressure to come back into the fold. Argentine loans from the Inter-American Development Bank are being blocked by the US.

The government has undone the privatisation of the national airline, national postal system, many city water services, and, critically for public finances, the private pension funds. All of this came at a very high cost to the Exchequer. Many services which were previously public remain privatised, their profits going to multinationals instead of being recycled in the local economy. The country faces countless litigations in the World Bank court (the International Centre for Settlement of Investment Disputes).

No one in Argentina would say that they wish to experience such a default ever again.

Unconventional Options for Irish Policy Makers

Unconventional economic thinking offers alternative policy options to Ireland's new government. These have been employed in South America with varying degrees of success. Use of similar strategies in an Irish context might at least offer Ireland a fighting chance of avoiding a hard default or paying back too much sovereign debt. Two unconventional options may have applicability in an Irish context:

- A government-sponsored national sovereign debt audit with subsequent debt reduction activities
- Alternative solidarity finance

Option One: Sovereign Debt Audits

The independent University of Limerick debt audit (completed in September 2011) was modelled on the debt audit used by the Ecuadorian government to their advantage in negotiations with the debt markets; as an independent audit it lacked access to certain information not in the public domain. An audit cannot itself reduce debt, but it can provide negotiators with arguments for doing so.

The Ecuadorian government began a sovereign debt audit under a presidential decree signed in the National Palace in Quito on 9 July 2007. President Rafael Correa had just been elected. He had run on a platform that included debt renegotiation. He created the Commission for an Integral Audit of Public Debt (CAIC in Spanish).[7]

The idea of a national debt audit is simple: pare back the nominal public debt to the essential debt that the public is legally obliged to pay. To do this it is necessary to audit the legitimacy and the source of the debt. The CAIC audit committee was made up of a team of government, religious and civic representatives, with both national and international participation. The Ecuadorian sovereign debt audit was followed by active debt restructuring. Reuters journalist Felix Salmon analysed the first phase of this restructuring in an article entitled 'Lessons from Ecuador's Bond Default' in May 2009. He cites Hans Humes, of Greylock Capital, who describes the Ecuadorian strategy as a 'great blueprint now of how to do it.' Humes called it, 'one of the most elegant restructurings that I've seen'. The bond dealers were sanguine; the party was over! 'The world has changed,' said Humes:

> ... we're now living in a world where not only Ecuador can default, but Iceland can default as well. And that's a world where defaults by small emerging-market countries simply don't have the systemic consequences that everybody thought they might have.

More information on the CAIC is available in the excellent Greek documentary *Debtocracy*[8] and the final report of phase one of the Ecuadorian debt audit (published in English in 2008) is down-loadable from the government website <AuditoriaDeuda.org.ec>.

Eric Toussaint of the Committee for the Abolition of Third World Debt (CADTM) was a consultant to the Ecuadorian CAIC audit in the sub-committee on multilateral debt. He argued in an article on 25 August 2011[9] that much of the peripheral unproductive (rescue) debt should be declared illegitimate. His argument goes as follows:

> It is obvious that the conditionalities imposed by the Troika[10] (massive layoffs in the civil service, the dismantling of social protection and social services, reduction of social budgets, increase in indirect taxes such as VAT, the lowering of the minimum wage, etc.) violate the UN Charter.
>
> [...] It takes us back to a question raised by the doctrine of odious debt: who benefits from the loans?

Option Two: Solidarity Finance

Another unconventional option for governments out of favour with the debt markets is to seek solidarity finance. In Ireland's case solidarity might be found within the European Union. Solidarity could preferably be coordinated with the other 'peripherals' like Greece and Portugal.

For a long time now the EU has been much more than just a common market. The EU is a political, monetary, economic and military community of nations. In fact it used to be called the European Community. It is in the interests of all community members to prevent a fellow nation's financial collapse, especially when most European nations have private banks that are (or were) bondholders of peripheral debt. Negotiating solidarity measures makes sense: it is part of being a good neighbour. It could demonstrate to the debt markets that speculative attacks would be unprofitable.

The ECB is currently providing essential liquidity to the Irish banks, thus bridging the transfer of risks from private European banks to community taxpayers (at the cost of Irish government guarantees). An argument could be made that some of this cost should be socialised to the community itself. Various suggestions have been made to do this including Eurobonds (EU bonds backed by institutions of the European Union, not national bonds denominated in Euro).

In late August 2011 Christine Lagarde, the new director of the IMF, had another suggestion. At the US Federal Reserve Symposium in Jackson Hole, Wyoming, Lagarde said, 'European banks may need forced capital injections to stop the spread of the Eurozone's sovereign and financial crisis.' In a curiously circular argument she added that European private banks would need this infusion of capital to '[be] strong enough to withstand the risks of sovereigns and weak growth [thereby] cutting the chains of contagion.' Lagarde suggested that the private sector could take its share of losses but also added that an injection of funds might have to come from public European sources:

> One option would be to use the European Financial Stability Facility to make direct capital injections into banks [so as to] avoid further stress on the finances of national governments such as Greece.

Presumably Christine Lagarde would also include Ireland in the list of peripheral governments with stressed financials, but Ireland is somewhat unique as much of the Irish sovereign debt (and guarantees) is the direct result of the rescue of Ireland's private financial sector. Lagarde suggests that private European banks need to have capital injected into them by the European

Financial Stability Facility (EFSF) so that they can improve their resilience to sovereign risks. In Ireland's case it is too late to do this; in fact the Irish 'sovereign risk' is the result of the private rescue. It could be argued that this new 'Lagarde doctrine', if put into effect, would imply that the EFSF should intervene after the effect in Ireland's case.

After the abrupt departure of Dominique Strauss-Kahn, Lagarde became the first female managing director of the IMF, having served as Finance Minister of France from 2007 until July 2011. The IMF is, as its name implies, an international monetary institution tasked with global financial stability (both private and public banks). Her call to save the private banks with public money in order to prevent risks to private banks from public defaults is a somewhat circular argument. In layman's logic it is somewhat absurd but the financial world has its own logic. It does not mean that, if implemented, the plan would not work.

Lagarde's idea to use the EFSF to protect Europe from a default on sovereign debt could be considered a call for an EU solidarity measure. In retrospect, implementing Lagarde's suggestion in Ireland's case would imply the use of European funds to rescue the private Irish banks (as against Irish state funds and guarantees). If the EFSF had intervened as Lagarde suggested in Ireland the Irish sovereign debt crisis would have been avoided altogether.

In other words, one way to save Ireland from default is to socialise the pain of rescuing the Irish financial sector. A transfer from the ESM could be used to partially eliminate the state guarantees and thereby pay down the sovereign Irish debt from the blanket rescue. The private sector could also be forced to share the pain. A default would be avoided. Problem solved! One could argue that Lagarde's suggestions give Irish negotiators further leverage in negotiations with creditors in Brussels and Frankfurt. The Irish, the Greeks and the Portuguese might even ask the IMF to broker such a deal. The fact that this announcement was made from Jackson Hole would lead us to believe that such a solution would be acceptable to Washington as well. It is an alternative means to rescue US holders of swaps at Europe's expense.

Regional solidarity was important to Argentina too. Unfortunately this solidarity came only after the political collapse when the new Kirchner government made new friends in South America. After the default, the private markets shut Argentina out of the 'conventional' sovereign debt markets. The government was in desperate need of financing to get out of the crisis so Argentina created peso bonds and sold them to Venezuela, who later sold them on at a profit.

Venezuela did not just buy bonds; it also offered up-front payments to prevent large Argentine companies such as SanCor (a dairy manufacturing cooperative) from economic collapse.[11] The Venezuelans receive future exports from SanCor in return. In effect, solidarity funding is being paid off in yogurt futures: a creative and healthy choice. Solidarity credit gave Argentina an alternative debt market; it provided crucial funds that helped the Argentine government get back on its feet financially and allowed it breathing space to correct budgetary problems.

Option Three: The Default Option

The new Irish government should try to avoid a debt spiral by whatever means necessary (conventional or not). Failing this, there is the worst-case scenario: a hard default on Irish sovereign debt. This was the fate of Iceland in 2008 and Argentina in 2002. The effect on the Irish economy of an uncontrolled default would be extreme and unpredictable. Ireland would also risk currency devaluation with the resultant loss in the purchasing power of citizens' savings and in difficulties paying off Euro-denominated debt.

Devaluation happened in both Iceland and Argentina. If it were to happen in Ireland this would imply a break with the Euro, analogous in some ways to Argentina's break with the dollar peg in 2002, but worse, as Ireland has no obvious currency to fall back on. In Argentina's case the peso dropped from $1.00 to

$0.30 in days (in September 2011, 1 peso was worth 23 US cents). In Iceland, 75 kroner bought €1 before the crisis; after the crisis €1 cost 180 kroner.[12]

In Iceland's case the country was able to return to debt markets within three years; not so Argentina. The markets were unwilling to accept peso-denominated bonds, especially after yet another Argentine default in 2002, and due to high internal Argentine inflation.

Some Irish pundits blame everything on the Euro but the Euro was not to blame for Ireland's financial problems. The problems in Ireland are not Euro–punt issues. The Euro is a competitive currency to the US dollar; the punt was always a dependent currency aligned with the British pound. Neither is Ireland's relationship with the Euro analogous to the peso peg to the US dollar in Argentina: for Argentina the dollar is a foreign currency. Membership of the Eurozone is, at least in theory, a more reciprocal relationship. The true extent of this Euro reciprocity still remains to be tested. Reverting to a new Irish punt would make Ireland more prone to speculative attacks against its new currency. It would be hard to convince financial markets of the stability of a defaulted and devalued currency. The resultant devaluation could be severe, making payment of Euro-denominated debt obligations more difficult in a weak new national currency. The state would have to maintain high foreign currency reserves to stabilise the value of the new punt. A break with the Euro is far from optimal, but it is possible. If it proves necessary it may be the least-worse scenario.

The Moral of Argentine Sovereignty

The fair distribution of the cost of debt restructuring gives governments a chance to recover by spreading the pain more equitably through society. Investor rights are important but so are human rights, as is national sovereignty. New human rights litigation was begun by former President Nestor Kirchner in 2003 and continues to this day under the presidency of his widow,

Cristina Fernandez de Kirchner (re-elected in October 2011). Most trials are for crimes during the last dictatorship but these are not unrelated to Argentina's sovereign debt. During Argentina's latest dictatorship, between 1976 and 1983, sovereign debt rose from $7.8 billion to $46 billion. Some calculations put this increase at about 20 per cent of Argentina's current sovereign debt obligations.

One of the most questionable economic measures was a law pushed though in the latter years of the dictatorship that effectively cancelled the foreign debt of much of the private sector. This has analogies in Ireland but the scale of the rescue of the Irish private financial sector is responsible for much more than 20 per cent of Ireland's nominal sovereign debt. A government-sponsored audit, like that which took place in Ecuador, has yet to happen in Argentina, but an extraordinary investigation was begun by an individual, Alexander Olmos, after Argentina's return to democracy in 1983. Olmos was so incensed by fraud during the dictatorship that he spent much of the last two decades of his life active in this prosecution.

In 1990 Olmos wrote an analysis of the fraud in his book, *The Sovereign Debt: All that You should Know but which They Kept from You*. The Olmos litigation[13] ended on 13 July 2000, just months after Alexander Olmos's premature death. It resulted in 470 commercial and financial proven irregularities. Criminal and correctional judge Dr Jorge Ballestero released his conclusive findings:

> Companies of significant importance and private banks with international debt, by socialising costs, even now compromise public finances servicing the sovereign debt .... The existence of an explicit relationship between the sovereign debt ... and the sacrifice of the national budgets since 1976 cannot have gone beyond the notice of the IMF who supervised international negotiations.[14]

The *de facto* government collapsed shortly after losing the Malvinas/Falklands war in 1982. Taking private debt public was a naked transfer of wealth from future Argentine taxpayers to influential private firms. Later studies indicated that this had negligible stimulus effects. The studies also showed that firms with the closest political contacts to the dictatorship received higher rates of debt alleviation. Much of the debt that companies claimed to have on their books (for which they received public guarantees) never even existed.

Redacted documents used by the Dáil committee investigating the bank rescue show that since early 2008 the Irish government had been debating how to rescue its financial sector. It received considerable advice from PriceWaterhouseCoopers, Merrill Lynch, Goldman Sachs and Morgan Stanley, and from the British government (which had the recent experience of nationalising the British bank Northern Rock).

On 19 July 2011, the *Financial Times* Alphaville blog published a story entitled 'Inside Ireland's Secret Liquidity' by Joseph Cotterill, which cited the same redacted documents used by the Dáil committee. Cotterill's examinations make Brian Lenihan's blanket rescue of the banking sector look even more like a rogue event, demonstrating that it flew in the face of direct advice from the secret overview of a financial stability resolution dated 8 Feb 2008, from the Irish Department of Finance. That advice included the following statement:

> As a matter of public policy to protect the interests of taxpayers any requirement to provide open ended / legally binding State guarantees which would expose the Exchequer to the risk of very significant costs are not regarded as part of the toolkit for successful crisis management and resolution.

Once the new government is clear as to why this advice was not heeded, they should be in possession of information pertinent to the tough negotiations ahead.

From Argentina we wish them well.

Endnotes

1 Sheila Killian, John Garvey and Francis Shaw (2011) 'An Audit of Irish Debt', available from: <http://www.debtireland.org/news/2011/09/14/debt-audit-gives-people-clear-picture-of-irelands/>. Anyone who reads this document will see that the access of the academics in Limerick to necessary information was only partial but it is a good start for a government-sponsored audit.

2 Downloadable from the Commission of Investigation into the Banking Sector in Ireland website: <http://www.bankinginquiry.gov.ie>.

3 Subordinate debt has less value than normal debt and is normally written off in liquidations.

4 Available from the Independent Banking Commission website at: <http://bankingcommission.independent.gov.uk/>.

5 This actually happened in 2011 when AIB defaulted on its debt, which triggered cash payouts of €500 million: <http://www.bbc.co.uk/news/business-13752758>.

6 See <www.clubdeparis.org>.

7 The results of the audit were published online here: <http://www.auditoriadeuda.org.ec/>.

8 To watch the film online with English subtitles please visit <http://www.debtocracy.gr/indexen.html> or <http://www.dailymotion.com/video/xik4kh_debtocracy-international-version_shortfilms>.

9 'Greece, Ireland and Portugal: Why Arrangements with the Troika Are Odious', *CADTM*, available from: <http://www.cadtm.org/Greece-Ireland-and-Portugal-why>.

10 The 'troika' is the European Commission, the IMF and the ECB.

11 The company Adecoagro, with investments from the Soros Fund, was reputedly interested in purchasing SanCor in its distressed state.

12 The Icelandic krona later rose in value against the Euro (in January 2012 €1 was worth approx 161 kroner).

13 For more on the financial irregularities of nationalising private debt see Anthony Phillips (2007) 'Fourteen Billions between Friends', *Project Allende*, available from: <http://www.projectallende.org/deuda/www-deuda/mdeh.pdf>.

14 Conclusions quoted in Spanish in full: <http://www.argentinaoculta.com/deuda/dictameno31.htm>.

10

Coring out the Big Apple: New York's Fiscal Crisis

Sam Roberts

Sam Roberts is urban affairs correspondent of the New York Times.

'I have been advised by the comptroller', the statement by the mayor began, 'that the City of New York has insufficient cash on hand to meet debt obligations due today. This constitutes the default that we have struggled to avoid.'

The prepared statement for Mayor Abraham D. Beame, a London-born immigrant and the city's first Jewish mayor, was ready to be released on 17 October 1975 if city and state officials could not persuade the teachers' union to invest $150 million from its pension funds in municipal securities. That's how close New York City came to bankruptcy in 1975: the margin between solvency and default by the largest city in the United States turned out to have been only paper-thin.

The city avoided a formal default, although the State Legislature imposed a debt moratorium that amounted to default in all but name. That moratorium was later declared unconstitutional by state courts, but only after it bought enough time for New York to restructure its debt and impose rigorous fiscal discipline that convinced a reluctant federal government to guarantee city debt.

Even without a formal default, the legacy of what would become known universally in New York as *The* Fiscal Crisis (like *The* War, even 70 years later no one would have to ask which one) would endure for decades with decidedly mixed results. The

173

formal fiscal discipline would persist, allowing the city to return to the credit markets within four years, but the impact of the first mass layoffs of municipal employees since the Depression and other budget cutbacks for vital services would within a decade or so precipitate social, financial and political crises that, arguably, were even more severe than The Fiscal Crisis itself.

'A crisis denotes a single incident', said Governor Hugh L. Carey, who was widely credited with rescuing the city. 'This was an atmosphere.'

The Causes

'The New York City fiscal crisis seemed at the time like a unique interplay of disparate forces', the journalist Steven R. Weisman, who covered the crisis for the *New York Times*, would later write:

> ... but it was quite similar to other modern debt crises. Like Latin America in the 1980s and Asian countries in the 1990s, and European and American banks in 2008, the city courted disaster by financing ongoing expenses with short-term debt. A reckoning almost always comes in such circumstances.

Lord Bryce, the British historian, wrote in the 1880s that municipal government in the United States was the most conspicuous failure of American life. That helps explain why no former mayor of any city has been elected President since Calvin Coolidge, of Northampton, Massachusetts, in 1924 and why, since the nineteenth century, the mayoralty of New York has been a political dead end. In their seminal *Governing New York City*, Professors Wallace Sayre and Herbert Kaufman wrote that while the presidency can elevate the most mediocre of men – even former mayors like Calvin Coolidge – 'the mayoralty is the highly vulnerable symbol of all the defects in the city and its government.' By the 1960s, New York was being widely denigrated as ungovernable, but some astute commentators reached that conclusion years earlier. After Fiorello H. La Guardia, a Republican, had been elected mayor of the heavily Democratic city in 1933, H.L. Mencken expressed the hope if La Guardia 'is well-advised he will make his will, get a shave and haircut, burn all the letters that he has ever received from women' and leap off the Empire State Building.

In 1965, the challenges facing the city seemed so overwhelming that New Yorkers were willing to gamble again on a maverick Republican, as they had with La Guardia three decades earlier. As the year began, a *New York Times* editorial expressed hope that one of the city's few phenomenal Republican vote-getters – perhaps that young East Side congressman John V. Lindsay – might be induced to go down what was admittedly 'suicide road toward City Hall'. That same month, the old *New York Herald Tribune* proclaimed 'New York, Greatest City in the World, And Everything Is Wrong with It'. When the year ended, John V. Lindsay would inherit what was, as the *Tribune*'s series dubbed it, a 'City in Crisis'.

That January, welfare workers struck for 28 days, disrupting relief to 500,000 New Yorkers. Twelve separate agencies were overseeing a vast array of anti-poverty programmes. Factories were haemorrhaging 18,000 jobs a year. One-third of the city's public schoolchildren were testing below the norm in reading and arithmetic. Antiquated garbage trucks were out of service 40 per cent of the time. Standard and Poor's lowered the city's credit rating and the city's comptroller, Abraham D. Beame, whom one Lindsay supporter, Democratic Socialist Michael Harrington, dismissed as having 'accountancy as a political philosophy', was warning about 'the treacherous fiscal path being followed by our city'.

New York was still reeling from riots that erupted in Harlem and Bedford-Stuyvesant the year before, after a 15-year-old black youth was shot to death by a white police officer on the Upper East Side. Major crime had soared by nearly 15 per cent in the past year alone. During the campaign, Lindsay visited the site in Kew Gardens, Queens, where 38 neighbours failed to respond to the screams of Kitty Genovese, a 28-year-old woman who was being attacked. What the murder 'tells us', Lindsay said, 'is that something has gone out of the heart and soul of New York City'. *Time* magazine grimly concluded:

> New York seemed a shiftless slattern, mired in problems that had been allowed to proliferate for decades. Its air was foul, and so were its surrounding waters – and there was barely enough water to drink. Its slums rotted away undisturbed, its new apartment buildings and public housing were as shoddy as rapacity and bureaucracy could make them. The city was deep in hock and going deeper; interest on its debt alone was $1.4 million daily – more than the cost of police, fire and sanitation services combined. More and more, it was a place where only the rich and the welfare-dependent poor could afford to live. Its crime rate was rising as inexorably as its traffic slowed down. East Side, West Side, male and female prostitutes seemed like shades of prewar Berlin. Even the fabled skyline had lost much of its old majesty. As Architect Edward Durrell Stone lamented: 'If you look around and you give a damn, it makes you want to commit suicide.'

The problems, nor the solutions that would lead to more problems, did not begin with Lindsay. Arguably, they could be traced to the New Deal, when New York became more dependent on federal largess, and to the reverberations of cyclical global economic upheavals. The publisher Jason Epstein wrote later that New York seemed to have survived only by dint of 'a kind of anarchic common sense'. But, Epstein continued,

> ... by the middle sixties you could see the city changing all around you. New construction was going up everywhere, herding the old residents and their businesses into ever narrower enclaves, or driving them out of the city altogether. Meanwhile, the expanding ghettos were overflowing with refugees driven here by the mechanization of Southern agriculture and by Southern welfare practices that made Northern cities seem deceptively generous by contrast. ... Between 1960 and 1970, the proportion of blacks in the city had risen from 14 percent to 21 percent, most of them trapped here by a city that didn't need their labor and that had, in fact, begun to export its menial and

routine work to less costly labor markets, often to the same areas which these new arrivals had recently abandoned.

The 1960 census was the first ever in which New York City registered a decline in population – the result of an exodus of mostly white middle-class taxpayers to suburbia. By 1965, exactly 100 years since the Civil War had ended, black impatience with the fruits of emancipation was coupled with another phenomenon, a profoundly divisive one, which Daniel Patrick Moynihan and Nathan Glazer astutely described in the preface to their updated edition of *Beyond the Melting Pot* in 1970: 'The Protestants and better-off Jews determined that the Negroes and Puerto Ricans were deserving and in need and, on those grounds, further determined that those needs would be met by concessions of various kinds from the Italians and the Irish ... and the worse-off Jews.'

Former Mayor Robert F. Wagner's credo that 'a bad loan is better than a good tax' was epitomised by his decision to issue nearly $256 million in short-term notes to balance the 1965–1966 budget of $43.9 billion – 'borrow now, pay later', the mayor explained. In effect, the city was taking out a loan against a property tax increase that had neither been imposed nor even approved. It was the first step on a slippery slope that would bring New York to the brink of default a decade later. Many of the costly 'good intentions' that ultimately got the city into trouble for overspending and that would be identified with Lindsay, began under Wagner. After he broke with the Democratic Party bosses in 1961, Wagner's progressive instincts were galvanised by his new alliance with reformers and their social agenda and with municipal unions, to which he had already granted the power to bargain collectively. His dependence on these 'expenditure-demanding political forces', Martin Shefter, the political scientist, wrote, 'helps explain why locally financed municipal expenditures rose twice as rapidly during Wagner's third term as during his first and second terms'. Short-term debt during Wagner's third term soared by what Ester Fuchs, the Columbia political scientist, wrote was 'an alarming' 79 per cent, adding:

'The city was saved from fiscal crisis during this period by new revenue in the form of inter-governmental aid, and a prosperous national economy.'

An independent commission – appointed by Wagner – was projecting a deficit of more than $315 million in 1965–1966. A *New York Times* editorial complained that 'the city is living on a credit card.' Less than four weeks into Lindsay's first term, the city borrowed $253 million, the largest financing in the history of the municipal bond market, and was forced to pay the highest interest rate since 1932.

Lindsay governed at ground zero of the 1960s culture wars. Even given Cold War competition from the Soviets, this was an era when, as Donald H. Elliott, the chairman of Lindsay's City Planning Commission put it, 'government was expected to make society better and everybody believed it could do so.' That was the underlying conceit of the Lindsay administration's 1969 futuristic strategic plan for New York. For all the administration's naiveté, its utopian illusions and its reputation for taking itself too seriously, the commission's master plan was paradoxical and prescient in defining Lindsay's constituency and in rendering its verdict on his mayoralty. 'We are, in sum, optimistic', the planners wrote. 'But we are also New Yorkers. We cannot see utopia. Even if all of these recommendations were carried out, if all the money were somehow raised, 10 years from now all sorts of new problems will have arisen, and New Yorkers will be talking of the crisis of the city, what a near-hopeless place it is, and why doesn't somebody do something.'

The fact is, the crisis came even sooner.

Budgets were generally balanced during Lindsay's first four-year term. By 1969, a recession struck; inflation rose. The budgetary gimmicks begun under Wagner were honed by Lindsay and his colleagues into an art. As Steve Weisman would later write, 'Though poorly understood at the time, these bookkeeping devices – like artificially deferring costs or borrowing against dubious or non-existent receivables – produced hidden deficits that drove up the city's short-term borrowing from a negligible amount in 1970 to more than $6 billion in 1975.' During Lindsay's two terms, the municipal budget nearly tripled to more than $10.2 billion, while the municipal work force grew from 247,000 to 291,000 (New York City is contiguous with its constituent five counties and performs many of the functions that other cities and counties do separately). Complicity abounded. Why cut budgets to demanding constituents when the day of reckoning could be postponed indefinitely? The city borrowed to pay for expanded welfare rolls and generous labour contracts. The banks looked the other way.

The budget would be balanced by what Charles Morris, in his *The Cost of Good Intentions*, described as $700 million in 'gimmicks and questionable borrowings'. The budget was adopted despite Lindsay's dissent. 'Over the next several years', Morris wrote, 'budget gimmicking was raised from the level of haphazard expedient to an arcane art form, and the practical limits of irresponsibility were pushed further and further out on the horizon.' Day-to-day operating costs were deftly shifted to the capital budget, financed by long-term bonds for major public works projects. Delivering a belated verdict on the fiscal crisis, the United States Securities and Exchange Commission staff concluded that Abe Beame, who succeeded Lindsay as mayor, had 'misled public investors'.

By 1975, the city's $12.3 billion budget was second in size only to the federal budget. The work force had soared to more than 300,000 in a decade and labour costs had doubled to $4 billion in just five years.

In retrospect, everyone saw it coming. Weisman quoted Edward V. Hamilton, a former deputy mayor now working in California, as likening the fiscal crisis to an earthquake: 'We know there is going to be a major earthquake in Los Angeles in 50 years', Hamilton said. 'But we really won't know until the earth starts shaking when it's going to happen.'

The Crisis

Hugh L. Carey delivered a blunt warning when he was inaugurated as governor of New York on 1 January 1975. 'The days of wine and roses', he said, 'are over'. Those halcyon days ended even sooner than he could have imagined. The press release on default that would be drafted the following October would be merely the midpoint in a crisis that had been percolating for months of debilitating death marches to the brink of bankruptcy and agonising negotiations over a longer-term solution. It began not with the city but with an agency of New York State, the Urban Development Corporation (UDC), created by Governor Nelson A. Rockefeller in 1968 in the wake of the Reverend Martin Luther King Jr.'s assassination to provide housing and other relief for the poor.

Most bonds issued by the state government in Albany were backed by the full faith and credit of New York State and were subject to constitutional limits. The UDC's commitment to repay its lenders was more creative and less binding. It depended on the state's 'moral obligation' to repay, a concept originated by a Rockefeller adviser, John Mitchell, before he became the Nixon administration's attorney general. 'This was one of the original "structured investment vehicles"', Weisman would write, 'like the ones that brought down several Wall Street houses in 2007–08 by establishing the principle of off-the-books debt'.

By January 1975, with revenues from its housing projects failing to keep pace with the expense of aggressive construction, the big banks informed Carey that they would no longer lend the UDC money or to underwrite its bonds. A month later, the UDC defaulted on a loan and on $100 million in bond anticipation notes. Carey recruited a prominent New York builder, Richard Ravitch, to bail out the agency out, meet its contractual obligations and restructure its debt by creating the Project Finance Agency to sell long-term bonds. That agency became the model for the Municipal Assistance Corporation (MAC) created later that year to save the city.

'We can't assume, as we did in the past', Ravitch said, who might just as well have been referring to New York City as to the state agency, 'that because a program is socially desirable it is credit-worthy'. New York, for the first time in a generation, was forced to acknowledge its limitations.

That May, Ravitch was again summoned to a meeting with the governor. Reeling from the UDC's default, the bankers were back. After months of warnings and after dumping their own holdings, they dropped a bombshell: they would no longer underwrite city bonds or short-term notes, which were being marketed at a rate of $600 million a month. The market was shut for what had been its biggest supplier. The bankers' decision triggered what became known as The Fiscal Crisis and immediately prompted the Beame administration to fire 20,000 workers, close eight fire houses and impose wage freezes and deferrals. Carey recruited the financier Felix G. Rohatyn who, inspired by Ravitch's Project Finance Agency, conceived the Municipal Assistance Corporation – Big Mac, it was soon dubbed – to lay legal claim to city tax revenues and restructure city debt. But by the summer, even the MAC was being shunned by the bond market. Washington spurned entreaties to help. Furtive hints were dropped about declaring bankruptcy and removing the mayor. Neither developed traction.

'The fiscal crisis was misnamed', Rohatyn would say later. 'It was a bankruptcy crisis', but without bankruptcy, because of the near-unanimity that the precedents for a government bankruptcy were so rare that the prospects made it the most alarming alternative. Nobody knew for sure what it would entail, but Rohatyn memorably likened it to 'stepping into a tepid bath and slashing your wrists: You might not feel yourself dying, but that's what would happen.'

Carey imposed an Emergency Financial Control Board, with himself as its chairman – 'my sign to Washington that the state was taking over', he would say – and accompanied his coup with higher taxes, an agreement with the banks to convert notes and bonds to lower interest rates and with municipal employee unions to purchase MAC securities and established a morato-rium on repaying the principal on short-term debt.

By 3 p.m. on 17 October, the city had to pay off $449 million to bondholders and a state loan, but Albert Shanker, the teach-ers' union president, was balking at investing the pivotal $149 million in union pension funds in MAC bonds. (Shanker had been immortalised a few years earlier in the Woody Allen film *Sleeper* when the protagonist travels to the future only to learn that the world was destroyed after 'a man named Albert Shanker got hold of a nuclear warhead'.)

The draft press release, which pointedly invoked the city comptroller, Harrison J. Goldin, a sometime Beame adversary, as the bearer of the bad news, went on to say that the city had applied for and obtained a court order to preserve its assets from creditors. It said that 'rational and humane' priorities had been approved to make payments in this order: police, fire, sanitation and public health services; food and shelter for people dependent on the city; hospital and emergency medical care for those with no other resources; bills from vendors of essential goods and services; school maintenance; interest on city debt; and payments due to the retired and aged, beyond those from pension funds. But Shanker finally relented (Beame would later reveal that another union leader was waiting in the wings just in case). A formal default was averted, but the city still had not resolved all of its $6 billion or so in short-term debt. After demanding more concessions, President Gerald Ford and recalcitrant members of Congress finally – if warily – went along with a programme to guarantee a $1.7 billion union pension fund investment in MAC bonds (at 7 per cent interest) after having been warned by, among others, Chancellor Helmut Schmidt of Germany and President Valéry Giscard d'Estaing of France that the bankruptcy by New York – jeopardising the investment of banks around the world that the city was indebted to – would trigger a global financial crisis.

'Bankruptcy was averted in stages over the following six months, finally with President Gerald Ford and Congress agreeing to participate with a package of short-term "seasonal" loans', Weisman wrote. Carey brought:

> ... unions, banks, and political figures together to accept a package of shared sacrifices. ... Could these steps have been taken in the absence of a crisis? That is highly doubtful. But the austerity and decline in city services (and quality of life) ushered in by the actions under Governor Carey probably contributed to the tarnishing of Lindsay's image in the eyes of New Yorkers, who also generally became disenchanted with his form of liberalism in later years.

The Consequences

The fiscal crisis cost tens of thousands of city workers their jobs, including Abe Beame, who in 1977 became the first elected mayor in half a century to be defeated for a second term. New Yorkers were also instrumental in the defeat of President Ford, whose onerous conditions for federal aid prompted the tabloid *Daily News* to famously proclaim: 'Ford to City: Drop Dead!' Other fallout from the fiscal crisis would be less dramatic, perhaps even invisible for a time, although there was ample physical evidence, too, that something had gone terribly wrong in city government. Construction abruptly stopped on thirteen schools. Enrolment at the City University of New York plunged by 70,000 to 180,000. Layoffs of police officers inflicted deep psychological damage on a force that considered itself immune from dismissals. The Narcotics Division would be decimated. From July 1975 to November 1979, no new police officers would be hired. The ratio of students to teachers in public schools soared by 5 to 25. The Fire Department scrapped a fleet of vans that ferried firefighters when shifts changed, forcing them to hire dial-a-cabs to race to fires. The police force shrank from 32,000 to 22,000. Crime went up, manpower went down, parks were transformed into dust bowls, maintenance was deferred ....

'If there are life-and-death services the city of New York provides – and there are – then you have to sort of assume a fire wasn't responded to as quickly as if you had 20 percent more fire coverage', Raymond D. Horton, a Columbia University business professor and research director for the Citizens Budget Commission, a business-financed research organisation, would say with a decade's worth of hindsight. 'You have to assume at some point in time a police officer couldn't get to a crime as quickly because he was answering another call, or you have to assume that a nurse didn't get to a patient on time because her patient load increased.'

Under Beame's successor, Edward I. Koch, the city adopted generally accepted accounting principles in 1980, a year earlier than required, and balanced its budget in 1981, also a year earlier than required. That same year, the private credit market reopened its spigot; the city sold $100 million in short-term notes backed only by anticipated tax revenue. The federally guaranteed loans were repaid eight years early. 'In the 60s, in the early 70s, there was a breakdown of any system of checks and balances', a Koch administration official, Robert F. Wagner Jr., a son of the former mayor, recalled. 'Nobody was able to say no. Institutionally built back into the system is not only the ability to say no, but the legal requirement to say no.'

By 1985, Comer S. Coppie, executive director of the State Financial Control Board ('Emergency' had been dropped from its title), would render this verdict: 'New York's is perhaps the most comprehensive and substantial recovery in the history of American cities and perhaps for any jurisdiction at the state or local level.' The continued loss of factory jobs was more than made up by the growth in finance, real estate and other white collar services (the strength of the dollar didn't hurt either). 'This is the city's best recovery record in the post-World War II years', said Samuel M. Ehrenhalt, regional director of the Bureau of Labor Statistics. 'The good old days really have been these days.'

But the payoff came with a stiff price, the result of a Darwinian accommodation to fiscal realities. Within a decade, the poverty rate rose from 15 per cent in 1975 to 23.4 per cent ten years later. Layoffs and attrition eliminated one in five municipal workers; the real earnings of those who survived were reduced by inflation, which also eroded welfare grants, frozen at pre-fiscal crisis levels, by one-third. Professors Horton and Charles Brecher of New York University, who would succeed him at the Citizens Budget Commission, would conclude that the Koch administration's forced austerity 'yielded a balanced budget, but at what cost? And to whom? The greatest burden was borne by the city's poor, whose standard of living was reduced.'

And by the late 1980s, with crack cocaine fuelling a crime epidemic and costs again outpacing tax revenues, the city was facing another crisis. A series of *New York Times* editorials branded New York as 'New Calcutta'. In 1991, the murder toll reached a record 2,245. The trailer for a film titled *King of New York* declared: 'Not everyone who runs a city is elected.' It wasn't about a banker. It was about a drug dealer. And this time there were fewer options. 'Last time, part of the solution was an unbalanced budget for a couple of years, but a mechanism to work your way out of the hole', said Philip R. Michael, the city's budget director. 'This time, there are no options to having a balanced budget.' But David N. Dinkins, who succeeded Koch and served as the city's first black mayor, cautioned: 'We know from our experience in the 1970's that the budget cuts of today lead to higher social costs a decade from now.' Felix Rohatyn would put it another way years later when the city again faced looming deficits. Were there some things the city could no longer afford to do, he was asked. 'It may not be able to afford to do them', Rohatyn replied, 'but if you stop doing them you may lose more than you gain'.

'Because of the fiscal crisis, there won't be another fiscal crisis', Dick Netzer, a New York University professor, concluded. 'Indeed', said John E. Zuccotti, who was recruited as deputy mayor to save Abe Beame from his complacency, 'maybe the things that had to be done could only be done by creating a crisis.' Still others expressed regret that despite the strict fiscal framework that was imposed on the city, more fundamental changes in productivity, privatisation and governance – and public expectations – had not been effected. 'We didn't change the way we provide public services', Professor Horton said. 'We simply shrunk the system.'

In his book *Political Crisis, Fiscal Crisis: The Collapse and Revival of New York City*, Martin Shefter, a political scientist at Cornell University, argued that the events of 1975 were merely the latest manifestation of a recurring dynamic between two sets of goals of government officials: getting elected and preserving civil harmony, on the one hand; and nurturing the local economy and maintaining the city's ability to pay its bills, on the other. In other words, there would be other crises, but they would manifest themselves in different forms. As Steve Weisman, now the editorial director and public policy fellow at the Peterson Institute for International Economics, wrote in 2011: 'It is amazing, in retrospect, how so much of that crisis foreshadowed the debt and deficit crisis in the United States and Europe today.' That year, several figures who were instrumental in resolving the crisis – Richard Ravitch, Felix Rohatyn and Paul Volcker, who was president of the New York Federal Reserve Bank in the mid-1970s – banded together to apply the lessons of The Fiscal Crisis to struggling state and local governments overwhelmed by public pension commitments. 'New York in 1975, is kind of a microcosm for what's going on in the U.S. generally now,' Volcker told the *Financial Times*. 'We borrow and borrow and continually spend and, so long as people are willing to lend, there is not sufficient pressure to do something about it in a timely way.'

11

When Cities Default ...

Marc Tomljanovich

Marc is associate professor of Finance at Drew University, New Jersey.

The sovereign debt crises in Greece, Ireland and Italy are in the gun sights of policy makers and news agencies alike. Their concern is well warranted. The effects of any developed country, even the smallest, being unable to fully repay its debts in a timely manner would likely have extreme impacts on many economies in Europe and across the globe, as well as on global financial markets. However, another debt crisis is looming, one that threatens to have more severe effects on individual households and local communities who only know about the travails of Irish banks through the late night news or online *Wall Street Journal*. This crisis involves municipal bonds, and is a tremendous example of trickle-down public spending gone wretchedly wrong. Though only a few US communities declared bankruptcy in 2011, these defaults may represent the dead canary in the coal mine. The next few years have the very real potential of bringing with them a cascade of new municipal defaults, and the combination of local and state tax hikes, alongside reductions or suspensions of local services, will make life much more difficult for these local areas for years to come. Nor is the crisis in locally-issued bonds limited to the United States. Whether the number of municipal defaults explodes across the United States and other countries depends on the extent to which national and regional governments are willing to step in and bail out struggling local governments facing challenging economic conditions and failing capital projects.

First, a very brief background on municipal bonds is in order. In the United States, municipal bonds are debt instruments issued by local governments, such as counties, towns and cities. It is an IOU – by purchasing one a municipal bond holder is entitled to the face value of the bond, which is paid back when the bond matures, as well as semi-annual coupon payments. Local governments issue these bonds for various capital projects designed to either repair deteriorating infrastructures, such as bridges and roads, or to create new infrastructures, such as a sewage treatment plant or new sports stadium. Municipal bonds fall into two main categories. The first type is general obligation bonds. With these bonds, the local government can raise taxes if needed to repay bondholders. These bonds are predominantly rated at investment grade status, since the municipality can almost always raise property taxes to repay the bonds. The second type is revenue bonds; for these bonds, only the revenue stream gained from the completed investment project can be used to repay bondholders. A good example of a revenue bond is a bond used to build a tolled highway – the government repays bondholders using the taxes it collects from drivers who pay exit tolls. Notice that there is one important feature of municipal bonds – they are not issued to cover operational costs. So, as tempting as it might be to try, a city cannot simply issue bonds and use the proceeds to pay workers their monthly salaries! The funding is to be used for capital projects only.

Why do investors like municipal bonds? There are two main advantages. The first is that, historically, municipal bonds confer a steady return to investors, unlike equities. Second, many municipal bonds also have a unique tax advantage in the United States. Interest received from municipal bonds is exempt from federal income taxes; this is not true for corporate or US Treasury bonds. And many states also allow interest payments to be exempt from state income taxes as well, provided the bondholder also lives in the state. What this means is that the returns gained from holding a municipal bond are in all cases exempt from federal taxes, and in some cases exempt from any US taxes at all. This tax advantage, combined with an overall stable performance, helps to explain why individual investors hold two-thirds of the $3 trillion of outstanding US municipal debt.

Historically, municipal bond markets have been wonderfully tranquil creatures. Secondary market trading is thin, since once investors purchase municipal bonds they tend to hold onto them until maturity due to their tax benefits. In addition, Lawrence Harris and Michael Piwowar found in a 2006 *Journal of Finance* article that municipal bonds are more expensive for retail investors to trade, so that, combined with the lack of price transparency, many investors take a 'buy and hold' attitude. However, municipal bonds certainly are not completely riskless assets. Bond holders may be exposed to multiple types of risk, including the risk that price levels may rise (inflation risk), the risk that market interest rates may rise (interest risk), the risk that municipalities may call their bonds early (call risk) and the risk that a municipality may declare bankruptcy prior to the bond's maturity (credit risk). The failures and near-failures are notable in part because they are so rare. The most widely cited municipal defaults in the United States include Orange County, California in 1994, the city of Cleveland in 1978, Washington Public Power Supply System in 1983 and the state of Arkansas in 1933 in the height of the Great Depression. And despite its eventual resolution, the near bankruptcy of New York City in 1975 serves as the highest profile cautionary tale of the short-term and long-term impacts a default can have on a local region.

Like many US cities in the post-World War II era, New York City experienced economic and social decay as both households and businesses began a flight to the suburbs in the 1950s and 1960s. Tax revenues dropped while crime rates soared, spurring on budget deficits by as early as 1961. By 1975 the city was on the brink of disaster, being unable to pay its daily operating expenses. It faced a $750 million budget deficit, and also had $14 billion in bonds outstanding, with almost $6 billion being short-term. By this time, the city also found itself shut out of credit markets, so new bond issuances were impossible. New York City avoided a full-scale default through a $2.3 billion three-year loan by the US federal government. New York City's services were reduced in noticeable and permanent ways. Many construction plans were halted, and the city's libraries, schools, parks and hospitals became more crowded and more poorly maintained. Programmes helping unemployed workers, such as weekly benefits and job retraining, were slashed. The city's free universities and open admission policy became a casualty of the new austerity plan, as restrictions were placed on who could get into the colleges and tuition was imposed for the first time. City teachers were forced to use $150 million of pensions to purchase city debt. Higher city taxes, including a 25 per cent increase in NYC's income tax, hastened residents' migration to the suburbs of New Jersey, New York and Connecticut, eroding the city's tax base. Of course, New York City's debt had been heavily downgraded by rating agencies, and the city was unable to re-enter the municipal bond market in any significant capacity until the end of the decade. Other related governments were also impacted by the de facto default. By also loaning New York City essential funding, New York State also suffered; being unable to raise money through new debt issuance for other needed projects. In a 1977 *Financial Analysts Journal* study, David Hoffland found that the New York City default resulted in credit spreads rising from 7 basis points (0.07 per cent) to 50–70 basis points (0.50–0.70 per cent) for a group of eastern cities including Pittsburgh, Boston and Philadelphia, raising borrowing costs for those cities and putting new external pressures on their budgets.

New York City's situation, though, appeared to be an exception to the norm. Moody's Investment Services discovered only 54 municipal bond defaults out of 18,400 rated issuances between 1970 and 2009. And Fitch ratings found that the cumulative default rate on municipal bonds issued between 1987 and 1994 was only 0.63 per cent. Furthermore, financial losses incurred by bondholders are rare, with Moody's reporting an average recovery rate of 67 per cent on defaulted municipal debt. In almost all of the cases listed above, bondholders were fully repaid at some point after the initial suspension of interest payments. The exception that perhaps proves the rule is Washington Public Power System Supply (WPPSS). Created in 1957 to bring affordable power to the northwest United States, WPPSS ambitiously issued $2.25 billion in bonds to finance the creation of five nuclear power plants, the proceeds of which would be used to repay bondholders. Environmental concerns and design changes led to massive cost overruns which forced the early cancellation of the project, and bondholders eventually received less than 25 cents on the dollar. Investors and the media quickly began pronouncing the municipal corporation's acronym as 'whoops'. One can thus see the allure of municipal bonds: credit risk is low, and even if default occurs, there is a high probability an investor will get back almost the entire principal. But the occasional defaults are also notable because they remind investors that if one municipality declares bankruptcy, it is entirely possible that any other municipality could do so. There may be key structural differences between the economies of Topeka, Kansas and Fargo, North Dakota, but they are likely lost on the average municipal bondholder who bought the related general obligation bonds based on after-tax rates of return. However, a municipal default that hits the news headlines can get investors looking at local communities with a more discerning eye, a requisite trait for successful long-term bondholders in coming years.

The financial crisis in autumn 2008 brought plenty of discerning eyes to every type of financial instrument. The implosion of the credit-default swap and structured products markets, in tandem with the heart-wrenching plunges in US, European and emerging equities markets, and topped off by spectacular bank collapses in multiple nations, meant that no asset class was completely safe. And it turns out that municipal bonds have many warts as well.

Municipalities in the United States have faced a perfect storm of financial horrors over the past three years. First, US property values began to fall by late autumn 2006, reversing a long-term trend and lowering local tax revenues. The meteoric rise in housing prices throughout the 2000s had led local governments to increase the depth and variety of their services, not to mention public salaries, and many were not equipped to quickly adjust to the new financial landscape. The presence of teacher, fire and police unions also tied the hands of many municipalities, which, due to long-term contracts, were forced to increase wages for public workers despite the deterioration in the economy. Second, in many states such as Florida, the fast pace of housing development required new infrastructures and new municipal bonds were issued to raise funds to build them. The assumptions of continued robust growth of new homes, and the associated revenue streams for the local governments, were decimated by the crisis. Third, as national consumer demand for goods and services slowed down in late 2008 into early 2009, millions of Americans were thrown out of work, eroding state finances as unemployment claims rose and income tax receipts fell. Fourth, beset by their own financial troubles, states reduced the amount of aid bestowed to local communities. The governors of Nebraska, Ohio, Wisconsin, Michigan, Massachusetts and New York are proposing deep aid cuts to their cities in 2012. Fifth, the rising number of foreclosures, with over 600,000 US foreclosure filings in the third quarter of 2011 alone, crimps both tax receipts and depresses home prices further. Foreclosures are an especially pressing issue for many high-growth areas, such as Nevada, that had to quickly construct new services like schools, roads and parks to accommodate the influx of families. These municipalities paid for these services through new bond issuances, expecting that tax revenues would continue to rise with the population and home values. Nevada now has the highest foreclosure rate in the country: as of the second quarter of 2011, an estimated 63 per cent of all homes in the state were 'underwater', and one out of every 75 residences was in foreclosure proceedings.

The time of reckoning has come for some municipalities in 2011. One well-publicised example involves Harrisburg, Pennsylvania, a city of 50,000 that is also the state's capital. The city has been in financial distress for decades with both low population growth and low per capita household incomes, including a 30 per cent poverty rate in 2009 according to the US Census Bureau. Adding fuel to the fire, the city guaranteed much of the $310 million in debt tied to a trash incinerator project that was envisioned to be self-sustaining but quickly turned into a financial morass. Members of the city council rejected demands from state officials that city assets be leased or sold. The city filed for bankruptcy protection in October 2011 claiming $450 million was owed to creditors, but just days later the state's governor signed legislation that would turn over the city's finances to state officials. The December holiday parade in the state's capital was one of the first items to be cancelled.

Sewage is causing mounds of problems down south. Jefferson County, Alabama began construction of a $3.2 billion sewage treatment plant designed to address population increases as well as environmental concerns. The project went awry as cost overruns and corruption issues mounted, and the county's decision to engage in interest rate swaps in 2002 designed to lower interest rate payments spectacularly backfired. Jefferson County defaulted on a $3.5 billion bond issuance in 2008, making it the largest municipal default thus far in US history. The county also tried imposing an occupancy tax to help pay for the project, which was ruled unconstitutional by the state's Supreme Court in mid-2011 and sent the county to the edge of disaster. In mid-September, following three years of tense negotiations with creditors, the county narrowly avoided filing for bankruptcy. One of the biggest holders of Jefferson County's bonds was J.P. Morgan Chase. The biggest impact of the bill is the effect on sewer rates in the county: 8.2 per cent annual increases have been proposed over each of the next three years, followed by 3.25 per cent annual increases until the debt is paid off.

In September, the small town of Center Falls, Rhode Island filed for bankruptcy. Budget deficits of $5 million are projected for the next five years. With a pension benefit plan promising $80 million in retirement benefits, over five times its general fund budget, and facing a payment instalment in October, the city had virtually no options left. Following the bankruptcy filing pension benefits were immediately cut by 50 per cent and a wave of layoffs within the town are imminent. Other municipalities under notable distress include Flint, Michigan; Camden, New Jersey; Detroit, Michigan; Riverdale, Illinois; and Pontiac, Michigan.

As these and other municipalities struggle to pay their bills, bankruptcy proceedings are certainly discussed by cities and councils, mayors, and local politicians. But in most cases, actual bankruptcy proceedings will not take place. Why not? First off, bondholders have appeared willing to accept alternative financing options in the current economic environment. Second, at some point, a higher level of government steps in to either take over a municipality's finances, or lend the municipality its needed funding, or both. In many cases it is the state government itself that saves the day by preventing a default. Though, really, it is a self-serving action. Municipal bankruptcies are expensive for the state and ultimately for taxpayers; a bankruptcy by the city of Vallejo, California in late 2008 ultimately cost $10 million in legal fees alone. A municipal default will raise borrowing costs for other towns and cities within the state, and perhaps for the state itself as well. In a 2004 article in *The Financial Review*, John M. Halstead, Shantaram Hegde and Linda Schmid Klein showed that the 1994 Orange County default was accompanied by negative wealth effects suffered by institutions that were unexposed to the original shock, a phenomenon they coin the *contagion hypothesis*. Preventing these negative spill-over effects that arise from a default, and the media news that accompanies it, is a chief goal of the state. The Harrisburg and Jefferson County cases are timely illustrations of this point.

Two critical factors will help to determine whether a large wave of municipal defaults is fast approaching in the United States and worldwide. The first involves state and federal aid, and directly ties in to the larger governments' budget realities. The US federal government's debt crisis in August 2011 will ultimately result in future cuts in government spending programmes, including aid to state and local governments. The trickle-down phenomenon passes through state governments beset by their own fiscal challenges, which in turn will be accelerating funding cuts to their municipalities. Further aid cuts to local communities will put additional strains on municipal budgets. Even though interest payments only average about 5 per cent of a US municipality's total expenses, the strong inclination to make these payments means that aid reduction will lead to cuts in other local services, including capital improving and preventative maintenance projects. How will a town pay for the rebuilding of a bridge that has become unsafe or a road that has been washed away by a mudslide? The putting off of these projects to future generations may be the only alternative given dire budget deficits, but will also lead to large challenges down the road.

The second critical factor involves tax receipts. The economic slowdown of the past three years has strained households and small businesses. Raising existing local taxes and imposing new taxes, then, is not a realistic option on both political and economic grounds. So what municipalities need is for tax receipts to remain as steady as possible. How can this happen? Certainly the stabilisation of housing prices would help matters. The current disturbing trend of falling home prices increases the chance of underwater mortgages; currently, 20 per cent of US households owe more on their homes than what they are worth at today's market prices. And as more mortgages go underwater, strategic defaults rise as homeowners walk away from their sinking investment. This is an especially common feature of homes that were purchased simply as a speculative venture, functioning not as primary residences but rather as a second, third or even tenth home. But strategic defaults are especially bad for towns and cities, since they are no longer collecting property taxes on those residencies. In addition, a house in foreclosure can hurt a neighbourhood's property values, which reduces tax receipts further. Coupled with foreclosures brought about due to the loss of jobs, falling home prices can cripple growth prospects for municipalities. Tax revenues are also determined by an area's tax base. Population and migration trends play a prominent role here. The cities of Detroit and Cleveland have seen their populations shrink since the 1970s due to the decline of the manufacturing sector in America. Their tax bases are steadily falling; a substantial problem given that the cities themselves, with their sizable and aging infrastructures, remain relatively intact. Rapidly fluctuating populations can also put severe strains on towns and cities. Reflecting a general migration pattern over the past decades from slow-growth manufacturing and north-eastern states to the sunbelt states in the American south-west, Arizona experienced annual population growth of 3 per cent from 1980 to 2010, well in excess of the 1 per cent national population growth rate. However, over the past three years, population growth has slowed substantially. Projections that municipalities used in determining future cash flows to help make interest payments have become worse than worthless.

In today's world, municipal bonds are still considered relatively safe investments. Out of 7,800 bonds backed by state or local governments in 2011, only 25 are rated speculative grade (Ba1) or lower, according to Moody's Investor Service. But local policy makers are facing financial pressures not seen in the United States since the Great Depression. Balancing long-run economic development with short-run solvency requires shrewd insights that are, quite frankly, beyond even national leaders. It seems clear that for many communities in the coming years, the only way to stay fiscally solvent will require shedding valuable local services, and reducing the number of teachers, sanitation workers, police officers and fire-fighters. Higher local taxes will also be a fact of life. Hopefully these painful adjustments will be enough to put municipalities, along with their households and businesses, back on the path of long-term sustainability.

PERSPECTIVES

12

A Market Participant's Perspective on Debt and Default

Peter Brown

Peter is founder of the Irish Institute of Financial Trading, and was formerly chief dealer and head of treasury for Barclays Bank.

To understand the market's perception of the current Eurozone crisis and how it might react to the eventual solution, one needs to understand the mindset of the trader. While the financial markets provide the products that industry needs to grow, and the products needed to control risk, once invented these products are subsumed by the traders in the market as a means to speculate. So despite foreign exchange being a means to eliminate risk for exporters and importers, foreign exchange turnover is dominated by speculative activity. The same goes for commodity futures, bonds, etc.

The financial market lives in a realm of perception and not reality. Traders who wait for the reality of the situation to occur have lost the profit opportunity of the journey. Reality is fully priced, whereas the move from the perception of the outcome to the reality of the outcome is where the money can be made. This is the world where speculators live. Speculation dominates the financial markets and traders have little or no sympathy for the outcome. They just want to make profits. This is a cold, calculating environment which has an effect on the world we live in. Politicians have little control over markets which can visit hardship or benefit on many. I have always maintained that the bonus culture is responsible for many of the disastrous products that financial markets invent. If you pay multi-million bonuses to individuals, they have no downside risk to their actions. It was out of this culture that sub-prime mortgages were created.

On the positive side, markets fight against poor political economic policies. Politicians have failed to understand that the markets will not be fooled by spin. If a policy is viewed as flawed, the market will attack it relentlessly and in most situations force a change. The currency crisis in Ireland in the early 1990s was a classic example. Rather than accept a 10 per cent devaluation of the punt, the authorities embarked on a ridiculous policy of defending an overvalued currency with exorbitant rate hikes. Those who remember will recall rates of 40 per cent and more being charged on corporate loan rollovers. A six-month standoff ensued before the realisation set in that to let the currency go might be the correct solution after all. Politicians lose when they take on the market with flawed policy. And the present Eurozone crisis is exactly that.

We have a Eurozone that simply has too much sovereign, corporate and personal debt. The solution being pursued to reduce the debt is austerity and economic growth. Austerity without growth leads to lower growth and increased debt. The Eurozone crisis is not a complex one but it is massive. The debt of nations is held by banks and it is the fear of sovereign default on bank balance sheets that is so serious. Weak banks cannot borrow money and therefore cannot lend. Lack of credit leads to lower economic growth which leads to increased sovereign debt and the spiral continues. No doubt the solution to the Eurozone crisis is debt forgiveness, restructuring or default. No one envisaged a haircut on sovereign debt within the Eurozone and the present market reaction reflects the enormity of such an event.

All banks are required to hold liquid assets so that they can raise money quickly in unforeseen circumstances. Historically the most liquid assets have been sovereign bonds. After the introduction of the Euro, bonds within the Eurozone could be purchased and held without the historical foreign exchange risk. For example, a bank in Ireland could hold French sovereign bonds in Euro and not francs as was the case previously. With the elimination of currency risk, the only thing that became important was the yield. Because default was never envisaged and Euro sovereign bonds were regarded as zero risk, the 20 basis points premium being offered on Greek bonds over their core European counterparts was irresistible. So began the ability for smaller nations to borrow at virtually the same price as Germany. We know it was the access to this funding that fuelled the high level of debt in the periphery countries, leading to the disaster that is now Greece and the property bubble that now defines Ireland.

Bonds are the integral part of this story and it is important to understand their various uses in bank balance sheets. Traders buy and sell bonds for speculative profits but banks also hold bonds for liquidity on what they call their back book. The important feature of a bond is that it is a negotiable instrument and is normally marked to market every day. This means that it is re-valued every day at the current price versus the original purchase price; the resulting profit or loss is set against the bond in the banks' accounts. Bonds are issued at par. Therefore if you purchase €1 million worth of a ten-year bond with an interest rate of 5 per cent on the first day of issue it will cost you €1 million. If interest rates fall the bond will have a value greater than par due to the attractive 5 per cent rate on the bond you bought. Because interest rates move continuously, bond prices change daily. However, because banks' back book holding of bonds were never for trading, historically they were never re-valued. The principle was that because they were zero risk, the money paid for them would be re-paid at maturity. And because they were being held for liquidity, the bank could envisage holding them to maturity. Because of this, back book bonds were not taken into account in either of the Europe-wide banking stress tests.

As I mentioned, markets deal in perception. Despite the authorities stating that the vast majority of banks passed the stress tests, the market's perception was different. If you have Greek bonds on your back book, you may not be getting all of your money back this time! So despite the authorities assuring us the banking system in Europe was sound, the market speculated that it wasn't. This is when the crisis moved from a sovereign debt problem to a banking problem. Sovereign debt can be solved over time while a banking problem is immediate. Banks are dependent on the inter-bank market for funding. When suspicions arise that banks may be in trouble the interbank market dries up. Confidence is hit and banks are unwilling to lend to each other as they are unsure as to who is badly affected. This leads to a credit squeeze between banks and ultimately between banks and customers.

Why did the authorities not see this coming and address the periphery bond issue earlier? Time and again, politicians and central bankers kick the can down the road, opening up opportunities for the speculators. As a trader myself I cannot complain but neither can I explain it. Most of the big successes I have had in my trading career have come from political misunderstanding and inaction. If the right decisions were made in a timely fashion, most volatility would disappear from the markets and speculation would diminish. Frankly this is unlikely to ever happen.

So where is the trader in all of this? Traders are opportunistic; they do not have a predisposed opinion on anything. Unlike economists who try to predict the future, traders react to the market in real time. While the market may go from A to B it will not do so in a straight line. So while the Euro may weaken as a result of this crisis, it is presently higher now at the time of writing (January 2012) than at the beginning of 2011. There is a saying: 'the markets can stay irrational longer than you can stay solvent.' Traders ignore this maxim at their peril. So the market today reflects underlying conditions today, while politicians would like the market to reflect where they believe their policies will take it in the future. This conflict is ever present and is why most politicians loathe and fear the markets.

The advantage of the trader is his/her ability to be either a seller or a purchaser, thereby having the ability to profit from a rising or falling market. Traders have a total lack of sensitivity to the direction of the market. The bonus culture overrides the fact that their actions may be affecting the performance of their pension fund. Indeed in the 1980s in Dublin you would have been hard pressed to find a trader affected by the recession. When Wall Street crashes it's an opportunity for the trader, despite the fact that the crash is devastating dad's equity portfolio. The mentality of the mob, some would call it. But mobs are hard to control and for the authorities they are hard to convince, especially with spin. So the market and the traders within the markets have the power to revalue equity assets, bond assets or property assets. And it is this power that will ultimately force some action to resolve the crisis.

So what opportunities exist for traders to profit from the present crisis? Bond traders are the highest paid in the financial markets. Anyone who read the book *The Big Short* will have some understanding of the millions these people earn. Buying bonds when yields are rising is loss-making so these traders need to be able to short the market to profit. There are two ways they can achieve this. They can borrow bonds from another institution for an agreed period of time, sell those bonds and buy them back before they have to be returned, hoping in the meantime the price of the bond has fallen. Or they can purchase a 'credit default swap' (CDS), which is basically an insurance premium against a default on the bond. You do not need to own bonds to purchase CDSs so the swaps can be a purely speculative instrument. The comparator would be a number of people having insurance policies on your house. Therefore the pay-out on the credit default swaps could be greater than the losses on the bonds. The point that a Greek default would lead not only to losses on the actual default but also to losses to the issuer of the CDSs is not fully appreciated.

Rating agencies have a major role in the bond market. They are tasked by the market to provide a rating on sovereign, bank and corporate bonds. Traders have limits on the type of bonds they can buy, so the rating of the bond has primary significance. Rating agencies have extraordinary powers and have in the past been heavily criticised for their performance. In the sub-prime mortgage meltdown of 2008 rating agencies had attached AAA ratings to mortgage portfolios which clearly were anything but AAA. They are playing a big part in the present crisis when adjusting ratings on sovereign debt. No doubt the authorities would like them to go away but this is unlikely to happen.

Traders can also profit from selloffs in the equity markets. Although there is a short selling ban on many financial stocks, that does not prohibit traders from profit opportunities. Banks are the engine room for any economy and any weakness in bank shares generally feeds into other areas of the market. Therefore even when traders cannot speculate on individual financial stocks, shorting indexes can still lead to handsome profits. Other markets open to speculation include foreign exchange, commodities and options. In all of these markets it is easy to be long or short and given the liquidity that is available it affords flexibility on risk. Traders can be bearish but swing to bullish easily if circumstances change. It is this flexibility that sets traders apart from traditional investors who by their long-only strategies get killed in bear markets.

So what is the trader's analysis of the current Eurozone crisis? Most traders think in the short term: weeks rather than months. The bigger hedge funds, because of their size, need to position themselves structurally long or short. This means they have to take a longer view of the market, much like economists do. If we take the longer-term view first, the Euro can only survive with closer economic integration. We need to become more like the United States, with one central authority overseeing economic policy for all the regions. Whether this will be politically acceptable to the diverse countries of Europe is a big call. Ireland, Portugal and Greece may accept this outcome because we are small and the fear of going it alone is too great. Italy may think differently.

The single currency has proven extremely unsuitable for small open economies like Ireland and Greece. The access to cheap funding was the cause of the debt problem. Time and again the European Central Bank (ECB) has set policy which is suitable to the core of Europe. Ireland, a small exporting economy, would prefer a weaker exchange rate and adjustable interest rates to control its boom and bust cycles. That will not be possible going forward and as closer integration comes the policies dictated to us will be designed to prevent us from being a problem rather than what is best for us as a nation. The call on whether the Euro survives will be a political one. The current policy of austerity and the hope for growth will fail for the periphery economies. The strains at political level are already starting to surface. Germany and France are dictating the strategies they feel will fix the problem. Smaller countries are expected to row in and have had little input of late. The main issue is not whether Greece will default – that is almost certain – but how will Italy fund itself at bond yields double last year's levels. To most commentators the problem is simple: there is too much debt. Either the Germans show resolve to keep the Euro by back-stopping the European Financial Stability Facility and let the ECB monetise sovereign debt, or the Euro is finished. This is a major policy shift but is the only sensible workable solution.

So is the Euro worth that much to Germany? Re-unification cost them €2 trillion and saving the Euro could cost them the same. You can be sure of one thing – if the Germans finally decide to back-stop the Euro it will come at a cost to the other members of the Eurozone. Germany is not going to allow a write-down of debt without the safeguard that it can never happen again. So the Euro can only survive if we hand over control to a central European authority that controls our finances, including our budgetary process. Will this be politically acceptable? I doubt it.

As you work through this argument most traders will reach the same conclusion. The Euro will not survive in its present form, if at all. Rather than showing unity, politically we are drifting apart. Ireland might be the good boy in the class but Greece and Italy are becoming pariahs. Will disharmony tear down the Euro and send us back in time? It would be a calamitous set of events. Prior to the Euro, banks were very insular because of the foreign exchange risk associated with cross-border deals. French banks tended to lend in France, and so on. With the introduction of the Euro, borders were blurred and now bank balance sheets resemble spaghetti in regard to where they have lent and borrowed. Unwinding these transactions after a Euro collapse would be a monumental task. Converting state balance sheets back to domestic currencies would be as daunting. Maybe the seriousness of the situation can drive the correct solution in the end.

13

A Mortgage Broker's Perspective on Debt and Default

Karl Deeter

Karl is operations manager of Irish Mortgage Brokers and a radio and newspaper commentator.

When I was a kid we used to play this game where you would stand in a circle and everybody would sit down at once; if you timed it just right everybody suddenly had a seat on the lap of the person behind you; if it didn't go right then you all ended up falling over in a mess of limbs and laughter. The mortgage market of the last five years reminds me of when that game didn't turn out right – minus the laughter part. If Ireland had a large credit event (in normal language it's called a 'default') what might the mortgage market look like in the aftermath? If we left the Euro what might happen to mortgage holders? How should mortgages work in the future? And should we ever 'forgive' debts? These are all questions I hope to put some perspective on in my contribution to this book; I cannot offer 'answers' because any prediction falls prey to the combined forces of the unforeseen, timing and the unique nuances that are particular to individual nations, markets and the formation of history. What I can do is lean upon historical precedent.

Taking the first idea of a sovereign default, we are likely to go into some form of negotiation in the future, not because we'll want to but because we'll have to. In part this has happened already with a reduction in our borrowing rates. However, in order to credibly access the markets again future lenders will need to be assured that we have the capacity to repay the debt. For now just be sure to add the acronym MYRA (Multi-Year Restructuring Agreement) to your vocabulary.

That a peripheral country could borrow at German rates was perhaps a mistake, but, equally, we won't have high odds of repaying if we borrow at high single digit rates either, nor will future lenders be willing to repeat that previous error of mistaking us for Germans when it comes to pricing credit. How this issue is resolved raises questions: will we get better terms such as longer maturities or more discounted rates? A partial write-off or accelerated amortisation (repayment of the loan) upon meeting certain criteria? Do we default?

The myriad of options boil down to a binary choice: do we repay our debts or not? If we do then it will need adjustment from its present guise, because things that can't happen don't happen, and we can't pay back the money we owe in full and on time under the present structure, so we'll likely face multiple rescheduling agreements in the future or go bang.

So what's on the other side for mortgages if this happens? I'll do my best to give you an idea ….

I have spent a little time in nations that have defaulted or had banking crises that brought them to the brink. Places like Indonesia, Argentina, Mexico, Brazil, Belize and a little more in Uruguay. One thing I have learned about default is that it is far from a 'painless' procedure, albeit at times a necessary one. And after default the mortgage market is generally all but defunct.

What happens to the mortgage business in the aftermath of a credit event? Normally lending to anybody becomes a bigger risk than not lending at all, a credit contraction occurs that would make our current 95 per cent drop-off in mortgage finance seem tame by comparison. Margins on lending shoot up – we have seen some of this already – but it is the 'pre-cyclone' version; credit-starved small and medium enterprises (SMEs) would go from a diet of bread and water to just water.

On my first trip to Uruguay I was going from the airport to downtown Montevideo; passing under a big cantilever bridge I remarked that we had two similar bridges in Ireland (the one near Drogheda and another in Dundrum). The taxi driver laughed; 'I helped design it', he said before producing his university degree papers, which he kept in the glove compartment. 'It wasn't always this way', he told me. I don't even know what the lesson in that is, but I can bet he didn't work on that bridge with a dream of one day driving an old beaten-up black and yellow cab.

If we default mortgage credit evaporates, and your humble analyst will become idle overnight. Even with the emerging duopoly that may happen, do people really need an intermediary to pick between two choices? In seeking two 'pillar' banks (one of which is only €9 billion 'less toxic' than Anglo) we will eradicate competition, allowing margins to rise to the point where an outside lender will come in and profit by charging less. That will stir competition, but there is no timeline on how long that takes. In the meantime expect to pay more for less, with higher charges on all aspects of finance.

And that is a frustrating thing about it: no matter how you deal with banks they can put up a toll on every road in the financial and payments system and extract money back out of an economy; in geek speak it is called 'economic rent'. Banks are the unforeseen monetary power in some respects, a second layer of interest rate setters.

Combined with a default, a sudden halt in credit for mortgages will damage confidence to the point that property prices plummet; we would probably overshoot the 'market clearing level' and that has benefits, but it would be at the cost of total household wealth destruction for a lot of people in the process.

We all lament the bank bailout, and that we won't burn bondholders, but nobody says the same thing about the final liability on bank balance sheets – the depositors. So let us not overlook that the government guarantee on deposits would be meaningless if we default, and if we reverted to the punt they might keep the guarantee but it would be in a devalued currency (no differ-ent than the traditional way of losing money). In the run-up to default and devaluation politicians would do all they can to play down the risk, but people would still panic and take their money out in Euro while they could. Thus far deposits in Irish banks are actually holding up well on the domestic front; it is the insti-tutional international depositors who have fled. Regular people would follow suit if they got wind of a default, and this would in effect 'create' a second banking crisis, for which there would be no bailout, just financial collapse; and as we saw from Asia in the late 1990s, decapitalised banks are also open to external shocks or speculative attacks, not a space one would ever envy.

There is something romantic about the idea of totally wiping the slate clean, but something quite impoverished about the real-ity of doing so; that's taking from first-hand experience. The upside is that the downside doesn't last forever, but the ensuing upside doesn't necessarily bring with it calm waters. The idea of 'leaving' the Euro on our own (as opposed to doing so if the Euro broke up) would put us in the driving seat, but of what car and where is it going? My inclination is that we'd be jumping into the back seat with Thelma and Louise during the final scene.

For the 400,000 tracker mortgage accounts a reintroduction of the punt and subsequent efforts to raise finance on international markets (bearing in mind that even within the Euro we are look-ing at high single digits at present) would destroy them, along with every standard variable rate holder. The vast majority of mortgage loans (circa 80 per cent) in Ireland are subject to changes in interest rates, meaning all of the interest rate risk is carried by the borrower. That is not to be confused with the 'cost of funds' to banks, that is a reflection of their own institutional risk and how the world sees them in terms of credit ratings versus their abil-ity to raise finance on open markets, rather we are talking about interest rates being set by the European Central Bank (ECB) and (if we left the Euro) potentially the Central Bank of Ireland. A sudden spike in those rates would be crushing; banks have the legal right to de-peg trackers from the ECB base rate if it is no longer an acceptable reference rate. It may be worse if there were grounds for continuing to pay in a new more expensive Euro versus our devalued punt! There is about €113 billion in home loan mortgage finance floating around this country, so the fall-out could be severe.

In the UK, Finland and Sweden property prices all remained undervalued for six to seven years after the bust hit their respective bottoms. In Finland the seven years after their crisis started were all years of deleveraging; we seem to be following that course. Finland didn't default, but it did devalue, and interest rates from 1989 to 1992 averaged 13 per cent. The experience in Mexico when interest rates shot up (due to currency devaluation in 1996) was that delinquent mortgages suddenly went from 4.1 per cent to 33.7 per cent, a massive 720 per cent increase!

From 1990 to 1994 unemployment in Finland went from 3 per cent to 18 per cent and resulted in a permanent increase in long-term unemployment and poverty. We are in a situation now where many people will simply never 'bounce back'. The debt to gross domestic product ratio in Finland increased almost fivefold from 13 per cent to 57 per cent in four short and very hard years; and it have never gone back to where it started; credit losses at banks were at 15 per cent. From 1991 there were seven years of budget deficits, with four of those years being over 10 per cent in the red. Look far away at Japan, currently more than half of mortgage loans are greater than 95 per cent loan to value (LTV), and even with borrower incentives like low interest rates and high LTV lending total mortgage lending is in decline, and property prices, after twenty long years, still haven't reached their previous levels.

But property prices be damned; I believe employment matters more. Employment in Finland has never recovered, and that is perhaps the worse fate. Even now unemployment is still twice as high as the pre-crisis 3 per cent. Since 1991 it has never dropped below 6 per cent (and has spent most of its time far above that figure). And the real kick in the teeth for the Finnish? Despite devaluation – which is oft trumped as an economic miracle – they still had six years of deflation and the same after that of disinflation. It's downsides like this that are conveniently brushed over in many debates. A big beneficiary was industrial production: the question for Ireland is do we have a manufacturing base that will do for us now what the Finnish one did for them nearly twenty years ago?

Reversing interest rates (along with currency devaluation) was vital for Finland, and in some respects we have benefited from this already via the ECB – current interest rates are at all-time lows. Simply put, if devaluation and default were as attractive in practice as they are on paper everybody would be doing it. It will hurt and hurt bad; that isn't to say it can't be a last-ditch option. Getting electrocuted isn't any fun (learned that the hard way) but defibrillators have saved a few lives too (thankfully haven't needed that yet!).

Which brings us to the next question – what about mortgages in the future?

If I had the ability to create their set up it would be as follows: mortgages are currently advanced at the outset on a 'one property – one loan' basis; granted you can split a loan with part on a fixed rate, part variable, but what I mean is that the loan is not tiered internally or spread amongst institutions. The structure of lending and the way people get paid to lend are the two things I would concentrate on the most. Imagine this: you buy a house for €100,000 and put down a 10 per cent deposit. Of the €90,000 borrowed is the riskiest bit the first €50,000, the 'middle' €30,000 or that final bit from €80,000 to €90,000? If property prices fall the borrower's €10,000 deposit is wiped out first and after that it is eating into the lender's money – *if* the loan goes sour and is never repaid. This doesn't encourage sensible risk pricing, the last (most risky) part of the loan is priced the same as the first (least risky) part. We don't think of a loan being broken up into sections, but what if they were?

What if you borrow 50 per cent of the purchase price with the rate at x per cent, and the bit from 50–60 per cent is x + 1 per cent and so on? The banks are pricing risk more effectively, and borrowers have an incentive to borrow less where possible and get a better price by doing so. Banks do 'tier' based on loan to value, but it's for the entire loan rather than for various strata of the loan. What if loans were split between recourse and non-recourse elements of the LTV? So the first 70 per cent is full recourse to the borrower but above that it isn't? The banks would then charge more for the loan over 70 per cent and would be more likely to insure against loss (as they largely stopped doing by opting out of mortgage indemnity guarantee bonds). If lending over 70 per cent was done on a non-recourse basis – meaning that if the lender repossessed the property the portion over this amount could only be realised via the property and not the person – they would share the risk with the buyer, which is far fairer than the present set-up.

It would result in future foreclosures forgiving parts of a debt over a certain amount. The national debate has proven this is a contemptuous topic; but it's damn effective. That is according to BlackRock, one of the world's largest advisory firms with over $3.5 trillion under management, which has shown that in every jurisdiction it has operated that reducing principal amounts works best when trying to avoid default and re-default. This is echoed by the behavioural finance experts in Loan Value Group – a company made up of mortgage bankers and behavioural economists from Wharton Business School – which offers back-ended incentives to borrowers who have not defaulted yet in order to avoid potential default.

Such a change may increase the likelihood of a strategic default, but acknowledgement and pricing of risk is precisely the point. It would also give investors in the bank a better idea of the type of lending they are doing because it could be broken down in the balance sheet. This would also mean that the cards are not stacked entirely in the bank's favour when people get into trouble with their mortgage, as it presently stands. Or they could spread it out, with different banks underwriting different parts: 'Bank A' shows the first lower-risk part of the loan on their balance sheet, with 'Bank B' offering the second unsecured lien and showing it on theirs. People can then gauge the risk of the institution in terms of their 'risk lending profile'. If one bank is saying 'all of our lending is less than 50 per cent LTV' that would make it a safer bet than one which is always in the 90 per cent or more LTV bracket, would it not?

Capital requirements could be weighted on the risk levels held by type and by size – this would be a far more dynamic and counter-cyclical approach, which would need some tweaking to stop an appearance of 'de-risking' during a property boom but that isn't insurmountable. Remuneration in lending is also a mess: brokers took a 50 per cent pay cut on loan origination, which used to be 1 per cent of the loan amount, and it got worse recently because there is a 'cap' on earnings with many lenders now, but this move to slash pay completely misses the point. The idea of 'money today' for a 25-year loan is insane. I even wrote a paper to the Central Bank about this (for which I got back a nice email). Payment should be aligned with the term of the product undertaken. If you write a 25-year loan then something like 0.2 per cent per year for every year the loan is performing is far more sensible and pragmatic, and, most importantly, it aligns the incentives of the seller with the principle; a non-performing loan offsets a performing loan, meaning banks and all of their sellers alike want to see the loan succeed. Quite frankly, it matters not to a person within the system if a loan goes bang two years down the line, and it should matter.

Many problems in this space will be resolved by the Personal Insolvency Act – at time of writing we have only seen the draft proposal, not the final version that becomes law. Outside of that however, debt will still be an issue and you can't fix one side of the equation (debt solutions) and avoid the other side (how the actual debt functions) or it's only a partial fix.

We have a view of what could happen and what could be beneficial if it were to happen, but what is actually likely to happen?

1. Credit will remain 'off the cliff', or widely unavailable, until our banks are either bought over by well-capitalised foreign banks or after several years of being competed against by new

entrants. Banks, despite the number of smart individuals in them, collectively act pro-cyclically or 'with the cycle', and lend a lot in booms and don't lend enough in busts; that trend will continue.

2. Government regulation will in hindsight be seen as a cause of protraction of credit contraction via higher capital requirements/stricter regulation, pricing control (recent Financial Regulator intervention)/increased rights for borrowers. The Regulator will also take a more prominent role in our history books for doing its job terribly in both boom and bust alike.

3. Changes to our bankruptcy and insolvency laws are long overdue; this may reduce the value of bank mortgage books – in particular their value if sold off if the underlying rights of the mortgage holders change significantly. This will affect both existing lending and future lending prospects.

4. Central banks are the last line of defence, and I believe they are fit for that purpose but it is not a mantle they necessary want to evoke; eventually a liquidity wall will need to be offered or uncertainty will remain.

5. Mortgage lending may eventually be a highly profitable and sought-after business in the future, but we need margins, money to finance lending and confidence in prices as well as the future or people will stay afraid.

6. The two aspects missing in the Irish market are a site value tax and a property database; without them we lack insight and the most important property-related fiscal tool available – this has to change.

7. Changing fiscal policy may also cause further issues, what about ending tax relief at source? And if we bring in a property tax (albeit needed) what effect will that have?

For now, banks must deleverage, lend to SMEs and lower their loan to deposit ratios. How? Easy, it's like trying to drink a glass of water, burp and sing a song all at once. In theory you may say it could be done; in reality you won't find a person who can do it. Our banks are bunched and will remain so for some time. Will this all happen again? You bet it will; that there are property and credit cycles is a given. Fred Harrison in the UK has traced the boom–bust back to the early 1700s, and it goes back further in many other countries. Eventually disaster myopia will set in and we'll forget about the time we are in; things will be different. The Reinhart and Rogoff book *This Time Is Different: Eight Centuries of Financial Folly* has an important hint in the title: it would seem that in almost a millennium (with the restriction on going back further likely being reliable data more than anything) we haven't learned to stop bubbles from forming, which is far more effective than fixing the aftermath.

Somehow I can't shake the feeling that we are merely on the line of track between two stations on the bubble express, a reflation (at least in this analyst's opinion) is not an 'if' event, just a 'when' and 'where' one.

At the same time I am hopeful, the natural tendency or inclination for the world and world economies is expansion; nobody wakes up hoping that their children have a fate or future worse than they do and that alone is a powerful positive force for an increased standard of living over time. What we call 'bad' now is not nearly as bad as many of the issues our ancestors faced, and, like a broken heart, with time, we'll all get over it and move on. A brighter future will also entail a lot of change, some of which you will see first as you read through this book. For my own part I don't know if there will be a 'mortgage broker' of the future, perhaps the biggest change in this industry will be to reinvent ourselves in some other space. Time will tell – the key is time – and time does fix everything (eventually). In Ireland it is just a question of ensuring we don't make it a longer process than necessary.

14

The IMF and the Dilemmas of Sovereign Default

Gary O'Callaghan

Gary is professor of Economics at Dubrovnik International University. He was formerly a member of the staff of the International Monetary Fund and, in that capacity, participated in negotiating a number of requests for sovereign debt reduction and rescheduling.

Introduction

'Sovereign default' is an intimidating term and conjures up images of riots in the streets, guards at the granary and gunboats in the harbour. Thankfully, any recourse to military methods of debt recovery is now frowned upon, but there is always a danger that aggrieved creditors could become forceful and that matters could get out of hand. As recently as 2008, the United Kingdom used its anti-terrorism legislation to seize the assets of an Icelandic bank that had frozen the accounts of British depositors. Iceland was outraged at what it considered an 'unfriendly act'.

The International Monetary Fund (IMF) represents many things to many people but its main purpose is to help sovereign member states run their economic and financial affairs in a proper manner and make the most of their own potential. The IMF is in the business of promoting stable growth so that a country's opportunities are maximised and its poverty is minimised. This also means that member countries are less likely to run into the sort of difficulties that lead to credit problems. In fact, the IMF strives for a quiet life where violent adjustments are avoided and trade and credit flow smoothly.[1]

Sometimes, however, member countries need help to repay their existing debts so that their access to international markets and financing is preserved for the future. And the IMF will often agree to bridge the financing gap, by lending its own resources, until solvency is restored. Unfortunately, this often requires recourse to a difficult path of adjustment for the country involved and it is these corrective measures that get most publicity. In these circumstances, the IMF is often portrayed as an enforcer for the great powers and their wealthy lenders – a surrogate for the gunboats of the past.

But, even in these situations, the IMF is more properly regarded as a credit resolution agency than as a debt collector. Some of the IMF's more recent attempts at credit resolution will be examined in this chapter and it will become clear that the IMF often proposes creditor contributions to an amicable debt restructuring in order to avoid either outright default or the imposition of repayment terms that are overly harsh. There is always the difficult issue of how much the country can repay, of course, and of how much debt might be 'forgiven' by creditors in order to make the solution more durable, but the intention is always to achieve a viable resolution to a difficult problem.

The word 'default' is uttered as a last resort at the IMF because the staff will always try to achieve an amicable accommodation between debtor and creditor – terms such as 'debt forgiveness' and 'debt restructuring' are used to imply creditor acquiescence to any necessary deal. And unilateral default is to be avoided at all costs because all parties lose out badly in such an event.[2] When a government does decide to proceed with a unilateral decision to default, the IMF will try to open negotiations as soon as possible with a view to resolving and normalising creditor relations.

As background, it is worth recalling that the IMF is an institution in the United Nations system and was established, at an international conference toward the end of the Second World War, to provide a framework for economic cooperation and development that would lead to a more stable and prosperous global economy. John Maynard Keynes was one of the main contributors to this conference; the same man who warned in 1920 that the harsh financial terms imposed on a defeated Germany after the First World War would foster resentment and lead to further bloodshed.[3] The IMF was founded, then, in a spirit of ensuring that punitive and unreasonable financial terms would never again lead to unfairness, instability and self-defeat on such a scale. The aftermath of the Second World War was marked more by the generosity of the Marshall Plan than the vindictiveness of reparations.[4]

The Default Dilemma: Time Inconsistency and Moral Hazard

Sovereign debt can lead to some very difficult issues but, at the core of any debt dilemma, there are two situations in social choice theory that present incentives for agents to act inefficiently. They are simple concepts but are often not fully understood:

- The first is *time inconsistency*, where one party to a transaction has an incentive to break its word and go back on a promise made at an earlier time. This danger clearly applies to debtors, who will always have an incentive to renege on debts once they are due. And the solution, of course, is to ensure that default carries such significant costs into the further future – including exclusion from future trade and finance – that the option will not be taken. Default must be a very costly choice.

- The problem of *moral hazard*, on the other hand, refers to a situation where a party who is insulated from risk behaves differently from how it would behave if it were fully exposed to it. If a creditor is fully isolated from risk, for example, there is a greater incentive to lend without appropriate diligence to potentially bad debtors. And, clearly, if default were never an option for a debtor, creditors would always be faced with moral hazard. The solution to this second problem is to allow the possibility of default in some circumstances – especially where the creditor may have been negligent and overly eager to lend – and encourage careful lending from the start.

So, the option of default can create a problem of time inconsistency but can also resolve a problem of moral hazard. And there needs to be a careful balancing act between the two consequences of default.

To make matters worse, these issues usually arise when some external shock has undermined the economic outlook that was shared when the loan was made. And it is often difficult – especially for opposing parties – to agree on whether, under the changed circumstances, the creditor is trying to take the easy way out or the debtor is trying to extract blood from a turnip. It is especially difficult when the turnip is a sovereign state and the IMF will try to assess what happened and what the debtor might reasonably be expected to pay in the circumstances. This requires a great deal of judgement.

The IMF's original mandate was to help countries overcome balance of payments problems in the context of a system of currencies with a fixed exchange rate to the dollar. Under that system, difficulties with debt repayment would first become obvious when central bank reserves began to drop. But, as time went on, the financial structure of the world changed radically and the IMF had to adapt and to expand its mandate in order to resolve the same basic set of problems. In fact, the IMF is constantly adapting to a changing world and there can be no IMF 'manual' on how to handle potential default. Rather, the IMF approach is inherent in how its financial instruments and conditionality have evolved over time; IMF principles are best observed in their application.

Complications have multiplied in recent years as private financial markets expanded and became more global in nature. And this gets to a third problem in social choice theory that the IMF must confront:

- The *free-rider* problem refers to a situation where a party tries to reap the benefits of a resource without having to pay for it. This concept can be applied to the benefits that ensue when a country returns to financial health: all market participants can benefit from this – especially any creditors that will be repaid

– but each will have an incentive to avoid making a contribution to the recovery.

Increasingly, then, the IMF has to ensure that, where appropriate, all beneficiaries make an adequate contribution to the resolution of a debt problem. This can be difficult with very disparate lenders.

It is worth noting at this stage that the IMF is never an endangered creditor when it is trying to resolve a debt problem.[5] The money is always due to somebody else and the IMF tries to act as an honest broker. In such circumstances, it is very difficult to create an *ex ante* rulebook for creditors. As will be seen below, there were attempts to create a code of conduct a decade ago, but this was rejected by creditors who wanted to retain flexibility. It is also difficult to impose universal rules in advance because the financial world is changing so quickly and any rule book could quickly become out-dated.

Instead, the evolving IMF approach is set out below. It should become obvious that the IMF always tries to achieve a balance between attaching sufficient costs to default, on the one hand, and imposing a meaningful duty of care on a complete group of international creditors, on the other. This is never easy and, sometimes, the IMF will get it wrong and will have to review its approach. However, the evolving nature of the IMF approach also allows one to speculate on how it might apply to the Eurozone crisis, and this exercise is undertaken in a concluding section.

An Evolving Approach to Debt Resolution

The IMF consults with member states every year on how their economies have progressed, where problems have emerged and what policies or corrective measures will be pursued. A 'surveillance' report is prepared and discussed at the IMF Board so that all member countries know what is going on with one another and can make comments. This process aims to impart good advice to members and to create an open and collegial environment in which countries can discuss their common problems.

This most basic function of the IMF already sets the stage to resolve any difficulties that might emerge. If a country has been honest and open in its discussions with the IMF, and has followed any advice that was offered, it is immediately in a better position to appeal for help should something go wrong. Any adverse events or shocks will more easily be recognised as something beyond the control of the country that is in trouble. After all, any country can encounter unexpected and adverse events.

Then, if necessary, the IMF can make a loan to the afflicted country to allow it to repay its debts while it makes the necessary corrections to the economy; the country will be given room to breathe while it adjusts to its new situation. Loans are approved by other member states and are sometimes offered at cheaper rates and better terms when the country is particularly badly afflicted, like Haiti in 2010. However, in most cases, the country will have to make difficult corrections so that its public finances and balance of external payments will be put on a stable footing into the future. An IMF 'programme' will establish a medium-term schedule of loans and corrective actions and policies to be adopted.

Very soon after the IMF was established (in 1946), and its basic surveillance and lending practices were set up (as described above), Argentina got into serious financial difficulty. It could not repay its debts, even with assistance from the IMF, and arranged to meet its assembled sovereign creditors in Paris in 1956. The debt was rescheduled and led to the setting-up of the Paris Club: an informal group of countries that 'seeks coordinated and sustainable solutions for debtor nations facing payment difficulties.' The Club has no formal legal basis but adheres to an evolving set of principles and has reached 422 agreements covering 88 debtor countries since its inauguration.[6] It is chaired by the head of the Treasury section at the French Ministry of Finance.

The Paris Club normally requires that countries have an IMF programme in place in order to qualify for a debt rescheduling agreement. The IMF monitors the capacity of the debtor to make repayments and, as a result, the Paris Club became the IMF's forum for the rescheduling of debt between countries. Until the mid-1970s, private commercial lending to non-industrialised nations was not common – most non-industrialised countries borrowed from richer nations only – so the Paris Club was the main venue for resolving debt problems. With a few exceptions, debt rescheduling during this early period was short-term and did not involve significant write-offs or relief.

From 1956 to 1980, the number of Paris Club agreements signed with debtor countries never exceeded four per year. But, during this period, procedures were put in place and the notion of 'burden-sharing' became an important element of any rescheduling. According to this concept, the creditor countries, the IMF and the debtor country would *all* share the 'cost' of resolving a debt problem. In practice, the IMF calculated a debtor's 'financing gap' and proposed a level of burden sharing – involving IMF loans, debt rescheduling and adjustment policies – that would bridge the gap into the future.

The Paris Club played a very important part in the transition of communist and socialist states to market economies in the early 1990s and this marked an important episode in the evolution of attitudes to debt restructuring. It was clear from the outset that these countries would have to undergo a very difficult period of adjustment and it was also true, of course, that the old debts had been accumulated by non-democratic regimes. Therefore, the problem of time inconsistency was somewhat diminished. Moreover, Western countries would benefit greatly from new markets. In these circumstances, very generous terms were offered, with Poland getting half its debt written off, for example, and most of the republics of the former Yugoslavia having two-thirds of their debt forgiven.[7]

During the 1970s, global finance began to change. Commercial banks took large deposits from oil exporters and lent these recycled 'petrodollars' to oil-importing and developing countries, usually at floating interest rates. When interest rates soared in 1979, and the price of commodities from developing countries slumped because of the associated recession, a serious crisis broke out and the IMF led the global response, actively engaging with commercial banks for the first time in Mexico in 1982.[8] In 1976, the London Club – an informal group of private creditors – had been assembled in response to Zaire's payment problems and this became the IMF's main private sector interlocutor as it confronted an increasing number of crises involving significant private sector lending.[9]

The first half of the 1980s saw an explosion in the number of debt restructurings, including Turkey in 1982 and virtually the whole of Latin America.[10] The IMF played a critical role by providing crisis lending to members, securing commitments from debtors that set the stage for financing a recovery, and assessing countries' ability to repay their debts. It prevented many countries from defaulting outright and contributed to the US-led Brady Plan in 1989 that eventually resolved the crisis.[11] The Plan offered liquid bonds to banks in exchange for their illiquid claims on insolvent nations, so long as banks accepted a substantial haircut on their existing claims and suffered delays in repayments.

The IMF certainly contributed to the resolution of the Latin American crisis but found itself criticised from both sides of the debt dilemma. On one hand, creditors accused it – somewhat ironically – of contributing to a series of short-term fixes in the early stages that held out the prospect of a complete bail-out and, therefore, delayed the harsh settlement that was ultimately required. On the other hand, the IMF was accused of acting as a debt collector for the banks, mainly because it insisted that countries had to clear any existing arrears to creditors before they could negotiate. In response to these accusations, the IMF became more conservative in its lending in the 1990s – insisting on early debt rescheduling before lending its own money – and became more lenient in its treatment of debtor countries – insisting only that they demonstrate 'good faith' before entering negotiations.[12]

More generally, charges that creditors from the developed world, led by the IMF, heaped debt on third world nations for their own enrichment became increasingly vocal in the early 1990s. This led to a realisation that some countries were indeed overly burdened and had little chance of escaping from an effective 'debt trap', where any growth was halted by debt service. In response, the Heavily Indebted Poor Countries (HIPC) Initiative was launched in 1996 by the IMF and World Bank. A comprehensive approach to debt reduction was designed to ensure that no poor country would face an unmanageable debt burden. To date, debt reduction packages under the HIPC Initiative have been approved for 36 countries, 30 of them in Africa, and a further 4 countries are eligible for assistance.[13]

The Fallout from Globalisation

But the sovereign debt problem only got worse as the millennium approached. A severe financial crisis hit Asia in 1997 and, even though only one country in Asia defaulted (Indonesia in 1998), the repercussions, direct and indirect, were felt across the globe. The governments of Russia (in 1998) and Ecuador (in 1999) were forced to default on parts or all of their debt while Pakistan (1999) and Ukraine (2000) sought a restructuring in the face of imminent default. These events, and an evolving crisis in Argentina in 2001–2002, prompted the IMF to undertake a comprehensive review of sovereign debt crises in a globalised world. And some surprising conclusions emerged.

First of all, the review prompted a rare statement of the principles guiding the IMF's approach to (especially commercial) debt restructuring, including avoiding the risk of contagion to other countries from undermining obligations to repay debt where possible, preserving market discipline by making creditors bear the consequences of the risks they take, a clear recognition that debt restructuring can often be a necessary solution, and the need to continually promote dialogue and regard all creditors as equal. The review noted that private sector creditors did not expect to be bailed out every time and were more concerned with establishing an efficient process to achieve debt restructuring. It repeated the need for the IMF to support problem countries, even when they were in arrears to creditors.[14]

The IMF looked closely at some recent episodes and concluded that the potential costs of sovereign default had risen to catastrophic levels. Many countries were reluctant to embark on a restructuring because domestic creditors also held local debt and there was a danger of the economy imploding due to secondary effects in domestic markets. Whatever about the damage to reputation and external financing prospects, it was increasingly difficult to target a restructuring at foreigners only, and countries hesitated until it was too late. At that stage, a country could lose the ability to control the domestic fallout from its own actions and the ability of the international community to soften the impact was also limited.[15] There was a danger of complete collapse and capital flight could suddenly reveal an economy that was highly indebted, uncompetitive and unable to meet its obligations.

The main lesson the IMF took from these episodes was that countries delayed debt restructuring for too long. '[T]he negative implications of a forced debt restructuring for the domestic economy [were] perceived to be so traumatic that policy makers [would] delay this option until all other possibilities [were] exhausted.' And attempts to resolve the problem in other ways – such as a fiscal contraction in Argentina in 2001 – could be counterproductive and simply delay and magnify the inevitable credit event.[16] Of course, the interests of creditors were also undermined by such delays: the more catastrophic the economic decline, the more severe the erosion of the government's revenue base and the less would be available to contribute to repaying even some of the debt.[17]

So, the IMF's long-standing policy of striking a balance between preserving the obligation to repay and insisting that some risk remain had effectively been turned on its head. Now, because of the spread of private financing into every corner of the globe, the potential costs of default had soared and *debtors* were reluctant to default while *creditors* had a greater interest in securing an early rescheduling. Anne Krueger, the Deputy Managing Director of the IMF, noted that like 'a toothache sufferer delaying a visit to the dentist until the last possible moment, governments frequently try to put off the inevitable. The result is that the citizens of the defaulting country experience greater hardship than they need to, and the international community has a tougher job helping pick up the pieces.' The lesson was that 'we need better incentives to bring debtors and creditors together before manageable problems turn into full-blown crises.'[18]

Procedures to Restructure Debt

Not only had the debt dilemma been turned on its head, but countries increasingly relied on bond markets for financing and its creditors were, therefore, 'more numerous, anonymous and difficult to coordinate'. This magnified the free-rider problem, and made it difficult to reach agreement with creditors, even if most of them would benefit from a collective restructuring. Moreover, individual creditors increasingly resorted to legal gambits that would give them an advantage; a 'vulture fund' held Peru to ransom by preventing it servicing its debts to other creditors. There was a need to 'create stronger incentives for creditors to stay engaged, rather than rush for the exits'.[19]

So, in 2002, IMF staff proposed the setting up of a Sovereign Debt Restructuring Mechanism (SDRM) that would encourage an early restructuring when 'there [was] no feasible set of sustainable macroeconomic policies that would allow the member to resolve the current crisis and regain medium-term viability without a significant reduction in the net present value of the sovereign's debt.'[20] The staff argued that the 'current process imposes undue costs on both the debtor country and its creditors, because it is prolonged and unpredictable. It may also risk contributing to contagion, with associated costs and risks for the stability of the international financial system.'[21]

This second concern – that a delay in default could lead to contagion – ran counter to the traditional argument that default in one country would lead to speculation against others. However, it recognised that markets are spooked more by the prospect of a large default – when they will bear most of the costs – than by the need for a small adjustment, which can usually be handled with the help of friends. To avoid panic, markets needed to see that a credible resolution mechanism was in place.

In designing the mechanism, the IMF looked to corporate bankruptcy regimes for inspiration. It sought to:

> [P]ut a better set of incentives in place by creating a predictable legal framework ... [where] ... a country would have legal protection from its creditors for a fixed period while it negotiate[d] a restructuring. In return, it would be under an enforced obligation to negotiate in good faith and to adopt policies that [would] get its economy back on track. Finally, once a restructuring [had] been agreed by a big enough majority of creditors, any dissenters would have to accept the same terms on offer.[22]

Countries would themselves activate the mechanism and put into motion an agreed set of procedures and conditions that would be recognised in international law.[23]

IMF staff were essentially proposing that there would be international legal protection for bankrupt sovereigns while they undertook negotiations with creditors and this major departure from existing practice would have significantly increased the power of the sovereign *vis-a-vis* its creditors. At the same time, the IMF recognised that this would only be one element of the strategy needed to resolve capital account crises — it would need to be 'complemented by measures to resolve balance sheet problems confronting the financial and corporate sectors'.[24]

The IMF was encouraged in late 2001 when US Treasury Secretary Paul O'Neill 'surprised the world, and his own staff, with his call for a new international sovereign bankruptcy law'. The US had long been opposed to such a regime, however, and 'O'Neill's isolation inside the Bush Administration made it impossible for him to ever close the deal.' Six months later, 'his own deputy for international affairs, John Taylor, made it clear that O'Neill had not brought the rest of the Treasury department along with him, let alone the broader Administration. Taylor's speech effectively signaled that no IMF design was ever going to win the support of the Bush Administration, let alone the US Congress.'[25]

Taylor admitted that reform of the existing uncertain process was long overdue but suggested market participants were simply too divided in their approaches to make such a significant and centralised proposal acceptable. In his view, 'the most practical and broadly acceptable reform would be to have sovereign borrowers and their creditors put a package of new clauses into their debt contracts.' These collective action clauses would 'describe as precisely as possible what happens when a country decides it has to restructure its debt' and would include provisions for a majority of bondholders to change the financial terms that would apply to all. The free-rider problem would be solved, but in a decentralised manner that was 'determined by the borrowers and lenders on their own terms.'[26]

The joint opposition of the US, major emerging market economies and private creditors doomed the SDRM proposal in the spring of 2003. In any event, Mexico led a series of other emerging market countries to introduce collective action clauses and this became the accepted approach, by default. And while it could be claimed that such clauses would help resolve the free-rider problem, it was clear to some observers that they would 'not fundamentally transform the existing sovereign restructuring process'. The IMF, these observers noted, might have more important goals than quick agreement on an external debt restructuring, such as 'financing to support macroeconomic stabilization and [trying] to mitigate the loss of output'.[27]

In other words, collective action clauses would not define a clear process to resolve sovereign insolvency in a very dangerous world where everybody needed to proceed quickly and carefully. For the IMF, this had been the lesson of the 1990s: that, left to their own devices, debtors and creditors could increase the cost of default. But this lesson was lost on some who still believed that prevention could obviate the need for a cure. Anna Schwartz, the well-known monetary economist, argued that 'when a financial crisis exposes a sovereign debtor's bankruptcy, it seems wrongheaded to focus on resolving its dishonored obligations rather than expanding efforts on preventing debtors from accumulating excessive obligations.' She, and others, berated the IMF for trying to reduce the cost of default and encourage reckless lending![28]

In an intriguing postscript to this debate, the main author of the IMF staff proposals on the SDRM in 2001–2002 was Timothy Geithner who, at the time of writing, has become the US Secretary of the Treasury. He must be exasperated that the world economy has stalled on his watch, mainly due to Europe's failure to resolve its sovereign debt problems.

Conclusions and Interpretations

The main conclusion about the IMF's approach to sovereign default is that it is ever practical: it tries to resolve problems with as little overall cost as possible. There can be no absolutes in the process of debt resolution – it is not a morality play – and a constant balance must be struck between the rights of creditors and the necessity for debt restructuring; when it is required and when creditors have been negligent. There is no IMF manual on sovereign default because its approach has to evolve over time.

Moreover, the IMF does not always get its way, as demonstrated by the SDRM debate. It tries to be forward looking and clearly saw that in an era of global and liquid credit markets sovereign default could become a very serious problem and that there needed to be more immediate access to debt restructuring – both to streamline the resolution process and to act as a deterrent to exuberant lending.

Few people thought that these lessons might apply to the Eurozone, but some have now argued for the introduction of a Eurozone SDRM to make debt restructuring more efficient and avoid the 'gambles for redemption' that have pushed many countries to the limit.[29] The Eurozone had been blind to the possibility of such problems and there was an implicit ban on default that saw most countries pay similar interest rates and, in some cases, accumulate too much debt. This was bad enough, but Germany and France then agreed to introduce debt restructuring as an option – to be known as 'private sector involvement' – before later insisting that it would only apply to debt issued after 2013. The Eurozone got stuck in the horns of the debt dilemma – it first exacerbated the debt problem by scaring capital away and then ruled out the obvious solution: selective default.

And it was an open secret that the IMF was frustrated by a ban on sovereign default in the Eurozone that, eventually, wore very thin. Default is not the enemy, the IMF probably said, because it sometimes cannot be avoided. Disorderly default is the enemy and must always be avoided. And often, when you rule out the option of an orderly debt default, or delay it for too long, you can make a disorderly default inevitable.

Endnotes

1   See <www.imf.org> for a description of the work of the IMF.
2   Even countries that do not repay the IMF on time are denoted as being 'in arrears' rather than 'in default' because the IMF is always confident that it will be repaid some day, when the countries have sorted their problems out. At the time of writing, the Sudan, Somalia and Zimbabwe are 'in arrears' to the IMF and have been so for many years. (See <http://www.imf.org/external/np/fin/tad/extdbt2.aspx?valueDate=2011-09-30>).
3   John Maynard Keynes (1920), *The Economic Consequences of the Peace*, New York: Harcourt, Brace and Howe.
4   The London Conference on German External Debt of 1953 took into account the repayment capacity of Germany's economy and its debt was reduced to about one-third of its nominal value (Enrique Cosio-Pascal (2008) 'The Emerging of a Multilateral Forum for Debt Restructuring: The Paris Club', UNCTAD discussion paper no. 192, available from: <www.unctad.org/en/docs/osgdp20087_en.pdf>, p. 5).
5   Even if the IMF is owed money, it is always regarded as a 'preferential creditor' and will be the first to be repaid and will be repaid in full. This is because the IMF's resources belong to all countries and because the IMF is always the first to lend into a difficult situation. If Zimbabwe comes back into good standing with the world, for example, it will first have to

repay the IMF what it owes – even if this involves getting a bridging loan from another country.

6   <http://www.imf.org/external/np/exr/facts/groups.htm#CC>. Also, <http://www.clubdeparis.org/sections/composition/historique-50-ans>.

7   Cosio-Pascal, 'The Emerging of a Multilateral Forum for Debt Restructuring: The Paris Club'.

8   <http://www.imf.org/external/about/histdebt.htm>.

9   Other private sector creditor forums are established from time to time, including the Institute of International Finance that negotiated private sector involvement in the Greek debt restructuring of 2011.

10 Carmen M. Reinhart and Kenneth S. Rogoff (2008) 'This Time is Different: A Panoramic View of Eight Centuries of Financial Crises', NBER working paper no. 13882, available from: <http://www.nber.org/papers/w13882> provide an extensive guide to debt defaults and restructurings. See, in particular, Tables 4 and 5.

11 Federico Sturzenegger and Jeromin Zettelmeyer (2006) *Debt Defaults and Lessons from a Decade of Crises Cambridge*, MA and London: MIT Press, pp. 21–22.

12 *Ibid*, pp. 22–23.

13 <http://www.imf.org/external/np/exr/facts/hipc.htm>.

14 IMF (2001) 'Involving the Private Sector in the Resolution of Financial Crises—Restructuring International Sovereign Bonds', available from: <www.imf.org/external/pubs/ft/series/03/IPS.pdf>, pp. 27–28.

15 IMF (2002a) 'Sovereign Debt Restructurings and the Domestic Economy: Experience in Four Recent Cases', available from: <www.imf.org/external/np/pdr/sdrm/2002/022102.pdf>, pp. 32–33.

16 *Ibid*, p. 3.

17 IMF (2002b) 'The Design of the Sovereign Debt Restructuring Mechanism—Further Considerations', available from: <www.imf.org/external/np/pdr/sdrm/2002/112702.htm>, p. 5.

18 Anne Krueger (2002) 'Should Countries like Argentina Be Able to Declare Themselves Bankrupt? A Commentary', *El Pais*, 18 January, available from: <www.imf.org/external/np/vc/2002/011802.htm>.

19 *Ibid*. A 'vulture fund' is one that buys up shaky, and cheap, bonds on the secondary markets and then tries to force the debtor to make a complete payout.

20 IMF, 'The Design of the Sovereign Debt Restructuring Mechanism—Further Considerations', p. 4.

21 *Ibid*, p. 6.

[22] Kreuger, 'Should Countries like Argentina Be Able to Declare Themselves Bankrupt? A Commentary'.

[23] IMF, 'The Design of the Sovereign Debt Restructuring Mechanism—Further Considerations' for a full set of proposed procedures and principles.

[24] *Ibid*, p. 73.

[25] See Brad Setser (2006) 'The Political Economy of the SDRM', *Council on Foreign Relations*, pp. 1–2.

[26] John B. Taylor (2002) 'Sovereign Debt Restructuring: A US Perspective', speech at the conference *Sovereign Debt Workouts: Hopes and Hazards*, Institute for International Economics, Washington, DC, 2 April 2002, available from: <http://www.iie.com/publications/papers/paper.cfm?ResearchID=455>.

[27] Nouriel Roubini and Brad Setser (2003) 'Improving the Sovereign Debt Restructuring Process: Problems in Restructuring, Proposed Solutions, and a Roadmap for Reform', paper prepared for the conference *Improving the Sovereign Debt Restructuring Process* co-hosted by the Institute for International Economics and Institut Français des Relations Internationales, Paris, 9 March 2003, available from: <http://www.iie.com/publications/papers/roubini-setser0303.pdf>, pp. 25 and 28.

[28] Anna J. Schwartz (2003) 'Do Sovereign Debtors Need a Bankruptcy Law?', *Cato Journal*, Vol. 23, No. 1, pp. 87–100, available from: <http://www.cato.org/pubs/journal/cj23n1/cj23n1-10.pdf>, p. 87.

[29] Beatrice Weder di Mauro and Jeromin Zettelmeyer (2010) 'European Debt Restructuring Mechanism as a Tool for Crisis Prevention', 26 November 2010, available from: <www.voxeu.org/index.php?q=node/5845>.

15

A Politician's Perspective on Debt and Default

Peter Mathews

Peter (BComm, MBA, AITI, FCA) is a chartered accountant and banking and finance analyst. In 2011 he was elected TD (Member of Parliament) to Dáil Eireann, the lower house of the Irish Oireachtas.

The Keane Report on distressed mortgages was a missed opportunity to face up to reality. Households are drowning in debt that is crushing our economy. This harsh reality will not disappear by ignoring it or putting it on the long finger. It can only be resolved by writing down mortgage debt across the board. We need to have an honest discussion about the levels of debt in Ireland. The central question that needs to be answered is this: how much debt is too much for the country to handle?

Central bankers from across the world discussed the international debt crisis at a meeting in Wyoming in August 2011. A keynote paper presented by Bank of International Settlement economists to the conference analysed the impact of the combined debt levels of governments, households and businesses on economic growth across a number of countries. It concluded that government debt in excess of 100 per cent of national income damages growth, household debt in excess of 85 per cent of national income damages growth and business debt in excess of 90 per cent of national income damages growth.

These figures are striking because Ireland exceeds these levels for government, household and business debt. Government debt in Ireland stands at 137 per cent of national income, household debt is 147 per cent of national income and business debt is 210 per cent of national income. The combined total for these three debt elements is 494 per cent of national income.

The report continues by listing the combined debt – the sum of government, household and business debt – for eighteen developed countries. Ireland was not included on this list. However, the Department of Finance provided me with the Irish figures in a response to a parliamentary question. Combined debt levels in the Irish economy are almost twice those of the Greek economy. For every €1 billion of debt in the Greek economy, there is €1.8 billion in the Irish economy. If debt levels in Greece have reached the point that a sovereign default is imminent, what does this mean for Ireland and what should Ireland do about it?

It is even more disturbing to see that Ireland tops this league table ahead of Japan. Japan's combined debt levels have flattened its economy to the point that the period since 1990 is frequently referred to as 'the lost decades'. It is crystal clear that the current Irish combined debt levels will suffocate any chance of a robust economic recovery. It is clear that we must reduce our overall debt burden.

The high private debt levels in Ireland are very noteworthy. They place a limit on the amount of austerity that is possible. It is often commented that Irish public sector wages and social welfare rates are far too generous. Between them, they account for two in every three Euro that the government spends. If we are to balance our budget through austerity alone, it is most likely that spending will have to be slashed in both of these areas. To analyse the impact this will have on the economy, take the example of a family comprising of a Garda and a teacher with two children who bought a modest house in recent years. They are receiving wages that, by international comparisons, are very high. They are receiving child benefit that, by internal comparisons, is remarkably generous. The austerity approach is to slash public sector wages and social welfare spending, perhaps down to the Western European average. Out of context, this seems entirely reasonable. Why should European taxpayers provide us with cheap loans to pay social welfare benefits and wages at levels that they cannot afford? However, the impact that this would have on the family in this example must be considered.

Their take-home pay will be drastically reduced along with the income they receive in child benefit. This is likely to mean that they will be unable to meet the repayments on their mortgage. Their disposable income will shrink towards zero. Any discretionary spending they did will end immediately. When you consider that there will be a similar effect in every similar household in the country it is clear to see the economic collapse that would occur. The amount of bad loans in the banks would explode. The amount of spending in the economy would dry up to a trickle, forcing businesses to lay off staff or go out of existence. All of these consequences would cost the government more money. More mortgages in default will force the government to pump more money into the banks. More unemployment means that tax revenue will fall and social welfare expenditure will increase. This makes it impossible to balance the budget. This is the dilemma that Ireland is in. Without robust economic growth, we are stuck between a rock and a hard place. We need to balance our budget, but implementing austerity measures in the absence of robust economic growth is damaging our economy to the extent that it is impossible to balance the budget. Grafton Street is bustling every weekend. If we were to balance the budget in a one-off swoop, tax increases would be so penal and reductions in social welfare payments and public sector pay would be so crippling that few would have the cash to shop. Grafton Street would be empty of people and full of boarded-up shops. Its atmosphere would resemble that of a ghost estate rather than a bustling city street.

The high private debt levels in Ireland place a definite limit on the amount of austerity that can be introduced. Once this point is passed, further austerity will simply cause more mortgages to become bad loans. This will force the government to provide further recapitalisation to the banks. This will put the country into a hopeless downward spiral. What proponents of endless austerity do not understand is that you cannot get blood out of a stone. There is a limit to the amount of austerity that an economy can take. We need to ask ourselves whether we have passed this point. Ireland's budget deficit peaked at €23 billion in 2009. €21 billion of austerity measures have already been implemented. Despite this, our budget deficit is stuck at €15 billion, excluding the cost of the bank bailout. Clearly, austerity isn't working.

The reason that austerity is taking place over a number of years is so that economic growth can return and lessen the impact of austerity. However, the domestic economy seems dead on its feet and will remain so until austerity ends. Exports are remarkably strong but our export partners are now facing very problematic economic problems of their own. If their demand for our goods dries up we are unlikely to experience any significant economic growth. Without robust economic growth austerity simply will not work. Austerity will not work unless it is accompanied by a huge stimulus to the economy to keep money circulating around the economy. The most obvious source for this stimulus was the National Pension Reserve Fund. However, this has now been almost entirely emptied into dead banks. The only possible way to have a stimulus in the Irish economy is to write down bank debts to the European Central Bank (ECB) and, in turn, pass these write-downs onto Irish households and businesses.

It is acknowledged that loan losses in the banks are in the order of €65 billion. Over a period of eighteen months up to March 2011, while the scale of losses had been denied by the previous government, the banks found themselves unable to repay in full the claims of senior bondholders which were becoming due for repayment. Were it not for ECB funding, the bondholders would have been largely wiped out. The ECB took a decision to protect the bondholders and loaned to the banks the €70 billion needed to redeem in full the bondholders. As the scale of losses became clear, deposits started to fly out of the banks. The combination of replacing deposits and repaying bondholders left the banks owing the ECB and the Central Bank of Ireland in excess of €140 billion. The scale of loan losses blew a hole in the banks' balance sheets to such an extent that the banks could not repay their bondholders. Without ECB funding, the bondholders would have been largely wiped out. The ECB took the decision to protect the bondholders. Clearly, this was inappropriate and therefore we can say with justification that half the money owed by the banks to the ECB and the Central Bank of Ireland is odious debt. Through a political chain of events it has ended up on the backs of Irish citizens and this is patently unfair. In a nutshell, the senior bondholders have received a get out of jail card and the Irish citizen has been locked into an austerity jail. The ECB's treatment of Ireland amounts to making Ireland the sacrificial lamb for European financial stability.

Many commentators believe that the government's hands are tied and that we must accept diktats from Frankfurt because we have no room for manoeuvre and no cards to play at the negotiation table. Nothing could be further from the truth. The ECB has lent almost €100 billion to the Irish banking system. They did this to ensure that European banks could be repaid the full value of their bonds with interest. The collateral on this emergency funding can be removed. The Credit Institutions (Stabilisation) Act 2010 allows the Minister for Finance to force burden sharing onto the ECB. The then President of the ECB, Jean Claude Trichet, was so disturbed by this Act that he signed off on a seven-page opinion criticising the legislation.

By moving loans to a newly established bank, the Minister for Finance can remove the ECB's collateral on emergency funding to Irish banks. This puts the Irish government back in the driving seat. It allows for burden sharing to be forced on the ECB and remaining senior bondholders, resulting in a realistic and workable resolution to Ireland's banking crisis. In turn, it allows for write-downs on unsustainable mortgages, at no further expense to taxpayers, which would provide a vital boost to an economy suffering from years of austerity.

There is precedent for this. It is precisely the approach that Iceland took in dealing with its banking crisis, with the blessing of the IMF. Iceland moved banking loans to entirely new banks and wrote down the principal on mortgages by 30 per cent. The bondholders were forced to pay for these write-downs. Moving Irish loans to new banks would effectively remove the ECB's collateral and allow the Minister for Finance to force burden sharing on the ECB.

The ECB is reported to have forced the previous Irish government into a bailout by threatening to cut off funding to the Irish banks. No other central bank in the world behaves like this. It is inconceivable that the Bank of England could bully the British government like this or that the Federal Reserve could treat the US government like this. The ECB has turned into an over-domineering central bank and need to be reined in. We should remind them that with a stroke of the Minister for Finance's pen, their collateral on the funding to Irish banks collapses and their power over our country disappears.

Yields on Irish government bonds fell by almost 40 per cent in the aftermath of Europe reversing its intention to charge Ireland the original draconian interest rate on its bailout loans. Forcing burden sharing on the ECB and passing this on to mortgage holders through loan write-downs would have a far greater positive impact on Ireland's solvency. If yields were to fall substantially again, Ireland would be very close to leaving the EU/IMF/ECB bailout and re-entering the markets. It's time to challenge the ECB's 'no bondholder left behind' dogma. We must assert ourselves to defend our economy and protect our people.

Minister Noonan is quite right to continue raising bondholder burden sharing with the ECB because it is no longer just an economic problem. It's a political problem. The banking losses were incurred and should have been recognised long ago. The long loan loss denial was extremely damaging. Now, the crunch issue is who pays the bill. This is a political issue. It is unreasonable and wrong to expect the Irish public to pay the entirety of the bill for the bad investments of European banks. The Irish bank rescue will add at least 40 per cent of gross domestic product (GDP) to Ireland's debt burden. To put this into scale, it's the equivalent of expecting German taxpayers to provide over €1 trillion to foreign banks to protect their solvency. It's the equivalent of French taxpayers paying over €800 billion to foreign banks to protect European financial stability. The German and French people wouldn't tolerate this. They would insist on burden sharing and write-downs. If the ECB doesn't agree to a realistic and fair solution, we have to ask whether it's time for Ireland to take firm action.

The European attitude to burden sharing with the private sector is schizophrenic. European leaders insist that purchasers of Greek government bonds must face the consequences of their poor choice of investment. There will be a write-down of 50 per cent on Greek government bonds. Speaking out of the other side of their mouth, European leaders insist that purchasers of Irish bank bonds must be protected from their poor choice of investment at all costs. Those who invested in an insolvent Greek state must share the pain whereas those who invested in insolvent Irish banks must be repaid in full with interest. There is no economic or moral logic to this whatsoever. The problem is not economic, it's political. The Irish government is being forced, under duress, to repay the bank bonds because many European banks are as stable as a house of cards.

Banks increased the risks that they took with their customers' savings in the hope of making more profit. If all the depositors of any bank in the world wanted to withdraw all their savings on one day, the bank would collapse. Banks do not have their customers' savings. They have lent them out to make profits on loans. Banks do not retain their customers' deposits in cash balances. They lend most of the deposits out by making loans to customers in order to make profits. In order to meet the normal calls by customers on their deposit accounts they retain a fraction of the overall deposits, called the fractional reserve, and only lend out the balance. Over the centuries, banks established tried and tested prudential principles of having a fractional reserve rate at least 10 per cent of their customers' deposits and only lending, safely, the other 90 per cent. Unfortunately, these rules were well and truly thrown out the window during the recent hyper credit bubble years and not just in Ireland.

Concern has been expressed by some observers at the levels of leverage by Germany's Deutsche Bank and France's Credit Agricole. In fact, they are leveraged to an even more dangerous level than Lehman Brothers was when it collapsed. It is worth pausing and reflecting on this point: French and German banks have been run as recklessly as Lehman Brothers. Numerous other French and German banks are in trouble to a lesser, but still very serious, extent. These are the banks that provided the funding to Irish banks to drown the Irish economy in debt. These are the banks that the Irish government is forced to repay under duress every time it ensures that the bondholders in Irish banks are repaid in full.

Neither Germany nor France is in a position to bail out its banks. The assets in Deutsche Bank are very questionable. They contain government debt that is likely to be written down and loans that could go sour. Deutsche Bank's assets are the equivalent of 80 per cent of Germany's GDP. German national debt is already close to damaging levels. It is very questionable to assert that the German government is capable of bailing out Deutsche Bank in the event of a crisis.

France's situation is even more dire. Its three main banks have assets that are twice as large as the entire French economy. It is simply impossible for the French government to bail out these banks. The French economy is just too small and their government debt is already at levels that are damaging to the French economy. The truth that Europe dares not speak is that there are Anglo Irish type banks everywhere which could bring down their countries and the clock is ticking.

The German people and government are terrified that this crisis will lead to what they call 'a transfer union'. This means that German taxpayers will provide annual transfers of cash to *flathulach* members of the Eurozone. However, the harsh reality is that the only transfer union that has been created is from Irish taxpayers to the worst behaved and most insolvent banks in the world. The Germans are adamant that solutions to the Eurozone crisis must not contain 'moral hazard' – they must not reward countries or banks for bad behaviour. Surely the transfer union from Irish taxpayers to some of the world's worst banks is moral hazard at its most extreme. This is law-of-the-jungle politics with every country fending for itself. It is precisely the type of narrow nationalism that the European Union was established to eradicate. The Euro currency remains a worthy and worthwhile ambition but the tendency towards narrow nationalism must end swiftly if the currency is to be saved. Realistic solutions must be found for all of the countries in difficulty.

The Irish economy needs two simple things to bring it back from the brink. We need a functioning bank and a huge stimulus to the economy. A functioning bank will provide credit to the economy and a huge stimulus will give people the encouragement that they need to start spending again. Standing up to Europe by enforcing write-downs on the amounts of money our banks owe the ECB and remaining senior bondholders across the banks will provide both of these medicines. Reckless lending by Irish banks only began this century. Moving the outstanding loans from the last century into a new bank will provide the first building block to a stable, functioning Irish bank. These assets are safe, secure and reliable. Writing down the odious debt to the ECB, and in turn, passing this write-down onto struggling mortgage holders and also to businesses under severe, unsustainable financial pressure will provide a huge stimulus to the economy. The cost to households of servicing loans will plummet, allowing people to spend again and create jobs in the domestic economy.

Greece is on the brink of collapsing because its government debt levels are impossibly high. Ireland is on a slippery slope to becoming Greece. The Irish economy cannot take as much austerity as the Greek economy because our private debt levels are too high. The growth targets in the bailout programme are very ambitious and may not be achieved. This, combined with inevitable losses from the National Asset Management Agency debacle later this decade, will force our government debt levels to unsustainable levels and we will end up in a similar position to Greece with a high probability of default. This would be a tragedy. Instead of defaulting on bank debt for which the state bears no responsibility, we would have a sovereign debt default that would damage our international reputation for decades.

At 494 per cent of national income, Irish combined debt levels are the most crushing in the world. We must resist being forced to bear impossible levels of debt overhang which expert economists have shown to be the main cause of contraction and stagnation in an economy. We must insist on write-downs totalling around €75 billion on amounts due to the ECB, the Central Bank of Ireland and outstanding bondholders across the banks. These write-downs must in turn be passed onto households and businesses. This would provide a huge stimulus to the economy. Write-downs of €75 billion may appear large and suggest that Ireland in some way is being let off the hook. This is far from the case. It would result in Ireland moving only one place down the league table, putting us just one place below Japan. We would still be carrying a huge load but at least it would be somewhat more manageable than where we stand at present. We must insist on putting this case forward to the ECB and unilateral action must not be ruled out if a sensible, workable, realistic agreement cannot be reached.

16

A Financial Journalist's Perspective on Debt and Default

John Walsh

John is editor of Business & Finance Magazine.

A default on either sovereign or bank debt would be a disaster for Ireland. Those advocating such a move are a bunch of snake-oil salesmen who either don't fully understand the facts or are cynically exploiting an emotive and complex issue for self-serving reasons.

If the country doesn't default on at least some of its debt obligations, then the country faces at least a decade of stagnation or sclerotic growth at best. The social consequences would be devastating; mass emigration, stifling taxes and endemic levels of social exclusion. Not only is a default inevitable, it should be welcomed.

These two narratives are at the extreme ends of a debate that is likely to convulse the country over the next few years. Ireland is facing into one of its most challenging periods since independence. A credit bubble and property bust has lumbered it with a debt burden that may or may not cripple the economy. This chapter will deliberately not take a position on whether it is in Ireland's interests, or not, to default. There are plenty of economists and other commentators who will slug it out on this issue in other chapters. But the media will play a crucial role in shaping public opinion. In an era of soundbite culture is that possible given the complexity of the issue?

Former Taoiseach Bertie Ahern has made some very withering comments about the state of the Irish media. In July 2007, during an address to the Irish Congress of Trade Unions, Ahern took a swipe at journalists and commentators who were wondering aloud whether the economy was about to hit the buffers. In an unfortunate turn of phrase, the then Taoiseach said, 'Sitting on the side-lines, cribbing and moaning is a lost opportunity. I don't know how people who engage in that don't commit suicide because frankly the only thing that motivates me is being able to actively change something.'

Ahern subsequently apologised to families bereaved through suicide for his injudicious comment. His hostility towards journalists lingered, it would seem. In an interview with Dublin City University (DCU) student radio in October 2011 Bertie had some choice words for the media and in particular its role in the financial crisis:

> There should be an investigation into it. They [the media] should have been following the economy from August 2007, but they weren't, they were following me. I think a lot of these guys really should have looked at themselves.
>
> The government were following the economy but the media weren't. It was a very poor job by the media really. They were shown to be incompetent and that was the trouble – everything was on me.

The former Taoiseach's comments are most revealing in many different ways. In September 2006, the *Irish Times*' journalist Colm Keena reported that the Mahon Tribunal was investigating payments made to Bertie Ahern. It turned out to be one of the most important scoops in this country for a decade or more. In a subsequent interview on RTE's *Six One* news programme with Bryan Dobson, an emotional and sometimes tearful Taoiseach offered a series of credulity-defying explanations about his labyrinthine personal finances. Moreover, Ahern blithely dropped into the interview that he appointed people to state boards because they were friends, not because they had helped him with 'dig out' payments. It was a comment that underscored how much cronyism had become embedded in the highest office in the land. Indeed, it is not too much of a leap of faith to argue that cronyism as much as anything else stopped the Celtic Tiger in its tracks.

Investigations thus far into the cause of the banking crisis have revealed a world where the Financial Regulator did not have an objective and arms-length relationship with the institutions under the watch of that office. There was no proper risk management and corporate governance practices in the banks. Non-executive directors didn't seem to be doing their job. But as dismaying as it may be to the members of the Irish media, does Ahern have a point about the journalists not meeting the standards tradition-ally associated with the fourth estate?

The Irish banking crisis is one of the biggest in the history of the world economy. It is a small country. How could this have happened? How could possibly the biggest story since inde-pendence unfold before the mainstream media, yet hardly a coherent analysis of why the country was heading to financial ruin emerged when it really mattered? It is true that it wasn't exclusively domestic factors that caused the crash.

In August 2007, the US financial media reported difficulties in the banking system. The US had experienced a building boom for much of the previous decade. Less creditworthy citizens had been granted access to mortgages through the subprime sector. These subprime mortgages were securitised and given AAA ratings by the credit rating agencies. These products had been hoovered up by investment banks. When the property market turned, the assets that backed these securitised products were in some cases not worth the paper they were written on. If there is one thing markets hate it is uncertainty. Yet it was impossible to tell the scale of losses sitting on the balance sheets of banks because of the opaque nature of these asset-backed securities. Uncertainty reigned.

The global economy was on the verge of the biggest financial crisis since the Great Depression. But not only did the mainstream media not pick up on this story well before it became a crisis, even the most prominent financial commentators were caught wrong-footed about the nature and scale of the problem when it became obvious that the banking system was under serious stress.

The economist Nouriel Roubini earned the derisory soubriquet 'Dr Doom' when he estimated that subprime-related losses could reach $1 trillion in the banking sector. Initially this was dismissed as alarmist scaremongering. It would prove to be a conservative estimate. Six years ago, Ireland was the fastest growing economy in the Eurozone. It had one of the soundest fiscal positions and one of the lowest debt–GDP ratios. The fact that there is now a debate about whether the country could or should default is testament to the reversal of fortunes for the now lamented and once mythologised Celtic Tiger.

But how could the Irish financial media get it so wrong? Journalists in the US can point to the truth lying beneath a maze of extremely opaque credit instruments that nobody seemed to understand, including the regulatory authorities. In Ireland, the story was much more straightforward. The banks had access to a plentiful and cheap supply of money. Surging population growth caused a demand for houses. The government played its part by offering massive tax concessions to property developers. The traditional banking model of scaling the loan portfolio in proportion to the deposit book put a brake on the almost limit-less lending opportunities to the property sector. The short-term wholesale money markets provided a lucrative alternative source of funding to the banks. As it now obvious, not only did Irish banks have a massive sectoral exposure to one asset class, the collateral backing up these loans was not properly drawn up and very often completely inadequate.

Investors were lured by the enormous returns generated by property deals. The more leverage in these deals, the bigger bang for buck invested. The regulatory authorities did nothing to stop the party. One *aperçu* that I can personally volunteer involved the developer Sean Dunne's acquisition of the landmark Jurys Hotel Ballsbridge site in August 2005 for €375 million. I wrote an editorial for *Business & Finance Magazine* at the time asking whether this represented the top of a dizzying and unsustainable market. I made an analogy with the dotcom bubble and Japan in the 1980s. I had recently returned from seven years in London. Many things about the Irish economy just didn't seem to add up – not least people on average salaries getting access to mortgages that made no economic sense. Yet less than a month after penning that editorial I was in a corporate box in Croke Park watching the 2005 All-Ireland Hurling Final between Cork and Galway with David Drumm and most of the senior management team from Anglo Irish Bank.

There seemed to be an intimacy between journalists and senior businesspeople in Ireland that didn't exist elsewhere. The objectivity I had brought back from London would soon desert me.

The closeness between journalists, bankers, politicians, economists and market sources militates against what John O'Sullivan, a lecturer at the School of Communications at DCU, describes as the 'holy grail of neutral, balanced, objective information'. When in 2007 market volatility pointed to potentially big problems coming down the tracks, the Irish media did take notice. In March of that year the well-respected journalist and deputy editor of the *Sunday Business Post* Richard Curran fronted a seminal documentary, called *Futureshock*, on RTE One, which posed extremely uncomfortable questions about the soundness of the property market and the wider economy. He concluded that it was all a house of cards.

For his efforts, Curran was subjected to a sometimes personal and vitriolic backlash. The chorus from the banks, in particular, was that this was no time for this sort of scaremongering. Green jerseys were needed to get through this temporary rough patch. Large parts of the mainstream media answered this clarion call. But by 2007 the damage had been done. The Irish domestic banks had mortgaged the house on the Irish property market remaining buoyant for the foreseeable future. Why had the Irish financial media not been much more critical of the reliance on property and the banks' dangerous over-exposure to this sector in the years leading up to 2007? That is not to say there weren't any dissenting voices. There were, but they were very much on the margins of the debate.

The failure of the media to put any brake on the frothy excesses of boom years points to systemic problems that don't augur well for the future. The print media has come under intense pressure in the age of the internet. Newspapers and magazines are no longer the only medium through which news, opinion and analysis can be disseminated. Far from it. There are a plethora of low-cost online news portals and blog sites that vie with traditional media outlets for readers.

The consequence for the print media sector has been declining readership and a marked deterioration in advertising revenues. Now the future of the print media sector is under threat and the type of journalism that goes with it. Should anybody care? Paul Starr, a lecturer in media studies at Princeton University penned a lengthy analysis of the impact the crisis in the print industry was having on US society for *The New Republic* in an article called 'Goodbye to the Age of Newspapers (Hello to a New Era of Corruption)'. He concluded that without the proper investigative journalism that newspapers specialise in there will be huge and damaging implications for US democracy because it removes a vital source of information needed to make informed decisions.

Over the past twenty years, stories about the economy and business have become much more prominent and important in the Irish media. The former *Guardian* journalist Nick Davies has popularised the pejorative term 'churnalism' to describe the state of mainstream journalism and in particular financial journalism. He argues that most financial journalism is now PR driven. The news agenda is shaped by journalists rewriting press releases. This is in part explained by the financial pressure experienced by news organisations. There are not enough resources to fund in-depth investigative journalism. Staff positions are steadily being replaced by contract workers, who are very often employed on a shift basis. Consequently many of the skills and knowledge acquired through full-time positions are lost. In other words, where will the Colm Keenas of the future come from?

'One view is that the media is owned by large businesses which have a conservative agenda. It is a reasonable position to take but it is far too simplistic. What we have in Ireland is a very monotone media. There is very little divergence from the central thesis', says DCU's O'Sullivan.

'It isn't just about where journalists and reporters come from – it is about how they work. If you look at any economics, finance or business story, the people mediating these stories are business journalists. They have come centre stage over the past twenty years, but they do not grow up knowing what a credit default swap is. They rely on bankers and stockbrokers and market analysts for their stories, so there is a circular flow of information.'

There is also intense competition between media outlets, which means the scramble to attract readers and viewers has introduced an entertainment dimension to the news-gathering process. Contributors are judged on who gives the best sound-bite. Very often, it is not about who can give the most nuanced and balanced account of the issue, but, rather, commentators who are the most headline grabbing. Yet many of these commentators, while very good at generating publicity for themselves, are often unburdened by in-depth knowledge of the issue at hand. And that is not to say that it was a peculiarly Irish phenomenon. Kevin Hassett wrote a book called *Dow 36,000* in 1999. His argument was that the Dow Jones was on an ineluctable rise and would hit 36,000 sometime in the early 2000s. The Dow Jones subsequently crashed to below 2,000 when the dot com bubble burst in 2001. Yet Hassett continued to remain a TV pundit in much demand by mainstream US business channels. In fact he found his way onto 2008 US Republican presidential candidate John McCain's team of economic advisors.

So, what role does the media play in the default debate? Is it there to shape public opinion or reflect it? O'Sullivan argues that the financial crisis in this country is discussed in very narrow terms:

> The paradigm of the debate is that we must be good boys – we have to be the best in class in Europe. There is almost an infantile mantra about this. Nobody says why? We are still concentrating on being the best boys and girls in Europe because we are not Greece. We have a very conservative dumbed down mainstream media, complemented by voices in the wilderness. ... It is not a point of view that will find favour with the markets or advertisers but I think we need to rethink public sector journalism – whether it exists and whether we want it? We don't have any money so it is a vicious circle. Moreover, is there an appetite for it? Is it about what sells or is it about journalism itself?

Sean Kay is a political scientist at Ohio Wesleyan University who has been observing Ireland's changing economic fortunes over the past number of years. He argues that it is incumbent upon the media to play a responsible role in the forthcoming debate:

> I think one of the dangers of the Irish media is that it could become very inward looking when what is really needed is balance. I would be extremely sceptical about default as an option, particularly if it is presented as some quick and easy and straightforward solution that would be good for Ireland. If the Irish media is going to make a case for default, then it is going to have to walk the reader or listener through what it means when it happens.

Then again, there are other commentators who claim that what is needed is a bit of creative destruction. The free market should be allowed to take its course; banks should be allowed to collapse and a series of defaults should happen across Europe. In a way there has never been more of a need for balanced, informed journalism. Ireland's membership of the Eurozone is likely to come under intense scrutiny over the next few years. It is an issue that will be closely related to whether the country defaults or not.

The stakes could not be higher. Can the Irish media step up to the plate?

17

A Behavioural Economist's Perspective on Debt and Default

Michael Dowling

Michael is a lecturer in Finance in Dublin City University.

What happens to a society that undergoes a profound shock to its normal way of living? A society, like Ireland in the 2000s, which finds its highly materialistic existence offers just transient comfort and no real protection against times of crisis? What insights does the intersection of finance and behavioural science provide in how this society might respond? This chapter explores this question using a behavioural perspective and draws on cultural, psychological and historical lessons to suggest a movement towards re-engagement with community (with a modern twist) as the key societal outcome of the crisis.

There seems to be a collective shudder going around the country at the moment as we remember some of the more embarrassing excesses of the boom years. The hot tub in the back garden (usage ten days a year), the many €10 sandwiches and €5 coffees, the fawning over which bottle of expensive wine tastes slightly different to the usual plonk, the €1,000 Jacuzzi bath that clogs up at the first sign of soap. The list goes on …. The raw materialism of the time, perhaps best epitomised by those glitzy €3 million weddings that littered the insides of the likes of *Hello!* magazine, is now viewed with a mixture of anger – as it turns out we ended up paying for those shows of fake wealth – and still a bit of envy – well, that doesn't vanish overnight; but also distaste.

The presence of distaste is new. As families across the country are finding out that those smiling bank manager adverts just covered up for organisations that would cut and run at the first sign of trouble, there are also discovering that their friends, family and community will go out of their way to selflessly help them if they can. There is a realisation that there is 'fake social' – companies don't *really* want to be our friends on Facebook – and there is the 'new social' – a vibrant mix of traditional community spirit and new communities of common interest formed through the social internet. We are learning that as much as that Jacuzzi bath might provide a few minutes of comfort before the inevitable breakdown, the power of being part of a strong community is something that won't grind to a halt even in the tough times.

The end result is that Irish society is moving from one that appeared to value raw materialism above all else to a re-imagined community-centred society. The traditional media, a vital voice for materialism, is in accelerated decline, being rapidly replaced by an internet where choosing to view advertising is optional and community-building is *de rigueur*.

This distaste of raw materialism provides an impetus to community-based initiatives; leading to a re-envisaging of how we want our society to progress. This has potent implications for how Irish society will develop post-crisis and this change is already well underway. Community engagement is currently undergoing its own tiger-like boom; but in ways in which an older generation of traditional physically based communities could never have imagined. These changes hold the potential to drive policy for at least the next generation, making them probably the most significant long-term outcome of the crisis.

Too much of the public discussion of the debt crisis has been couched in opaque, complicated, legalistic and economic terms that are largely meaningless to the majority of our day-to-day lives. We need to look at the individual and community level changes that are having a real – and surprisingly positive

– impact on Irish society. This chapter begins by charting some of the reasons for the decline of materialism and explores how Irish society is beginning to re-engage with community initiatives, including what this suggests for a post-crisis/debt/default Irish society.

Materialism in Decline (Thanks to the Decline of Traditional Media)

Apart from 2,000 daily calories of (ideally) unprocessed food, clothing, shelter and the occasional drop of medicine, there is very little we actually *need* to buy. The role of advertising is to convince us to add desires to our shopping list alongside these needs, and it is particularly effective at doing this. Consider that about 55 per cent of Irish families buy expensive powdered baby milk despite ample supplies of the natural variety and the evidence that breastfed babies are healthier and perform better in school and later life. Leaving aside the medical cases requiring bottle-feeding, advertising has apparently convinced Irish families to spend money on something where the alternative is free and demonstrably better. Advertising is clearly a powerful tool in the arsenal of materialism.

This materialism has a significant impact on communities. Materialism doesn't easily co-exist with community involvement. A research paper from 1997 by Ronald Inglehart, a noted culture researcher, contrasts materialism with post-materialism, and is of relevance to our discussion. Materialism, he says, is associated with emphasis on economic well-being, working hard and survival; while post-materialism – where material possessions are still valued, but not prioritised – is associated with political participation, taking pride in things like a clean environment and living in pleasant surroundings, and openness to people from different backgrounds.

These post-materialist characteristics are clearly drivers for community involvement. A materialistic society is too busy working hard to earn money to acquire more possessions to be involved in the community. It is for this reason that this section charts the threats to materialism, particularly the threat to advertising effectiveness. If materialism is finding it harder to maintain its message of 'more possessions equates to a happier life', this can provide a rationale for the re-emergence of community involvement and suggests that the rise in community interest is not just a temporary blip in the otherwise dominant advance of the desire to acquire.

The traditional media plays a vital role in materialism given that it serves as the main platform for advertising of products and services. However there are strong indicators that traditional media is under threat from alternative media sources, particularly through the internet. As traditional media declines and advertising becomes optional we should see a decline in the ability of companies to influence the consumption behaviour of the population. As noted already, this loosening of materialism's grip plays an important role in allowing the new community-centred society to emerge.

At the beginning of 2011, Irish television ownership stood at an impressive 106 per cent (due to multiple television sets in some households), and our newspaper readership numbers are high with 573,630 buying a daily newspaper and 991,697 buying a Sunday newspaper as of December 2010; although these newspaper numbers are a drop of 11 per cent in daily newspapers and 14 per cent in Sunday newspapers compared to December 2008. But overall there doesn't seem to be any shortage of interest in traditional media.

However, there is an underlying change in the consumption of traditional media that is not reflected in the raw numbers. No one would expect that people would throw out a perfectly fine television just because of their newfound distaste for materialism; but what has changed significantly is the interest displayed in traditional media's messages. People are increasingly watching television with less focus due to watching while also engaging in internet-based activities. A 2011 experimental study by two Boston University researchers, S. Adam Brasel and James Gips, notes that for the key advertising demographic, the under 30 age group, 40 per cent of internet and television viewing is simultaneous – people are browsing and watching TV at the same time. The researchers find that people who watch television while also browsing the internet concentrated most of their time on their internet activities and were constantly flicking back and forth between the two activities. This form of television viewing is hardly optimal for a television advertiser wishing to embed their product message.

With the decline in television attention has also come an acceleration of availability of alternative media sources which have either reduced or no advertising. YouTube, for example, is twice as popular in Ireland in 2011 as it was at the beginning of 2008, and carries minimal advertising. News can be freely read online without intrusive advertising, compared to an estimated €700 annual cost of buying the advertising-heavy *Irish Independent/ Sunday Independent* every day. Media piracy is another source of viewing that poses a threat to advertising effectiveness through traditional media, given that pirated material rarely contains advertisements. Reliable statistics on media piracy in Ireland are not available, but we do know there is an increasing (unsuccessful) effort by digital rights holders such as the Irish Recording Music Association to persuade internet service providers to disconnect persistent illegal downloaders of media material, indicating their concern over piracy. The managing director of Xtravision also partially blamed internet piracy for the national entertainment chain being pushed into interim receivership in April 2011 and subsequent examinership.

It is possibly too early to say, but materialism does appear to be on the wane in Ireland. While wages dropped 14 per cent from 2008 to the middle of 2011, retail sales suffered a 20 per cent drop over the same period, according to Central Statistics Office data. Certainly lower disposable income and reduced lending will be the primary causes of the drop, but the excessive drop suggests more factors at play than merely the amount of money in our pockets. At the least we can say that there is a reduced focus on material goods acquisition among the population, which suggests greater available time to focus on post-material ambitions, such as community engagement.

Society Responds: The Re-Emergence of Community

Being part of a community offers a wide variety of benefits. At an important basic level, the work of Robert Putnam demonstrates that people who are more socially active are not just happier, they are also healthier. Community involvement also offers us coping strategies in times of crisis and need that are an improvement over how we could cope if we just had to handle problems by ourselves. This section discusses the power of community and charts how Ireland is now re-engaging with community; the concluding section discusses the future possibilities from this shift in attention towards community and away from materialism.

Sociologists frequently refer to 'social capital' when discussing community. Social capital is the value of the 'goodwill that others have towards us'. This is an inherently community-based concept that conceptualises the idea that there is value in our social connections, such as being able to rely on friends, family and neighbours in difficult times.

A mid-2011 story in the *Irish Times* epitomises the power of social capital and tells of a Galway family having to stay with their seriously ill daughter in Our Lady's Children's Hospital, Crumlin, in Dublin and the mother thinking back over her experience of that time:

> She thought about the small, constant kindnesses of friends and neighbours that had sustained the family through their struggle: a lit fire when they returned on winter nights; meals prepared; someone to look after their younger child, then just a baby.

International researchers have documented how strong social networks can work together to overcome even the worse disasters. Thus, researchers Emily Chamlee-Wright and Virgil Storr show how strong community ties helped a collection of small towns in New Orleans recover after Hurricane Katrina, and an associated spill of millions of barrels of oil, had devastated their community. Other researchers have found similar stories in the wake of the disastrous earthquakes in Kobe, Japan in 1995 and Gujarat, India in 2001.

An interesting 2001 study by World Bank researchers Michael Lokshin and Ruslan Yemtsov provides more details on how such social capital works. They studied the 1998 Russian currency crisis and its impact on households using survey data from approximately 3,000 Russian households. A key finding is that households that are socially excluded, such as the elderly, relied on passive coping strategies – mainly cuts to expenditure – to handle the crisis, whereas more social households adopted a variety of active approaches to cope with the economic turmoil; including relying on help from neighbours and finding supplementary work. This suggests that households strong in social capital are able to utilise this resource in times of need to actively manage their problems and find positive solutions.

One of the issues with social capital is understanding the 'investment' required to build this capital. While people generally show a willingness to help other people, the level of help is usually mediated by the closeness of their ties to a person. For example, a 2007 paper by Canadian researcher Brenda Murphy examined community responses to an electricity blackout that affected approximately 50 million people across Canada and the US and found that people's help of others was strongly mediated by familiarity. One-quarter of the sampled population had helped neighbours, 15 per cent had helped family and friends, and only 2 per cent had helped strangers. This suggests benefits to investing in social capital. The following quote from a 2004 paper by Charles Kadushin whimsically illustrates this idea:

I am baking a cake and have run out of sugar, but I can go to my neighbour next door to get some. It was worth being nice to that neighbour even though I did not particularly fancy her. Do I have to return the sugar? Maybe she can borrow my lawn mower the next time she needs to mow her lawn and that will count as a return of the favour. Maybe the value of the sugar is trivial enough not to require repayment in kind.

It sounds distasteful to view community involvement as an investment (one book on the topic suggests regularly culling unproductive contacts from your network!), and this has been a common criticism of social capital theory. However, we are not really talking about investment in the traditional financial sense of seeking to optimise returns from time spent, but instead just noting that social capital can deliver strong benefits in terms of overall life satisfaction and help in times of need, but it does need time to be spent in developing this resource. That might just be time spent with friends in the pub, or helping out with refereeing matches in the local club or volunteering in a community organisation. This is time that just isn't available where materialism is a driving force and working to acquire material possessions is considered of paramount importance.

Having set out some of the benefits of community, we can now look at some of the evidence of community involvement taking hold in Irish society. For this we can look at community involvement statistics and also some broader measures of the importance attached to being socially active.

Irish society has always been highly community oriented. Researchers of early Irish history such as University College Dublin's (UCD) retired Professor of History, Francis John Byrne, and the late Professor Daniel A. Binchy described in vivid detail the role and importance of clans and tribes in early Irish history, and the importance this system attached to community cooperation and ties. Thus, Professor Binchy refers to the early Irish as 'tribal, rural, hierarchical and familiar'. Rural Ireland also has a long-established tradition of 'meitheal'; a Gaelic term used to describe volunteer labour groups who would assemble to help members of the community, for example to bring in the harvest. References to meitheal on paper are fleeting despite the widespread nature of the event, but the following gives some flavour of the idea:

> At harvest time neighbours would combine together to help one another make hay or gather other crops. This co-operation was a great way of fostering neighbourliness and a spirit of togetherness in the community. Those in the 'meitheal' joined the host farmer for a meal at the end of the day's work. Kitchens in the old farmhouses were very big so as to accommodate the large numbers. Every farmer would repay his neighbour by taking part in his meitheal next time round.

There are indications that Irish society is re-discovering its social roots. Although we would expect this to be a gradual process, especially given that people are quite naturally currently pre-occupied with handling the personal impact of the crisis on their lives. But the signs of a growth are there. The Tidy Towns community improvement initiative had 821 entrants in 2011; the highest number of competitors in its 53-year history, and compared to less than 700 entrants in pre-crisis 2006. The Social Entrepreneurs Ireland Awards and Pride of Place awards, two national schemes that are heavily focused on community initiatives, both reported record interest in their 2011 awards. There has been a doubling of participation in sports volunteering amongst the unemployed. Interestingly, the growth in sports volunteering has only been seen in team sports. The importance of building social capital appears to be slowly being re-discovered.

However, the real social revolution is not happening in physical communities, but through the social internet. The powerhouse of internet social communities in Ireland is a website called Boards.ie. This website has 435,000 members – overwhelmingly Irish – and 2.2 million unique visits every month, with discussions spread across 600 different sub-communities. Google Trends suggests the website is about three times more popular in 2011 as it was at the beginning of 2007. Want to talk about a personal problem? There's over half a million posts on people's problems and the associated advice given. Got a stutter? Have a read of the stuttering sub-forum. 200,000 posts on transport; 100,000 on parenting; 800,000 on politics …. Interested in scuba diving, mythology, the weather, palaeontology …? Communities of interest representing nearly 10 per cent of the Irish population have self-organised themselves around every possible interest, and Boards.ie is just one example, albeit a highly prominent one, of this new social movement.

Initial fears that physical communities would suffer from people spending more time online have been dismissed by studies of what actually happens. Thus, Andrea Kavanaugh from Virginia Tech University in the United States and her colleagues found in a 2005 study that being part of an online community for a town strengthened the feeling of belongingness to the linked physical community. Similar findings have been reported for users of Facebook – people are building social capital online that can be utilised offline. A 2010 study published in *American Behavioral Scientist* finds that people living in rural communities use the internet to maintain and build social capital in their physical communities, thus overcoming the hampering effect of distance between households in a typical rural community.

An Irish example of this online–offline linkage can be seen in Ballymacarbry Community Centre in Waterford, which won a 2011 Pride of Place award and was described by the judges as 'the best they had ever seen in nine years of judging the Pride of Place Competition. … The judges were witness to how clear vision and single mindedness can create a cohesive community.' Despite Ballymacarbry only returning a population count of 436 in the 2011 census, they have 220 followers of their online page on Facebook. The local population can blend offline with online and be kept up to date on the schedule for community meetings, news on the latest bake sale (proceeds of €330 for donation to the Irish Society for the Prevention of Cruelty to Animals), and progress in having concerns addressed about a wind farm planned for construction in the near future. This is the new post-materialistic Ireland slowly emerging from the dust of materialism's failed promises.

Debt and Default: The Inadvertent Route to Societal Happiness?

Materialism is in decline, and community involvement is increasingly moving centre stage, helped by the recognition of the power of social capital and the boom in internet-organised communities. Of course, it would be naïve to assume that this is an entirely willing move on the part of Irish society; a large number of people who are no longer driving materialism forward are presumably inhibited from doing so due to a decline in their disposable income. Thus, it is quite possible that the 'stick' of debt and default has brought us to where we are, rather than the 'carrot' of putative benefits. That does make the suggestion of a societal value shift a bit more tentative. We can though speculate as to what a future community-centred Irish society would mean in terms of well-being and involvement.

Research in countries across the world shows money to be important in terms of national happiness, but only up to a certain level. Someone in abject poverty will be less happy than someone who can put food on the table. But the benefits of money level off quickly and benefits can easily be nullified if the more qualitative influences on life satisfaction fall as a result of economic development. Thus, China's tripling of household incomes for its population between 1990 and 2000 actually resulted in lower reported levels of happiness among the population.

Irish people report one of the highest levels of life satisfaction in the world. In 2007, 46 per cent of survey respondents claimed to be very happy with their lives. This makes us one of the happiest countries in the world. A 2011 research paper by Professor Brendan Walsh in UCD charted the long-term well-being of the Irish population from 1975 to 2011 and found very little increase as a result of the boom years in the 2000s, and only a minor decline in reported life satisfaction caused by the debt crisis. There was even an uptick in happiness reported in 2011.

Yet nearly every public discussion about the crisis seems to concentrate on gross domestic product, or debt or the possibility of default. The boom in doom-laden words in the media is in huge disparity to what's happening in people's lives. Clearly something is missing from the public debate. Could the Irish people have already discovered what policy makers are so desperately fumbling to find? – That just having money to spend on material goods is not really the route to societal happiness.

Ireland's future, if we continue along the route we have commenced, is to move closer to the Scandinavian countries – the happiest countries in the world. Ronald Inglehart and his colleagues in 2008 studied why these countries were so happy and found that what distinguished them was not their high income but their high levels of social capital. They had the highest reported levels of trusting other people, of openness, of prizing living in pleasant surroundings, of a wide range of social activities. In short, they attached greater importance to living in a community rather than an economy. We ideally wouldn't have chosen debt and crisis to get us to this same realisation, but now that we're here let's enjoy what we've inadvertently started – a renewed joy of social living.

18

A Political Activist and Businessperson's Perspective on Debt and Default

Declan Ganley

Declan is an entrepreneur and political activist.

12 July 1776, at the tip of Lower Manhattan, where the fast-flowing Hudson meets in confluence with the East River and opens out into the wide expanse of New York Harbour, standing in the pre-dawn darkness, was the figure of a young captain of artillery. Dressed in the attire of a local officer of militia, he was guarding the most important commercial hub of his nine-day-old country, the United States of America. His name was Alexander Hamilton. His small command consisted of six cannon and a small cadre of unruly men, some still suffering the early morning effects from a night of whisky and a deficit of sleep. Looming toward their position were two of King George's finest ships of the line, HMS *Phoenix* and HMS *Rose*, their combined 72 cannon primed and loaded to deliver His Britannic Majesty's first kinetic response to America's rebels. Other American founders would shortly and irrevocably put their necks on the line, affixing their signatures on 2 August to the Declaration of Independence, with the words of Benjamin Franklin ringing in their ears: 'we must all hang together, or most assuredly, we shall all hang separately.'

As dawn broke, Hamilton's position came under the Royal Navy's guns and they opened fire with a thunder that witnesses were to attest was the most terrible and mighty sound to have ever been heard across New York up until that time. Hamilton's position was pummelled and yet, with comrades dead or dying around him, he stood his ground and returned the fire. This was the first of many heroic actions throughout Hamilton's life but I recount it here to underline that this was a man of extraordinary courage, honed in action to take risk and prepared to make any sacrifice for his country. Very many years later, Talleyrand, the famous French statesman, diplomat and manipulator of eighteenth and early nineteenth-century Europe, said of Hamilton, 'I consider Napoleon, Fox and Hamilton the three greatest men of our epoch and, if I were forced to decide between the three, I would give without hesitation the first place to Hamilton.' Talleyrand had known all of these men on a personal basis and I believe that his measure of Hamilton is not without merit.

So what was it that Talleyrand recognised which marked out Hamilton from all the other leaders of his age and what lessons can we learn that might be applicable to Europe's current crisis? Hamilton after all, never got to lead his country; however, he did get to serve George Washington in a position that was to become absolutely pivotal to the survival of the United States of America, that role was as America's first Secretary of the Treasury.

On taking office shortly after the conclusion of America's War of Independence, Hamilton found himself with the challenge of shaping the economic framework upon which the nascent and very bankrupt United States would either perish or prevail. Hamilton's country had been ravaged by war and saddled by debt. On top of that, he had to find a way of paying off a well-armed army that in many cases was awaiting years of back-pay. In addition to domestic concerns, there were major foreign lenders, including some of the very largest and most powerful players in global finance at the time – French and Dutch bankers. With British Red Coats on the Canadian border and still holding western forts and the Royal Navy ruling the Atlantic waves, Hamilton quickly understood that the Union's credit rating would play a large part in deciding whether or not America really had a future.

Hamilton was a protégé of George Washington, commanding general of the Continental Army and the first American President. The young Hamilton was perhaps the closest to him of all his military officers. Washington was not just his commander, but more like a father. Hamilton was brilliant but sometimes divisive, viewed suspiciously by Jefferson, Adams and many others as a treacherous manipulator intent on creating a central power over the people and ruining the purity of the agrarian republic in favour of urban creditors and big money interests. It was a sort of Old Virginia v hustling New York conflict. Washington was trusted by, and stayed above, the factions. He backed Hamilton against his own Virginians and perhaps was the only man who could make Hamilton's ideas stick. It's remarkable that Washington, himself a devoted farmer and son of Old Virginia, with no finance or business experience, could make this choice so decisively. Hamilton, under Washington's protection as Secretary of the Treasury, was given the scope to establish the economic structural basis of America. That simply would not have been possible had Washington and the other 'Founding Fathers' not already put in place the initial mechanisms for government by consent. Washington, a titan of history, also left on record his wishes to see Ireland with freedom to legislate and trade: 'I would felicitate the Kingdom of Ireland on their Emancipation from British Control, and extend my pious entreaties, that Heaven may establish them in happy and perpetuated tranquillity, enjoying a freedom of legislation, and an unconfined extension of trade, that connecting link, which binds together the remotest countries'.[1]

Without Hamilton, or his patron Washington, the superstructure facilitating the fantastic nineteenth century burst of American economic growth would simply not have occurred. As an aside, Franklin was maybe the first to see the vast economic potential. Long before Hamilton or Washington, he was a businessman with interests throughout the colonies: his 'Almanac' and postal delivery service were everywhere, slightly altered for each colony. His argument to the British in the 1760s was that a unified America would be an economic powerhouse, and they would be foolish in the extreme to risk losing it for the few seats the colonists wanted in the British Parliament. That hard-headed denial by the British elite, to bow to granting their colonies government by consent of the governed, was to have major consequences. There is no reason to doubt that a similar resistance by European elites could also have long-term consequences.

On dealing with the most pressing matter of government debt, Hamilton was faced with the fact that the thirteen founding states of the United States all had separate and disparate debts, built up during their times as separate colonies during the course of the War of Independence. As the war had been waged in some states more than others and as the contributions of the states to the war effort and cost had varied greatly, even that portion of debt that was directly attributable to a form of 'joint enterprise and expenditure', was not evenly or proportionately disbursed across all of the states. On top of the states' debts, there was already a federal debt, which had been used to finance some of the cost of Washington's triumphant Continental Army, as well as some other federal borrowings.

Hamilton knew that he possessed limited short-term financial resources and that these many debts would have to be re-structured while enhancing the United States' reputation as a borrower. One dilemma was that many securities had changed hands at significant discounts, raising potential moral dilemmas. Weighing his options, Hamilton decided that security of transfer and its repercussions for private property were paramount to establishing credibility and thus assist a favourable credit rating. He then made the bold decision to federalise all of the state debts in distress, doing so to ensure the survival of the whole rather than the sacrifice of any member state.

Interest on the already incurred federal debt was at between 4 per cent and 5 per cent and Hamilton understood that, for the sake of American credibility, this debt, all owed to foreign lenders and primarily made to finance America's war effort, must be paid in full. The various interest rates on the debts of the thirteen states were high at 6 per cent and greater. Hamilton knew that his ability to raise revenue was simply not sufficient to allow the servicing of the combined states' debts. He also knew that bond-holders sitting on state debts were exposed to a broad range of growing risks, of which they were well aware. Hamilton also saw the opportunity to shift the loyalty of those creditors by giving them a stake in preserving a federal government by having it federalise the state debts and thus make those creditors commit 'risk on' to the new United Sates. However, given the fact that combined state debts and interest were just too high to sustain, Hamilton decided to deliver a federal 'haircut' on assumption of the states' debts. Hamilton took the path of offering 'volun-tary' haircuts in a variety of options that largely boiled down to a partial payment at 6 per cent interest, a partial 'equity swap' (in Hamilton's case, for western land that at the time was relatively valueless but had prospects), or payment at a lower interest rate over a longer term but sweetened by quarterly payments (rather than yearly) and paid from taxes specifically earmarked for the purpose of paying those bonds.

The creditors did the pragmatic thing and accepted Hamilton's offers; Hamilton drew those creditors into supporting his new country while at the same time rescuing many of his thirteen member states. Through his federalisation and re-structuring of unsustainable state debts Hamilton helped cement the disparate states together to form their 'more perfect union'.

Hamilton's hands-on experience with a potentially catastrophic sovereign debt crisis provoked him to leave some wise advice for posterity that growing debt 'is perhaps the natural disease of all Governments. And it is not easy to conceive anything more likely than this to lead to great and convulsive revolutions of Empire.' He also wisely advised that he 'ardently wishes to see it incor-porated as a fundamental maxim in the system of public credit of the United States that the creation of debt should always be accompanied with the means of extinguishment.' That is to say, you don't take on a sovereign debt without also having in place a specific revenue stream with which to pay it down. Europe of 2012 should duly take note. As a means to finance debt, Hamilton set up 'sinking funds': revenue that was stored up to service debts and which he prudently and quietly used to buy back large amounts of government debt at bargain prices (Hamilton understood the central banker's art of 'creative ambiguity').

When considering Hamilton's approach, bailouts were not his *modus operandi*. Hamilton's King's College (later to become Columbia University) friend and early companion in the Treasury Department was one William Duer. Early on, Duer had departed his assistant secretary role at the Treasury in order to engage in private banking and speculation, becoming a major New York 'market maker' in the process. In 1791 and 1792, Hamilton was faced with the US's first banking and government securities crisis. Amongst the financial fallout, his powerful financial industry friend Duer had ended up in the position of needing a government bailout for his banking and financing interests or he would ultimately face debtors' prison. Hamilton, though empathising with Duer, would not provide the bailout. The end result was that Duer ended his days in a debtors' prison, sometimes visited by Hamilton but paying the ultimate price for Hamilton's allowing 'the freedom to fail', which in the eighteenth century had steeper consequences than the more risk-friendly world of today. Given Hamilton's actions, it is hard to imagine why the principle of 'freedom to fail' is not more readily afforded to European banks and institutions that held entirely private failed risk. The idea that any government would (like the Irish governments of 2010–2011) ever contemplate pledging taxpayer resources to fund already failed private bank risk, where the initial loans were not made to, nor expended by government, would have struck Hamilton as beyond absurd.

Hamilton's most recent (and excellent) biographer, Ron Chernow, summed up the completion of Hamilton's time in office as follows:

> Bankrupt when Hamilton took office, the United States now enjoyed a credit rating equal to that of any European nation [back then, that was a good thing]. He had laid the groundwork for both liberal

democracy and capitalism and helped to transform the role of the president from passive administrator to active policy maker, creating the institutional scaffolding for America's future emergence as a great power. He had demonstrated the creative uses of government and helped to weld the states irreversibly into one nation.[2]

It is popular today for Europeans to look back at the early formation of the United States of America and to say that it was inevitable, unique and took place in an already cohesive and homogenous society. The facts of the matter are more complex. The thirteen colonies that made up the first states were disparate in their make-up and had regarded their existence in relation to their ties with London more than with each other. American cities were filled with immigrants from all of Europe's cultures, speaking a multitude of languages, with English and German being the most dominant. Great cultural differences existed between the states, perhaps the most acute being on their attitudes to slavery. In summary I would say the early institutional success of America's union was more due to the willingness and courage of a principled minority of gifted leaders, formed in a more meritocratic environment that, for its time, was somewhat less constrained by the sclerosis that often afflicts old establishments, and who were motivated by a common bond of morals and a pioneering willingness to make sacrifice and take risk for the greater good. This character served the United States well when, time and again, as its leaders were faced with seemingly insurmountable challenges, they took bold risks and eventually met with success (the revolutionary war at first consisted of a succession of military defeats for George Washington's army. Where others would have accepted the 'inevitable' Washington and his men did not).

An observation of what some might consider a root of 'American exceptionalism' was made by Alexis de Tocqueville, the great French statesman and writer of the nineteenth century. In his 1835 book *Democracy in America* de Tocqueville, observing the new American Union from the perspective of a European, made incisive observations on the American appetite for risk in commerce, first noting that although American seamen were paid higher wages, their way of business was more competitive. He went on to say:

How is it, therefore, that American's navigate more cheaply than we do? ... The European navigator ventures on the seas only with prudence; he departs only when the weather invites him to; if an unforeseen accident comes upon him, he enters into port at night, he furls a part of his sails, and when he sees the ocean whiten at the approach of land, he slows his course and examines the sun.

The American neglects these precautions and braves these dangers. He departs while the tempest still roars; at night, as in day he opens all his sails to the wind; while on the go, he repairs his ship, worn down by the storm, and when he finally approaches the end of his course, he continues to fly toward the shore as if he already perceived the port. The American is often shipwrecked; but there is no navigator who crosses the seas as rapidly as he does. Doing the same things as another in less time, he can do them at less expense.

Before reaching the end of the voyage with a long course, the European navigator believes he ought to land several times on his way. He loses precious time in seeking a port for relaxation or in awaiting the occasion to leave it, and he pays each day for the right to remain there.

The American navigator leaves Boston to go to buy tea in China. He arrives at Canton, remains there a few days and comes back. In less than two years he has run over the entire circumference of the globe, and he has seen land only a single time. During a crossing of eight to ten months, he has drunk brackish water and lived on salted meat; he has struggled constantly against the sea, against illness, against boredom; but on his return he can sell the pound of tea for one penny less than the English merchant; the goal is attained.

Then in summary de Tocqueville tells us:

I cannot express my thought better than by saying that the Americans put a sort of heroism into their manner of doing commerce. It will always be very difficult for the European trader to follow his

American competitor on the same course. The American, in acting
in the manner that I described above, not only follows a calculation,
he obeys, above all, his nature.[3]

In essence, de Tocqueville assessed that if there was an American exceptionalism at that time (and he certainly concluded that
there was), it culminated in an exception to risk aversion. De
Tocqueville's observations of American commerce, when added
to the life stories of the founders of the American union such as
Hamilton, show an undeniable appetite for courage, boldness
and heroic self-sacrifice underpinned by Judeo-Christian values,
yearning for justice and the rule of law, and the exercise of classical liberalism. I find it mildly ironic that many of the same voices
in today's Europe that decry any concept of 'American exceptionalism' are often the very same voices that seek to tell us that
Europe can learn little from the American experience. I dare to
assert that Europe, facing our very own financial and political
crisis of union, has something to learn from the American experiment, which, after all, found its inspiration from the best ideas
imported from European history. What we need to learn most
of all is that which might define a 'European exceptionalism',
requiring a complete re-think about Europe's approach to risk,
political and financial, because unless we radically attack the
disease that has beset the idea of European unity this modern
European experiment with union will fail, with consequences as
yet untellable but that I believe may be severe.

It was the grand disaster of World War One that inspired the
early founders of the European Union idea, an idea that only
began to properly come into being following the disastrous
efforts to unite Europe under the not-so-varied totalitarian jack-
boots of National Socialism, fascism and communism.

Today, as we observe the now bizarre ritual of failed European
summitry, the uninspiring posturing of Europe's 'leaders' and
the short-term political risk aversion, leading to chronic errors
and splits with potentially dangerous long-term consequences,
one cannot but wonder to what extent these politicians grasp the

magnitude of what they are putting at risk by their petty politicking. For my small part, I have spent some time and resources in trying to draw attention to the sucking wound that is really eating away at Europe's vitality.

That wound is the chronic lack of democracy, accountability and transparency now rupturing the heart of the European project and manifesting itself in everything from the machinations of the Commission and the European Council's Committee of Permanent Representatives to the boardroom of the ECB and to the back rooms of Europe's newest self-styled elite: the so-called 'Frankfurt Club' encompassing a would-be Franco-German axis planning on turning the Eurozone into what effectively would be a collection of vassal states.

So what are Europe's options? Which path in this historical fork in the road are we to venture down? It would seem in their lack of vision our leaders want to either go in reverse or continue the practice of strong rhetoric backed by limp action, all of which compounds the growing type of injustice that we see in Ireland effectively being forced to spend billions to make good the losses of bondholders that we at no point ever borrowed money from.

Looking at the consequences of Europe's leaders' unwillingness to lead justly, or indeed at all, one is reminded of the words of Hamilton and de Tocqueville's contemporary, the great classical liberal and Irishman Edmund Burke, who said: 'Nothing turns out to be so oppressive and unjust as a feeble government.'

Given all that has happened I now see Europe's choice as this: we either learn from the lessons of history and take the calculated but worthwhile risk to fully unite in a democratic and federal union, or we will see this project fall apart. To believe that it can fall apart in an orderly fashion, reverting to a neat trading club, I fear is an over-indulgence in wishful thinking. It is at least as likely that a collapsing of the European project, made more likely by a collapse of the Euro, would result in a balkanisation of Europe as a return to some type of trading utopia that would be devoid of internal rivalries and outside threats.

For example, consider this. If the Euro's collapse were to destroy the political credibility of the union in the minds of the average European, what might a sundering of Europe mean for Europe's eastern borders? The issues arising are too many to detail here but they are deadly serious with all the potential to become another Yugoslavia but written on a much larger map.

The proposition of a fully federal European Union fills many Europeans with deep concerns and I must say that it should. The idea that we would further centralise power to the European Union in its current form should be an anathema to any right-thinking lover of liberty and democracy.

In the words of the eighteenth-century Scottish philosopher David Hume, 'it is seldom that liberty of any kind is lost all at once', but a further concentration of central power without accountability would be a very mighty step.

So Europe must now grasp the nettle of major reform – of 'treaty change' – to establish a Europe not of the now defunct and bankrupt Lisbon Treaty but one created 'by the people for the people' – a Europe bringing us that only form of temporal governance that should ever be acceptable to free peoples, government by consent of the governed.

In summary, this is the federalisation that Europe should implement now:

1. The position of President of the European Commission and President of the European Council should be merged into one office holder and should be made subject to a popular democratic election to be held not later than December 2013. Voters should be weighted in an 'electoral college' type format so that smaller member states' voters are not made irrelevant. This president would serve for one six-year term only and would be chairperson and chief executive in the same manner as the President of the United States of America. An accommodation might be made to remaining European monarchies in respect of their traditions, to allow for some ceremonial roles.

2. The Commission should become the servants of the executive arm and be filled by nomination of the democratically elected president, and ratification of a newly created upper house of the European Parliament.

3. An upper house or 'senate' should be created, with four representatives of each member state, each representative holding equal voting power. That is to say, Ireland will have four senators and Germany will have four senators, etc. This upper house will be given the co-right to initiate legislation along with the lower house, the current European Parliament.

4. The European Parliament should be reformed to give greater balance for population (which would favour larger member states) and should be given the power (along with its upper house) to initiate legislation.

5. All lobbying of the executive and legislative branch must be registered and transparent.

6. A full insolvency purge of all European financial institutions should be immediately undertaken. A liquidation and asset sale of all unhealthy institutions should take place forthwith. A write-down of significant size, together with a Hamiltonian-scale re-negotiation, should take place on all distressed EU member state debts. The federalising of all remaining state debt should immediately follow, backed by the issue of union bonds backed by the entire tax revenue of the Eurozone. (This can be altered later but will end market turmoil and establish real stability.)

7. The Union civil service should be kept small and highly efficient; this should be enshrined in Europe's new constitutional arrangement. A debt ceiling will also be set constitutionally.

8. The Union should have monopoly of external action, both in soft and hard power.

9. The ECB should be guaranteed full independence and a low inflation policy be pursued.

It is to be understood that the above model may be considered unfathomable to many. However, it is not unreasonable to suppose that anything less than a democratic federalisation of a similar form to that set out above will result in failure and a loss of confidence in European unity that may lead to this continent turning back the clock by 100 years. The price is worth paying; the risk is worth taking. As Europeans we should, in de Tocqueville's words, 'open all [our] sails to the wind' and seize this moment in history while always guarding our right to government by consent of the governed – essential to maintain our individual liberty – which can never be negotiable. As de Tocqueville also underlined with his explanation of the early Yankee Clipper shipping trade from China, fortune does indeed favour the bold. Time for Europe to put some 'heroism' back into politics.

Endnotes

[1] George Washington, letter to George Martin, 'Head Quarters', 10 August 1783.
[2] Ron Chernow (2004) *Alexander Hamilton*, New York: Penguin, p. 481.
[3] Alexis de Tocqueville (1835 [2000]) *Democracy in America*, Volume 1, Part 2, Chapter 10, Reprinted, Chicago, IL: University of Chicago Press, pp. 386–387.

Index

Note: Page numbers followed by 'f' indicate references to figures and by 't' indicate reference to tables.

Ahern, Bertie, 246, 247
AIB, 73, 74, 83
Almunia, Joaquin, 141
American International Group (AIG), 154
Anglo Irish Bank, 17, 18, 74, 78, 93, 143, 153, 155, 249
annual interest payments, 82
Argentina, 39, 149, 150, 153, 156–157, 167, 222
   lessons from Argentine default, 160–162
   privatisation of pension and energy assets, 160
   regional solidarity, 167
   sovereign debt, 169
   tequila effect, 157–158
Arizona, population growth, 196
Asian financial crisis (1997–1998), 19, 29, 38, 41, 225
asset bubbles, 30, 89
austerity, 99, 101, 106, 159, 200, 236, 238, 243
Austria, 60f, 61
   bond yields, 100

bailouts, 18, 73, 85, 100, 140–141, 270
balance sheet contagion, 35
Ballestero, Jorge, 169
Ballymacarbry Community Centre, Waterford, 262
bank balance sheets, 35

Bank for International Settlements, 94
bank guarantee, 8–9, 17, 89
bank lending, 28
Bank of Ireland, 73, 74, 83
bank rescue, 151–153
banking crises, 18, 131
banking sector debts, 65
bankruptcy cascades, 28
bankruptcy laws, 215
banks, 24–25, 96t
   interconnectedness of, 34–35
Beame, Abraham D., 173, 175, 179, 183
Belgium, 61
   bond yields, 100
bench-marking, 11
Binchy, Daniel A., 260
Black, William K., 152
BlackRock, 213
Boards.ie, 261–262
bond traders, 203
bonds, 200–201
Bord Snip Nua Report, 11
borrowing, 14
Brady Plan, 224
Brasel, S. Adam, 256
Brazil, 24, 38, 160
Brecher, Charles, 185
British Independent Commission on Banking Report, 153
Bryce, Lord, 174
bubbles, 29–30
burden-sharing, 223, 239, 241

Index

Burke, Edmund, 274
business debt, 235, 236
Byrne, Francis John, 260

capital controls, 21, 41
capital flow between countries, 35
capital linkages, 32
capital market integration, 35, 40
capital market liberalisation, 38–42
Carey, Hugh L., 174, 180, 181, 183
cash interest, 82
cash reserves, 83
Cavallo, Domingo, 161
Celtic Tiger, 19, 58
Center Falls, Rhode Island, 193–194
Central Bank Governor, 9
Central Bank of Iceland, 141, 142
Central Bank of Ireland, 74, 79, 93, 136,
   210, 238
Central Bank of Russia, 119, 124
central banks, 94, 215
central government bodies debt, 92
Central Office of Project Evaluation
   (COPE), 15
Chamlee-Wright, Emily, 258
Chernomyrdin, Viktor, 120, 126
Chernow, Ron, 270
China, 95
Chopra, Ajai, 140
churnalism, 250
city defaults, 187–196
Cleveland, 196
collateral, 26
COMECON trading block, 118
Committee for the Abolition of Third
   World Debt (CADTM), 164
commodity price indices, 116f
community engagement, 254, 255, 258
conditionality, 100
construction sector, 89
contagion, 17, 21, 32, 33–34, 35, 38–42,
   157
Coppie, Comer S., 184
corporate debt, 10

corporation tax, 129
Correa, Rafael, 163
Cost of Good Intentions, The (Morris),
   179
cost of living, 67
Cotterill, Joseph, 170
credit, 214–215
credit default swap, 203
Credit Institutions (Stabilisation) Act
   2010, 239
credit ratings, 27
cross-border financial flows, 36
Cuba, 95
Culliton Review of Industrial Policy in
   Ireland, 15
Curran, Richard, 249
current account deficits, 60
   1990s v 2000s, 62f
   reversal of, 63
current budget adjustment, 8
current budget balance, 8t
customer loans, 78t, 79, 80
Cyprus, 61
Czechoslovakia, 95

Dáil Éireann, 7
Davies, Nick, 250
de Kirchner, Cristina Fernandez, 169
de Tocqueville, Alexis, 271–273, 277
debt
   of central government bodies, 90t
   servicing of, 82
   sustainable, 81
debt audits, 163–164
debt forgiveness, 218
debt levels, 10
   unindexed, 26
debt overhangs, 54, 55f, 56, 58–59
   exports-led growth and, 59–63
debt ratio, 71–72, 79, 80
debt resolution, 221–225
debt restructuring, 53–68, 218, 226, 231
   procedures, 227–230
   selective restructuring, 64–68

default, 85, 86, 167–168
    definition, 87
    soft, 97
    uncontrolled hard, 160
default dilemma, 219–221
    moral hazard, 219
    time inconsistency, 219
deficits, 75
    reversal of, 61
Delors, Jacques, 12
Denmark, 91
Detroit, 196
devaluation, 56–58, 157, 167, 168
Diamond-Dybvig model, 28
Dinkins, David N., 185
disposable income, 67
distributional shock, 26
diversification, 20, 21, 22, 32, 40, 118
Dow Jones, 251
Drumm, Brendan, 11
Drumm, David, 249
Dubinin, Sergei, 121, 124
Duer, William, 270
Dunne, Sean, 248

East Asian crisis, 19
economic crises, 17, 18
economic growth, 238
Economist House Price Index
    1997–2007, 10
Ecuador, 225
    sovereign debt audit, 163
Educational Building Society (EBS),
    74, 93
Ehrenhalt, Samuel M., 184
Elliott, Donald H., 178
Emergency Financial Control Board,
    181
emergency liquidity assistance, for
    banks, 94
employment, 211
    see also unemployment
Epstein, Jason, 176
Estonia, 61

EU/IMF loans, 70t, 91, 92
EU/IMF programme, 75, 76, 85
Euro, 159, 168
Eurobonds, 165
Europe, Ireland's relationship with,
    99–108
European banks, 96t
European Central Bank (ECB), 84, 93,
    99, 136, 139, 155, 165, 204, 210, 238,
    240, 277
European Commission President, 275
European Council President, 275
European economy, effects of an Irish
    default on the, 87–98
European Financial Stability Facility,
    91, 92, 165–166, 205
European Financial Stability
    Mechanism, 91, 92
European Parliament, 276
European Stability Mechanism, 155, 166
European Union, 12, 99, 164
    Ireland's relationship with, 104–105
    response of leaders to crisis, 100
Eurozone, 12, 200, 230, 231
    break-up of the, 103–104
    exit process, 106
    prospects for the, 99, 100–104
    stimulating growth in the, 103
exchange rates, 20, 29, 31
exogenous shocks, 29
exports, 106
exports-led growth, 61
    and debt overhangs, 59–63
external balances, 63

Facebook, 262
Fianna Fáil, 7, 155
financial constraints, 33
financial crises, 17, 18
    active coping strategies, 259
    causes of, 23–32
    logic of, 22
    market and individual
        irrationalities, 28–31

market frictions, 25–27
market processes destabilisation, 31
mathematics of, 22
Mexican crisis (1994–1995), 23–24
multiple equilibria, 22, 24–25
passive coping strategies, 259
in Russia, 37, 38, 95, 111–134, 225
spread of, 32–38
systemic crises, 27–28
trend reinforcement and 'orbits of
    attraction', 31–32
financial integration, 40
financial liberalisation, 38–42
financial linkages, 33, 34
financial market, 199
Financial Regulator, 9, 215, 247
Fine Gael, 105
Finland, 61, 63, 211–212
fire sales, 36, 160
fiscal policy, 215
fiscal responsibility legislation, 14
fiscal union, 103
FitzPatrick, Sean, 155
Ford, Gerald, 182, 183
foreclosures, 192
foreign claims, 96t
foreign direct investment, 58
former Yugoslavia, 223
fractional reserve, 241
France, 60, 61, 96t, 205, 231
    bond yields, 100
    Credit Agricole, 242
free-rider problem, 220–221
Fuchs, Ester, 177
Futureshock, 249

Geithner, Timothy, 154, 230
general government debt (GGD), 69–
    70, 72–73, 74–75, 83
Genovese, Kitty, 175
Germany, 60, 61, 96t, 205, 231
    Deutsche Bank, 242
Gips, James, 256
Glazer, Nathan, 177

Goldin, Harrison J., 182
Governing New York City, 174
government bonds, 70t, 84, 89, 90t,
    91–92
government debt, 10, 56, 89, 90t, 235
government deficits, 60
government regulation, 215
Greece, 61, 99, 100, 101–102, 106, 138,
    156, 204, 243
    debt levels, 236
    debt ratio, 71
gross domestic product, 70
gross national income, 88
growth dynamics, 113

Hamilton, Alexander, 265–271
Hamilton, Edward V., 179
Harrington, Michael, 175
Harris, Lawrence, 189
Harrisburg, Pennsylvania, 192–193
Harrison, Fred, 216
Hassett, Kevin, 251
health service budget, 11
Health Service Executive, 11
Heavily Indebted Poor Countries
    (HIPC) Initiative, 225
herding, 28
Hoffland, David, 190
Honohan, Patrick, 136, 143
Horton, Raymond D., 184, 185, 186
house price index, 10
household debt, 10, 59, 65, 66, 235–236
housing prices, 10, 29, 211
Hume, David, 275
Humes, Hans, 163–164

Iceland, 135–147, 152–153, 167, 168, 217,
    239–240
    and Ireland, 137–140
Icelandic króna, 135, 138, 168
individual irrationalities, 28–31
Inglehart, Ronald, 255, 264
'Inside Ireland's Secret Liquidity', 170
insolvency laws, 215

institutional competitiveness, 57
integration, 41
interest bill, 82
interest rates, 210, 212
internal devaluation, 56–58
international bailout packages, 38
International Monetary Fund (IMF),
  41, 75, 91, 99, 120, 125, 136, 139, 155, 166
  conclusions and interpretations,
    230–231
  credit resolution, 218
  and debt resolution, 221–225
  purpose of, 217
  and sovereign default, 217–233
internet, 257, 262
investor irrationality, 29
investor rationality, 34
investors, response to shocks, 37
Ireland, 61, 99, 100, 204
  currency crisis in the early 1990s,
    200
  debt ratio, 71
  Iceland and, 137–140
  relationship with the EU, 104–105
  staying in the Eurozone, 107–108
Irish Bank Resolution Corporation
  (IBRC), 78, 79, 81
Irish Banking Crisis Regulatory and
  Financial Stability Policy, The,
  2003–2008, 151
Irish government bond yields, 240
Irish government debt, 56
Irish Nationwide Building Society
  (INBS), 74, 78, 93
Irish punt, 168, 200, 209, 210, 211
irrationalities, 28–31, 39
Italy, 61, 71, 96t, 99, 100, 138, 156, 205

Japan, 81, 96t, 211
  debt levels, 236
  general government debt (GGD), 71
Jefferson County, Alabama, 193
J.P. Morgan Chase, 193
Jurys Hotel, Ballsbridge, 248

Kadushin, Charles, 259
Kaufman, Herbert, 174
Kavanaugh, Andrea, 262
Kay, Sean, 252
Keane Report, on distressed mortgages,
  235
Keena, Colm, 246
Kelly, Morgan, 144
Keynes, John Maynard, 218
Kirchner, Nestor, 168
Kiriyenko, Sergei, 120–121, 125
Koch, Edward I., 184
króna, 135, 138, 168
Krueger, Anne, 226
Krugman, Paul, 159

La Guardia, Fiorello H., 174
Labour, 105
labour costs, 101
Lagarde, Christine, 165
Latin America, 97, 157, 224
Lavagna, Roberto, 158
Lenihan, Brian, 136, 143, 170
Lewis, Michael, 153
life satisfaction, 263
Lindsay, John V., 175, 178
liquid assets, 200
Lisbon Treaty, 104
loan losses, 80, 238
Loan Value Group, 213
loans for sale, 78t, 79
local government debt, 90t
Lokshin, Michael, 259
London Club, 115, 117, 224
long-term debt, 90t
losses, 80
Luther King Jr., Martin, 180
Luxembourg, 61, 63

Maastricht Treaty, 69, 70
macroeconomic shock, 26
Mahon Tribunal, 246
Malta, 61
market frictions, 25–27

market imperfections, 21
market irrationalities, 28–31, 39
market processes destabilisation, 31
markets
    interventions in the, 21
    rational participants, 21
materialism, 253–254, 263
    decline in, 255–258
    post-materialism, 255
    raw materialism, 253–254
McCreevy, Charlie, 137
McGuinness, John, 13
media piracy, 257
medium-term debt, 90t
meitheal, 260–261
Mencken, H.L., 175
Mexico, 39, 211, 224, 229
    peso crisis, 23–24, 161, 167–168
    peso devaluation, 157
Michael, Philip R., 185
Mitchell, John, 180
money, national happiness and, 263
Morris, Charles, 179
mortgage arrears, 66
mortgage lending, 215
mortgages, 208, 209, 212–213
Moynihan, Daniel Patrick, 177
multilateral banks, 155, 159
multinational companies, 100,
    106–107
multiple equilibria, 22, 24–25
Municipal Assistance Corporation, 180,
    181
municipal bonds, 187, 196
    advantages of, 188
    background on, 188
    defaults, 189, 190
    general obligation bonds, 188
    revenue bonds, 188
    risk, 189
Murphy, Brenda, 259
National Asset Management Agency
    (NAMA), 18, 56, 65, 77–78, 80, 81, 89,
    144, 154, 243

national debt, 89
National Pension Reserve Fund, 73, 74,
    83, 91, 238
National Treasury Management
    Agency, 76
negative shock, 31
net current expenditure, 8t
Netherlands, 61
Netzer, Dick, 185
Nevada, 192
New York City, 189–190
    1960 census, 177
    causes of the fiscal crisis, 174–179
    consequences of the fiscal crisis,
        183–186
    fiscal crisis, 173–186
    mayoralty of, 174
Nice Treaty, 104
non-bank private sector, 96t
non-European banks, 96t
Noonan, Michael, 76, 105, 240

Olmos, Alexander, 169
O'Neill, Paul, 228
optimal financial architecture,
    40–42
Orange County default, 194
O'Sullivan, John, 249
ouzo effect, 158

Pakistan, 225
Paris Club, 115, 117, 162, 222–223
pension funds, 160
Permanent TSB, 74, 83
Personal Insolvency Act, 214
Peru, 227
peso crisis, 23–24, 161, 167–168
Phanos, Theo, 153
Piwowar, Michael, 189
Poland, 97, 223
Political Crisis, Fiscal Crisis: The
    Collapse and Revival of New York City
    (Shefter), 186
political power transfer, 156

Portugal, 61, 99, 100, 101, 106, 138, 156, 204
post-materialism, 255
Pride of Place Awards, 261, 262
primary balance, 72
print media, 13, 250
private debt levels, 237
private sector involvement, 101
Project Finance Agency, 180
promissory notes, 68, 70t, 73–74, 78t, 90t, 93–98
property boom, 19
property database, 215
property developers, 27
property prices, 29, 211
public assets, sale of, 160
public debt, 69, 70, 80
  and economic growth, 71
public debt overhang, 56
public expenditure controls, 13
public finances, 63
public sector, 96t
public sector wages, 11, 236
punt, 168, 200, 209, 210, 211
pure contagion, 33–34
Putin, Vladimir, 127
Putnam, Robert, 258

Quarterly National Household Survey, 66
quasi-governmental debt, 56

rating agencies, 203–204
rational investors, 34
Ravitch, Richard, 180, 181, 186
raw materialism, 253–254
Real Effects of Debt, The, 53
Report of the Special Group on Public Service Numbers and Expenditure Programmes, 11
restructuring of debts see debt restructuring
retail debt, 70t
Roberts, Sam, 15

Rockefeller, Nelson A., 180
Rohatyn, Felix G., 181, 185, 186
Romania, 97
Roubini, Nouriel, 248
Russia, 38, 95, 111–134, 225
  1997–1998, 37, 117–125
  banking crisis, 131
  consolidation of banks, 133
  GDP, 115
  general government fiscal performance (1998–2008), 128f
  gross domestic product per capita, 112f
  post-crisis recovery, 126–133
  roots of the crisis 1995–1997, 113–117
  tax reform, 123–124, 127–129
  total deposits in credit institutions in, 122f
  trade balance, 114
Russian ruble, 119, 121, 123, 125, 130

Salmon, Felix, 163
Sayre, Wallace, 174
Scandinavia, 264
Schwartz, Anna, 229
secret loans, 155
selective restructuring, 64–68
semi-state bodies, debt levels, 81
Shafik, Nemat, 137, 139
Shanker, Albert, 182
Shefter, Martin, 177, 186
shock diffusion, 34
short-run exchange rate interventions, 38–40
short-term debt, 90t, 92
Sigfússon, Steingrímur, 137
Sinn Féin, 105
site value tax, 215
Slovak Republic, 61
Slovenia, 61
social capital, 258, 259, 260, 264
Social Entrepreneurs Ireland Awards, 261
solidarity finance, 164–167
South America, 149, 156

Southeast Asia, 38
sovereign bonds, 84, 200–201
sovereign debt, 150, 157, 202
sovereign debt audits, 163–164
Sovereign Debt Restructuring
  Mechanism (SDRM), 227
sovereign default, 95, 97, 145, 207, 217
Soviet Union, 118
Spain, 61, 99, 100, 138
Starr, Paul, 250
state bodies, debt levels, 81
state savings schemes, 90t, 92
Stiglitz, Joseph, 151, 159
Storr, Virgil, 258
Strauss-Kahn, Dominique, 166
stress tests, 80
structural deficits, 60, 63
subordinated debt, 151, 152
subprime mortgages, 247
swaps, 154
Sweden, 91
  property prices, 211
systemic crises, 27–28

tax receipts, 195
tax revenue, 8t
taxation, 159
Taylor, John, 228, 229
television ownership, 256
tequila effect, 157–158
Third World, budget deficits and
  government debt, 156
Thomsen, Poul M., 136, 139
Tidy Towns community improvement
  initiative, 261
Toussaint, Eric, 164
trade linkages, 32
traders, 202
  analysis of the current Eurozone
    crisis, 204
transfer union, 242–243
trend reinforcement and 'orbits of
  attraction', 31–32

Trichet, Jean Claude, 239
Turkey, 97, 224

Ukraine, 225
unemployment, 66–67, 130
  see also employment
unit labour costs, 101
United Kingdom, 91, 96t, 139, 217
  property prices, 211
United States of America, 247
  economic downturn, 37
  federal government debt crisis, 194
  municipal bonds, 188
  property values, 191
  War of Independence, 266, 268
Urban Development Corporation, 180
Uruguay, 209
USSR, 113, 118

Vallejo, California, 194
Venezuela, 167
Volcker, Paul, 186
voluntary debt exchange, 101
volunteering, 261

Wagner, Robert F., 177, 178
Wagner, Robert F., Jr., 184
Walsh, Brendan, 263
Washington, George, 266, 267
Washington Public Power System
  Supply (WPPSS), 191
Weisman, Steven R., 174, 178, 183, 186
Whelan, Karl, 88
Wolfensohn, James, 124
Wright Report, 9

Yeltsin, Boris, 120, 121, 125, 126, 127
Yemtsov, Ruslan, 259

Zaire, 224
Zuccotti, John E., 185